# SAVE ME FIRST

**200** WAYS TO SURVIVE A HOSPITAL
PHYSICALLY, MENTALLY AND SPIRITUALLY

BY
JACKIE TORRES

## SAVE ME FIRST

Title in Spanish: SALVAME A MI PRIMERO
Author: Jackie Torres
www.jackietorres.com
Cover Design: Mario Ramírez Reyes

© 2016, Torres, Jacqueline "Save me First" Library of Congress
© 2010, Torres, Jacqueline "The Violet Wall" Library of Congress
© 2008, Torres, Jacqueline "Miracle's Hospital" Library of Congress

Editorial Jakmar
P.O. Box 2771
Toluca Lake, CA 91602
jackietorresnet@gmail.com

First Published Edition: 2016 (Spanish) 2017 (English)
ISBN 978-0-9976270-3-9
Unauthorized reproduction of this book, partially or fully in any way, is prohibited.
Made in the USA

TABLE OF CONTENTS

| | |
|---|---|
| INTRODUCTION | 4 |
| HOW TO DEAL WITH EMERGENCIES | 7 |
| HOW TO OPTIMIZE THE PATIENT'S EXPERIENCE | 42 |
| PATIENT'S CONCERNS | 80 |
| HOW TO SURVIVE A HOSPITAL ROOM | 117 |
| THE ART OF CO-EXISTING IN A HOSPITAL | 153 |
| WHAT TO AVOID, ACCEPT AND FIND IN A HOSPITAL | 187 |
| WHAT EVERY PATIENT SHOULD KNOW | 226 |
| FIND ALLIES; ENEMIES WILL COME UNINVITED. | 260 |
| WHAT TO EXPECT DURING REHABILITATION | 296 |
| MASTERING THE ART OF BEING PATIENT | 323 |

## Introduction

LIFE IN A HOSPITAL is an experience most people do not want to go through but it is almost unavoidable for all, at some point in our lives. In my case, such emergency arrived on the morning of October 1$^{st}$, 2006. Back then, I was painting a wall at my home in North Hollywood, California, and since the ladder I had was too short I had the "brilliant" idea of improvising a taller one, placing a wood dolly with wheels underneath. I allowed my hurry and not my intellect dictate my destiny. As I was trying to reach the upper part of the wall, the ladder slipped; it fell from the wood dolly with wheels to the floor, and I fell with it. What would my school friends think of me? What were my diplomas good for? I was going to die in the most stupid way!

As I was flying in the air going straight to the floor, it felt like I was moving in slow motion, as if someone had turned me around in mid air so I did not fall over my back. My stomach landed miserably over a small tube the small ladder, of only three steps, had in its upper part; it did not penetrate my skin but it felt as though it was touching my spinal cord. I could barely breathe; I was grasping for air. I knew something inside my belly was broken. The smell of death filled the room; my spirit felt it was about to exit my body.

I slowly walked to a nearby sofa, feeling unbearable pain. From there, I tried to ask for help but only a whisper came out of my lips. I had to reach the door; otherwise, no one would hear me. I walked towards it, knowing that every step could be my last. I made it, barely able to breathe; I was able to leave the door open and asked for help with the little voice I had left. Several minutes went by but no one heard; the usually bustling hallway was totally deserted. My husband was not home; at that moment he was landing at the Los Angeles airport after having been working out of state for several months.

My intention was to give him a nice welcome back reception with a living room that had a new color. My negligence, however, put me at death's door and sent me to a hospital where along my relatives I experienced very challenging situations. Very often I wished I had a manual to guide me on how to face a hospital stay with the fewest number of setbacks. Since I did not find those instructions in writing, I had to experience them first hand and decided to compile them and present them in this book so that those who read them can be better informed about what to expect from a hospital stay and how to survive it. Hopefully, this book will be for you the manual I did not have, and it will avoid you huge headaches and will even save your life when the inevitable emergencies arise.

## Chapter 1:
## How to deal with emergencies

**1. 911 responds quickly, but it can cost you a fortune.**

After living a life surrounded by family and friends, I did not want to die by myself. In the worst case scenario, I had to die with someone next to me, holding my hand with a firm grip, showing me that I mattered that I was loved while I lived in this planet that I would be missed. By then, I was aware that perhaps no one would hear my cries for help. I considered another option; I could call 911, the number for emergencies in the United States. My cell phone was within reach; I only had to dial three numbers that could save my life.

Then I remembered: -who would pay the $2000.00

dollars needed to cover the expenses of the ambulance, the police, and the firefighters that respond to a 911 call? I have no clue why so many people respond to a 911 call but California is flashy; everything is done like in the movies. Just thinking about those expenses makes you think twice about staying alive. I guess you must be thinking I am just cheap. How can I put a price on my own life? Well, I must tell you that not long ago, just like anyone else, I saw everything the American way: buy now, pay later, until a day came when the expenses piled up and there was no money left to pay later.

I was dying but my brain was still aware of my debts, especially payments to credit cards with interest rates suddenly increased by banks from 7 or 9 to 19 or 24 percent. There was no budget left to pay for 911 or a health plan. What would kings and queens do in a situation like this one? They would probably call their royal consultants.

## 2. If a friend or relative helps you, your chances of survival increase.

That was just what I needed, a royal consultant to guide me about my course of action. I remembered that my friend Elba had called minutes before the accident. Who better to help? My friend was an employee of the USC hospital of the Los Angeles County for 33 years so chances were she was equipped to deal with these types of emergencies. Her small height, of almost 5 feet, contrasts with the aplomb of her dominant personality. She is the same age as my mother, but she behaves with the energy of someone younger. Just like the royal consultants, she always has a solution for everything, so I called her to help me out.

Pain had left me without strength to dial a complete phone number, but I only needed to press talk three times, and my friend would be at the other side of the line. As soon as I dialed, Elba responded. A relief feeling invaded my whole being and I rushed to tell her: - I just fell. –Come and help me please. I whispered. Elba laughed; she did not believe me. I knew I had to be quick to call her attention in a more dramatic way, or I would not live to tell about it. –Come quick, I am dying. I told her with the dramatic tone of soap operas and my drama had quick results. Elba understood and with the nervous voice of someone about to cry responded: -I'm on my way. My heart seemed to beat faster; soon my salvation would come.

Soon after, I hung up and prayed silently. This is the moment when believers pray to what they believe in, the point at which we cry to the most high spiritual force, whether we call it God, The Lord, or any other name by which we identify the origin of everything that exists. In my case, I put myself in God's hand. I entrusted my life to him with the faith of someone who wants to live but recognizes the inability to stop death. At the same time, I kept on doing what I could to keep myself alive and conscious until my friend came, breathing as much as my hurting chest allowed me to and trying not to focus on my unbearable pain.

I could not avoid, however, thinking about consequences. What if I die? What needs to be done while I still breathe? What plan can my relatives use to pay for my burial? If I do not have a health plan for my life as a living person, my possibilities of having a plan to pay for my days as a dead person are even less probable. In this side of the world it is expensive to live but it is even more expensive to die, so we better concentrate on living. Hurry up Elba; I have no money for a burial!

### 3. Look for solutions; do not waste time on self-pity.

The phone rang; it was Elba again. She wanted to let me know she had called Manuel, a mutual friend that practiced alternative medicine. Coincidentally, Elba is not a fan of those remedies. She worked at a hospital for a great part of her life, perhaps because of that she thinks that the effective healing is the one provided by doctors. As per me, I love alternative remedies and that would be the first solution I would try. Perhaps a good therapeutic massage from my friend Manuel is all I need. I was thinking about this when my friend arrived. She looked nervous and had been crying; she was not the unshakable friend I had always known.

I told her not to cry and not to worry. My goal was not to waste a single ounce of my scarce energy reserves on self-pity, and I expected those around me to behave accordingly. I had no experience on being on the verge of death, but I had plenty of experience producing and directing TV, film and theater shows. I learned there that to get something done you develop a working plan that has to be followed by your team. My plan was to stay alive; my team was still in the selection process. To be a part of it a positive attitude was a requisite. My friend understood and while still nervous, within seconds she became the strong friend I needed her to be.

-Manuel is coming. Elba said to cheer me up. Meanwhile, she took my hand and gently patted it. Her love fed my hopes of survival. Suddenly, I remembered that my husband Mario should be waiting for me at the Los Angeles airport. What a nice welcoming reception am I going to give him after not seeing him for the past three months! He has been working in a movie as an actor in Phoenix Arizona. The worst thing is that if I make it alive out of this one, my husband will get even by constantly reminding me what I had done. Have you ever had an accident after someone warned you not to do what you were doing?

Well, my husband did not warn me since he was not with me, but he did not know I would paint the wall, so he will probably question me why I did it. I am not a psychic, but I predict the expression, "you shouldn't have," will be heard in many arguments. Hearing those words after falling, getting cut or simply having some sort of an accident almost hurts you more than the fall itself. -Are you okay? -What do you want me to do? Elba asked while caressing my hair. -Could you look for Mario at the airport? I told my friend searching for a solution. -He's coming home today, and I was going to pick him up. My friend did not hesitate: -of course. -Let's just wait for Manuel and then I'll go. That is the attitude I needed to see, the one displayed by those who find solutions. Within minutes Manuel was there, and Elba went to look for Mario at the airport.

### 4. In severe cases, massages should be avoided until the condition of the patient is known.

The specialty of my friend Manuel is healing massages and his dear friend Jackie desperately needed one. Without having to ask for it, Manuel gave me a gentle reflexology massage that began at my feet. I instantly felt the healing warmth of his hands but wished he rushed to massage my stomach; that is where it hurt, not in my feet. I realized my friend was in no hurry. His touch was so light that it felt like he was afraid of massaging me. I had no clue his brief massage of my feet had revealed to him that one or two organs where in bad shape.

How did he know, I had no idea. Some other times, he

had shown me an illustration of how the nerves in our feet are connected to other parts of the body. When he reached the central part of my foot and saw my painful reaction, he knew that an organ in the central region of my body was in bad shape. Because of that, my friend decided, without letting me know, to wait for some X-rays before conducting a complete massage. It was a good thing that he knew when to stop. Had his pride guided him, perhaps he would have done more harm than good. Other people who practice alternative medicine are not so cautious and this works against the patient, since he or she looses valuable time and money in remedies that will not solve an emergency.

I had hoped that alternative medicine would be enough to make me feel better, so I could welcome my husband in a better condition, but I had to change my plans. My husband's welcome back celebration instead of consisting of an exotic dinner where I would accompany him with my glamour high heel shoes, a beautiful dress, jewels and make-up would consist instead of a yummy IV, a faded gown and an indefinite stay at a hospital room.

### 5. If alternative medicine is not enough, do not hesitate to go immediately to the hospital.

My husband arrived at the Los Angeles airport, probably with the smile of someone who finally reunites with his loved one after a long separation. One of our traditions as a couple was to go to a good restaurant after a plane trip; that way we felt like the "good life" continued even after the flight. Finally my king had arrived at his confused kingdom, but his queen could not welcome him, and my friend Elba had to tell him what happened. I am not aware of what she told Mario while driving to our home but based on my husband's look when he saw me, it seemed he was told I was dying. And Mario, with good reason, looked pale, as if he were looking at death itself; he seemed afraid of loosing his wife.

On top of it, not only was his beloved Jackie in bad shape but also the house was "upside down." It was not the glamour welcome the queen had planned; instead of a welcoming sign, there was a half-painted wall, a tray, cans of paint, newspapers, plastic paper covering the floor, paintbrushes scattered around, and a fallen ladder next to a mini moving dolly. The balloons and the happy atmosphere that usually surrounds a welcome back celebration were nowhere to be found. My husband immediately spotted me reclined on the sofa and cautiously approached me, as if he did not want to make a movement that would make me feel worse.

In many other occasions, he would have made a joke so that everyone relaxed, but he seemed too worry to make use of the great humor that characterizes him as a comedian. I think he kissed me on the cheek but it was not the warm welcome we always had. He rapidly went to look for some herb that Javier, a naturopath that was also our friend, had recommended to Manuel so that I drank it to avoid sudden diabetes. It tasted horrible but I drank it, convinced that it would help me.

Up until now, I had hoped I could deal with my accident at home. That wishful thinking had come to an end. Two hours after the accident, I had to accept that I was not feeling better that the possibility of dying was still very real and that alternative medicine would not be enough to save me. At this moment, I needed drastic medical intervention. -Take me to your hospital. I told Elba. -If someone can save me, it will be them.

### 6. ER employees can seem cold; do not take it personal.

We entered the emergency parking area of the USC Medical Center through a small street, reserved only for ambulances. Not thrilled to see a non-emergency vehicle entering the ER vehicle area, one hospital employee told us to remove the car immediately. We all agreed that Elba would come in with me, since we thought I would get a quicker admission that way; meanwhile, Mario and Manuel quickly removed their cars to park them in a "legal" area, far from the angry employee.

At the ER lobby while Elba explained what had happened to an employee, another one brought a bed and asked me basic questions: name, age, what happened, and what I felt. In great pain, I answered all the questions. Elba wanted to add more information but the employee, who behaved more like a robot than a human, did not pay attention and pushed my bed to another area. Elba was not allowed inside; her connections did not take us any further. I had no other choice but to go in alone.

### 7. The emergency rooms of public hospitals are always crowded.

While entering the ER area, I felt overwhelmed. More than a hospital it looked like a war zone, just like the ones shown in films; people screaming in pain, doctors running to save someone, nurses pushing beds with patients with many tubes attached to their bodies as well as their IV's, Intravenous therapy; the infusion of liquid substances directly into a vein. This was, after all, the second busiest ER of the nation. Apparently, the busiest one is in New York, but I could not visualize another emergency room with bigger chaos than this one, unless war zones count. There were people with heart attacks, with bleeding open wounds, with third and four-degree burns, people that had to be saved right now or they would die, and I, so it seemed, could spare a few more minutes.

This was nothing like that "ER" seen on TV where I had worked as an actress once. This was the real deal and it was by far scarier, busier and more intimidating than the TV show. No acting here; this was life and death in the making. This ER was 100 times busier than the one on TV. I had always thought that television exaggerated the ER panorama. Now a reality check was putting everything into perspective. The attendant left me in a corner, next to the door of a bedroom where an elderly man lay with a respirator and other medical equipment attached to his body.

The ER was packed. As they say in my hometown, Puerto Rico: -there is not enough beds for so many people. Actually, no beds and no space, to say that the room was crowded is an understatement. There were no empty rooms or space. Because of that, like most other patients, I had to settle for the only place the personnel found to position my bed: at the middle of a small hallway, next to many other patients. What would my subjects say if they saw me in such precarious condition? I guess appearances did not matter now. My pain was the one that concerned me; it was so acute that I could not contain my tears anymore. I had tried to show my strong side until now. I did not want any drama, but I could not control myself, and I cried like a Magdalene. I made sure I did not make much noise; class is the last thing you lose. My husband and my friend were not allowed in so crying by myself, without an audience, was not fun.

## 8. To get seen, if your case is not visibly severe, you must call someone's attention.

A male nurse attendant passing by saw me, and I pleaded for his mercy by grabbing his hand. I could not speak by now but my eyes were loud and clear: -help me, I'm in pain. He looked at me compassionately and patted my hand. My heart started beating again. This was the first sign of hope. I held onto his hand, just like a wounded person holds onto his possible savior, with the desperate grip of someone who fears proximate death. The nurse looked tenderly at me, and he let go of my hand after a strong grip that seemed to tell me he cared.

Desperate, I tried to grab him again. I did not want to be left alone in this painful place. More than an hour had gone by, and he was the first one to pay attention to me. I could not let go of him. In my mind, this moment felt like those lived by many soldiers in a war zone; this was the crucial point where the wounded soldier would be left behind by his friends or his enemies. If the bombs did not kill him, the vulture would. I was not planning on letting the vulture eat me alive, so I tried to grab the nurse's hand like there was no tomorrow for me if I did not. But I could not move, not even an inch, so I could not reach him.

## 9. You will not get pain medication until tests are made: hold on, it is for your own good.

I had to accept my fate. -Let me see whom can I get. The nurse tenderly told me and then he left. The only thing this patient wanted was a pain medication injection. Why was that so hard to get in a hospital? Doctors passed by me but as much as I tried to call their attention, I seemed invisible to them. Suddenly my bed abruptly moved. -At last, some help. I thought. The vulture would not be eating me after all. But much to my dismay, all I saw was an Asian nurse attendant who was moving my bed so that she could take her patient out of the room next to me.

Since I was situated in the hallway, I was obstructing the entrance of two rooms. As the saying goes: -when it rains, it pours. I was already feeling terrible and instead of helping me, this nurse moves me out of the way as if I were trash that needed to be removed. For what may have been less than fifteen minutes but felt like an hour because of my pain, several people moved me back and forth in the hallway to get me out of the way. I guess I would not have minded the "rides" if I would have been in a better condition but don't be cruel, this moving back and forth hurts. It is not a merry-go-round. Can't you see I am in pain?

Space was scarce; I never seemed to land in a "safe" place. Every sudden movement was total agony, and the attendants were anything but subtle. I guess it was because I did not look as bad as the patients in those other beds, and I did not externalize my pain with some moaning; not only because I did not have enough oxygen to do so but also because I refused to behave like noisy patients. Perhaps because of that the hospital personnel thought I was in better shape.

Suddenly, the nurse attendant I had seen before returned. -You're going in. He said. I smiled. He smiled back, knowing what those words meant for someone in my condition. My pain would soon go away. Even though I did not understand then why was not my pain taken care of as soon as I got to the hospital, I found out, later on, I was not given anything because my pain would let doctors know where to make their tests. In other words, having pain was bad for me but it was good for the doctors, it would tell them the precise location of my aches.

Unaware of that information, I felt great relief when another nurse attendant softly pushed my bed, to take me to the surgery room. A subtle smile covered my face. -I'll make it. I thought as we moved away from the disastrous war zone and headed for friendlier grounds: the surgery room.

## 10. The documents you sign determine your treatment: if you do not understand, ask.

If chaos ruled the hallways, calmness ruled the surgery room. It was like entering an oasis, after having crossed an inhospitable desert. There were many doctors, men and women, but they all looked in charge, no screaming and no drama. I was brought to a room with the most sophisticated medical equipment I had ever seen, huge medical machinery that I had no idea what it was for. A female nurse approached me and talked to me with a sweet tone of voice: -what happened? -I fell from the stairs while painting a wall in my house. I replied, my voice now only a whisper, and I started to cry. Here goes the Magdalene again. -It's going to be okay. The nurse tenderly told me while she held my hand. After that, she changed my clothes and cleaned me up. She did not ask me about the paint on my clothing. Very discreet! Just like so many people I know.

Quickly, a female doctor came and when she saw my tears she said: -Don't cry. -We'll take care of you. I felt relieved. That is exactly what I wanted to hear. -Who will give permission for any procedure? Another nurse asked. -Me. I answered without hesitation; they quickly brought some papers. At that moment my concern was to get rid of the pain; it was not the best time to fill any paperwork, but you are not given any treatment until you do. The documents are to define what is acceptable and unacceptable in the patient's care. This is when the patient decides whether he or she will accept or not blood transfusions, resuscitation and even artificial life. I did not feel well enough to read something so important or to even understand it. It was like signing a life contract without lawyers or people to advise you. But, in order to be helped, I had to express with my signature what I wanted in my treatment, so I received some orientation by asking what every question meant.

-What is this for? I asked. I was dying but still had some common sense in me. I wanted to make sure I was not signing my own death sentence. -In case you need a blood transfusion, you sign if you agree. The nurse told me. I signed. -And this? My interrogation continued. -In case you need plasma. The nurse clarified. I was in urgent need of getting rid of my pain, so I signed all the documents, once the nurse clarified what each question meant. It takes longer when you ask but it works in both parties favor: the patient and the hospital. Signing documents without knowing what they are for is not good for anyone.

After that, many doctors surrounded my bed, every new one with an even more compassionate expression than the next. I felt relieved. -I'm in your hands now, and God put you there, so I know I'm in good hands. I told them, moved by their undivided attention. All the doctors smiled; whether they believed in God or not, they knew I was paying them a compliment. The good chemistry was instantly felt. The pain medicine came or anesthesia perhaps; I could not have cared less what it was, I was finally liberated from my excruciating pain and could finally rest.

### 11. Until a room is assigned to the patient, someone must accompany him/her.

At the same time the hospital staff got ready to operate on me, another kind of operation was taking place in the hallways. Mario, my husband, was trying to get information on my location; but no one seemed to know where his wife Jackie had been relocated. For unknown reasons to him, finding out where I had been taken was practically impossible. No one seemed to know where I was. By then, 73 hours had gone by since my admission to the hospital, and I had already been given pain medication, but Mario had not been told where I had been taken. He had been next to me only a couple of minutes before and had gone to the cafeteria to eat something but when he returned, I had already been taken to the operation room. Since no one stayed with me in that brief period of time, there was no way the personnel could notify where I had been taken. Because of that, it is advisable that someone remains next to the patient at all times until a room is designated. If that someone has to exit, it would be best to leave another person next to the patient so that his/her location is always known. But since our marriage was a beginner in these types of emergencies, my husband had to face the agony of not knowing my whereabouts.

For Mario it was inconceivable that his wife had to sign hospital documents in her medicated state. The king had lost control of his kingdom. The queen had been relocated to another place, without his consent. For less than that, war would have been declared in ancient times. But this was another kingdom and another time; here my king had no power. He had to wait, just like any other plebeian, to find answers to his questions.

Mario asked the reception employees and everyone he found at the hallways, but no one seemed to know where I had been placed. The only thing he was told was that they asked for a relative and since no one answered, I was relocated. For Mario this was unheard of. How could the king protect his queen if he did not know where she was? It was then when he spotted a Hispanic janitor and his fuse as a strategist lit up. He had a plan; he would find me even if he had to hide behind the trash bin, in order to have access to places where visitors where not allowed at that time. It was not a glamour strategy, absolutely underneath his class and kind but in war everything is valid.

The king (Mario) explained to the plebeian (the janitor) his dilemma and luck was on his side; the employee understood his anguish and agreed to hide Mario behind his trash bin. This is how the fascinating journey of "The Quixote" (Mario) and "Sancho Panza" (the janitor) began. Every area they went to had its own "charm." They did not find mills to fight with like the Quixote, but they found far more dangerous obstacles.

Their first stop was the $15^{th}$ floor, to anyone who does not know the hospital simply the highest floor; for those who did know the place, like the janitor, the floor where prisoners of the county received medical treatment while chains and handcuffs restrained their movements. Lord have mercy! If the queen came here, she would surely die faster. Even though some of the prisoners did not look aggressive, a big group of them looked like hired assassins. Some had multiple tattoos that identified them as members of dangerous gangs. Almost all of them had their heads shaven. The vast majority were young men and their aspect was intimidating; many were offenders responsible for stealing or murdering someone. All the prisoners had at least two policemen following their every move. This was an intimidating place to be, and Jackie would certainly not be there, so Mario and the janitor only glanced at the place from the elevator and continued their journey to a friendlier floor.

Safe places were scarce in this adventure. If the $15^{th}$ floor left Mario speechless, for he was not expecting his wife to be treated in a hospital that had convicted felons so close by, what he saw on the next floor disconcerted him even more. It was a morgue; perfect for a horror film, with corpses fresh in their tombs, I mean, in the aluminum boxes or refrigerators. Mario's breathing also sounded as accelerated as someone who is in panic. He had never given any thought to it. The last thing you want to think about when you take a loved one to a hospital, is about the possibility of that person dying there. But that is precisely what happens to many patients and this is the room where they remain, until they are sent to the places chosen by their relatives for burial. Mario was in shock; he did not dare to take a peek at the corpses and quickly left the floor.

It was then when the janitor told Mario that a young lady was just going to the surgery room, and she was Hispanic, had long hair and short height. They both thought they had found Jackie and went there. The janitor then returned to his tasks while Mario remained at the hallway, looking through the glass of a door at a lady that apparently was his wife but was too far away to be recognized by him. He was not allowed in that area, but Mario remained keeping an eye on the young woman for some time. The last thing he expected was that his wife would actually be at the opposite hallway; there he saw Jackie by chance, when he turned his face to follow 4 male nurses that were pushing a bed towards a staff elevator that was nearby. The patient was his beloved wife.

When he saw me, Mario was in shock; I was swollen beyond recognition. Most of my face was covered by an oxygen mask. I had already been operated on and was being transferred to the intensive care room. The queen had been found, but the king did not know whether to celebrate or get ready for the worse.

## 12. Do not fear the machinery at the Intensive Care Unit: although intimidating, it saves lives.

Desperate, my Quixote continued his journey through unexpected kingdoms once more; Sancho Panza did not accompany him this time, there was no need. In this new adventure his Dulcinea was the only one requested. To reach her, his trembling legs cruised the hallway that led to his wife. It looked like an endless voyage to the thresholds of the restricted intensive care unit. Despite hastening his step to reach his wife, his fast walking did not warm him up due to the cold temperature of the hospital. The smell of roses or fresh herbs that he perceived in previous adventures was not present here; rather the funeral scent of alcohol, medicines and cleaning detergents, accompanied by the noise of electrocardiograph devices, went with him in his uncertain path.

His eyes examined each room he found on the way; there was a patient in severe condition in each one. The machinery in those rooms intimidated him more than any villain of his previous adventures; he feared that the claws of those cold devices would equally trap his Jackie. He finally found her; she had been placed in the last room of the hallway. The valiant spirit of my knight collapsed. Sadness invaded his whole being. There was his beloved, connected to several machines, with her abdomen opened up due to an exploratory exam. An artificial respirator covered half of my face. I was totally unconscious. Mario could only stay next to me for 5 minutes. Visits were restricted to give way to my intensive treatment.

Even though the equipment and the delicate state of the patients at the intensive care unit intimidated, knowing that the quality of the medical treatment his wife was receiving was great, was a relief. Mario kept going in and out of the room, without being able to see me awake, until he was no longer allowed to stay since visiting hours were over. His journey was no longer determined by his wishes but by a giant with more power, the hospital. He had to leave, place his lady in the hands of strangers, and hope that upon his return, next day, she would still be alive and perhaps a tender kiss from his lips would awaken her.

### 13. You might think some equipment is killing you, but it will be saving you.

When the sleeping beauty, which did not look so beautiful this time around, woke up, it was not the lips of her beloved what brought her back from the deep sleep. A weird-looking device with the shape of a duck's mouth, made up of hard plastic, abruptly brushed her mouth and woke her up. What an anti-romantic way to come back from a dream! What is that? My first reaction was to quickly remove that thing from my face, just like you get rid of a mosquito or a fly, but the device rapidly came back to me. An Asian nurse was holding it, so I could not remove it. Where did she come from? We had not been introduced, and she was already forcing me to do something I did not want to do. I struggled to remove the device; it gave me the chilling sensation of drowning with air. But the nurse was stronger than this patient. That is not fair! How can this be a fair fight? Can't she see I barely have the energy to keep myself alive? Where will I find the strength to defend me?

My heart was beating so quickly; it felt like it would pop out or even worse that I would get a heart attack. A sudden strong blow of air hit my mouth and nose; its pressure felt like an open fire hose. I had never felt such a strong air stream in my life. You feel like you are choking and your first reaction is to protect your life getting rid of it. Wait a minute, supposedly lives are saved here not taken away; either this nurse was not informed or else my worst enemy hired her. What a stubborn woman. Cannot she see my desperation? The skinny woman, without paying attention to my concern, placed the strange looking respirator on my face. Is she a serial killer or what?

Can you at least soften the rough moment with an explanation of your actions? Just be creative, give me a good reason to accept your device. The nurse totally ignored my concern, perhaps because I could not express myself with words but the desperate gesticulation of my hands was quite clear; I did not want that thing on my face.

I believe the crickets outside the hospital were more diligent paying attention to my concern. So that is your response? If you do not show your white flag, this means war. I thought. My arms served as shields to repel the approach of the trespasser and my hands were able to remove the artifact while my eyes filled up with tears. -You're mean. I told the nurse. These words seemed to have hurt the nurse more than a weapon, since she immediately stepped out with teary eyes while replying: - I'm not mean.

### 14. The patient is in a vulnerable condition: do not argue with him/her.

My husband Mario and Elba came in. Just about time! Some good allies came to free me from this unexpected villain. -What happened? Asked my friend. With the eloquence of a drugged dying person I told her, as best as I could, what just happened. With the understanding of someone who knows you well, they were both able to decipher my babble and upset with the incident, they exited to demand a better treatment for their loved one. If this nurse thought there was nobody to defend me, they will prove her wrong. I felt weak, out of breath and in pain. I was in need of all the understanding I could get; maybe that nurse would not give it to me, but my friend and my husband would. Good luck valiant warriors! Capture the enemy soldier and subject her to the rules of the new regime!

A few minutes later my friend and my husband returned. -Shame on you. They said. -That nurse, according to the doctor, is one of the best nurses in the hospital. -She just wanted to help you. They both said. Did I hear right? It turns out the villain of the novel is now the good one. What does that make me then, the villain? Those words, said in combination by both my friend and my husband, sounded like high treason to me. Red alert; there are two deserters in my battalion. In less than five minutes this stranger had more credibility than I did to my friend but most importantly, to my husband.

What about that violent drowning sensation I felt? Did not anyone care to find out what the patient was experiencing? Don't they know the world spins around me right now? Whether they are right or not is beyond the question. Would you tell someone who wants to commit suicide, go jump from a cliff? You probably would not because the person would follow your advice. Well, this was my cliff. I was in a severe condition, felt highly vulnerable and totally unstable physically, mentally and emotionally. So when my husband tried to add some words, regarding the angelical qualities of that nurse and my demonic traits, I exploded. —This is the second time you betray me. I told my husband. I sounded as tragic as the villain of a soap opera.

Mario was speechless; something not normal in him for he always has something to say. But he knew he was in trouble. I am not referring to any unfaithfulness on his side as a husband; I was referring to another kind of treason. Countless times, my husband has sided with me in all sorts of matters. Regardless of whether he agreed or not, he very often found a way to side with me. I have done the same for him, equally often. But this time, he did the same thing he had done many years before and this incident opened up that old wound.

## 15. Beware of volunteers; they can be the apple of discord between families.

Immediately remembered the time when my husband was the one in a hospital bed and a female volunteer approached him. Mario was really ill and needed to rest, and the volunteer started to talk about God and salvation in what sounded to me like a very aggressive and ungodly tone. I did not appreciate the aggressive intrusion and let the volunteer know that my husband needed to rest. She went nuts and told me that I was the devil and suggested to my husband that he would be better off without me. What did she just say? Instead of sharing God's love, this "preacher" is encouraging a divorce. Has not she read the phrase -what God has join together, let no man tear asunder?

I could not believe what I had heard. I was furious but kept my calm, even though the thought of breaking every bone in that woman's body felt like the right thing to do. Luckily for her, I was not the devil as she had suggested, so I did not defend myself with violence or cursing. I used something more civilized in my defense, the adequate use of conversing. With a philosophical tone, just like the ones frequently used in social media, I expressed to her that I was not even sure hell existed.

I did not tell her my true conviction; my goal was to discourage her quickly, so she would leave right away. Very often I have being successful getting rid of annoying people, so I was convinced my tactic of showing a cold attitude, accompanied by a rejecting language, would be enough to get rid of the intruder. I mean, after all, she is supposed to be a Godly woman and therefore would not offend me more than she had and would understand she had to leave.

How naïve of me or should I say, what a complete fool; my words did not appeal to her common sense, and my husband did not back me up. He was probably feeling as vulnerable as I felt now at the hospital so instead of telling this woman to go away, which would have probably been the right thing to do, he allowed her to stay, and his wife was the one who had to leave the room. What a great sight, the intruder stays, and the owner of the house has to leave.

Now the roles had switched; the wife was the one in a hospital bed. Mario had done exactly what he did years ago; he had sided with someone else he had just met, before he even listened to his wife's point of view. Troy will burn! Between the medications and my anger, I cannot recall if I was so politically correct as I was years ago. I did, however, make sure to ask to be left alone. I needed time to ease my fury or else the punches belonging to the careless volunteer, would be received by my loved ones instead: metaphorically speaking, of course.

## 16. Being PATIENT
### means to tolerate, endure, withstand.

My husband and my friend left. I have to give them credit for it; they perceived the tsunami before it annihilated everything: my anger would have created a catastrophe in my regular self. But now, my body was not in its optimal condition so continuing with my anger did not make sense. Because of that, I breathed as deeply as my aching lungs allowed me to, they hurt and angry even more! A few minutes later, the nurse returned. Oh God, I think you are testing my tolerance, and I am hanging myself. To tolerate: endure, put up with, resist, bear; I knew what the word meant but putting it into practice was a big feat. I assumed that if I did not agree it would be worse, so I remained still and with calmness, not frequent in me, allowed the nurse to place that horrible device on my mouth and nose.

I guess this was the fiery ordeal I had to pass, learning to tolerate. I felt like the victim that has no other option but to submit herself to the executioner. Fortunately, after the storm the sun comes out and mine came in the form of a beautiful and slender young nurse that came to my rescue.

### 17. Even though treatments hurt, bear them: in the long run you will feel better.

If angels were human, they would surely show up like Michelle did to me; a young nurse with Hispanic or Caucasian features, of a sweet and melodic voice. Looking very calmed, she approached me slowly, with a warm smile on her lips. She did not look like the menacing "killer nurse," the previous one. I immediately felt safe with her. That was, of course, until she showed me what she had in her hands. It was something that looked like wire hangers when they are fully extended, like aluminum wires. She showed them to me and warned me: -it's going to be very uncomfortable. Her soothing tone of voice was enough to convince me to calmly accept the procedure. After all, someone with that beautiful voice and presence would not hurt me, right?

A beat later, the painful and uncomfortable wire, with another metal at its tip, slowly went down my throat, without anesthesia or pain medication. Ouch, ouch, that hurts! It was, doubtless, the most uncomfortable pain I had ever experienced in my life. So much for trusting sweet voices and harmless looks! No wonder the witches in children's stories first appear as young, beautiful and sweet sounding women. As soon as you fall for their charm, they show their true dark side. Snow White, yeah right! You were the witch with the apple or the poisoned wire.

But I did not want to let the loving nurse down; after all, she had warned me. I patiently waited for the device to be removed; the same way injections are quickly removed. Am I passing my test, God? Look at how tolerant I have become; a minute has gone by. OK, the device is still there. I have already covered my tolerance dues. Please someone remove this wire from my throat! I opened my eyes as wide as I could, to let the nurse know that it was time to remove it. -Not yet, it has to remain there. She told me. The first thing that came to my mind was: -you tricked me. I thought you were the heroine of this story, only villains in this film.

I cried in desperation and tried to speak but the device did not allow me to. But I had to say something. This wire or cable was not going to prevent me from complaining. I managed to utter some words while trying to reach the device. —Remove it; it hurts. I told her. -I know. The nurse replied, undermining the importance of my complaint while preventing my hands from removing the device. -But it has to stay there for a while. She said without moving a muscle. She reacted with the same indifference of the previous nurse, have they been cloned? At first very sweet but once she got what she wanted, she did not want to please me. I had to put up with that wire because I had no other choice. With time, however, I realized how positive was the fact that I endured that wire. It freed my throat from having to undergo a tracheotomy, in other words, a process by which the throat is cut to make a hole that allows a person to breathe.

### 18. If you try to remove your equipment, you will be tied up to the bed.

The Magdalene in me came out once more but this time with desperation. Tears of frustration covered my eyes while I tried, with the little strength I had, to remove either the respirator or the wire down my throat. Fortunately, as the saying goes: "even the longest night comes to an end." My night did not last forever. Fatigue won me over enough to not realize I had been tied down to my bed, to prevent my urge to remove the devices I felt were killing me but were ironically used for keeping me alive.

My mind was unconscious but my body was not and my hands constantly tried to remove the equipment. I had to be tied down to my bed. In some way, I am glad I fell unconscious during the incident; it would have been a shame to witness being tied up.

## 19. You will ask many questions but will get few answers: you must be PATIENT.

Later on, when I regained consciousness and those devices were removed, I told Michelle, the nurse, how frightful my experience with those devices had been. –That tube down the throat, what does it do? I asked. The nurse hesitated a bit in her response. Then I continued: -because had I not controlled my heart with my mind, I would have had a heart attack. Yeah right, how knowledgeable; I had just arrived at the hospital and already was an expert in medicine and mind control. Since the nurse did not say anything, I continued talking with the wisdom of those patients that think of themselves as if they were doctors because they have already visited the doctor many times, those that self-proclaim themselves experts in medicine without studying it, doctor and expert in mind control with only one medical procedure.

-That tube has saved many lives. The nurse replied. That did not answer my question, so I tried to find another response. -And I'm sure it has caused a lot of heart attacks as well. I said, hoping to obtain an answer that would provide me with more information. The nurse only smiled; because of that, I decided to formulate the same question in a different way. -I just want to know if there is any other way to achieve the same result, without such a painful and risky procedure. Because if a device makes the patient feel so bad that she just wants to let go and die, then maybe it is time to find another device to cure her. At that moment, I was seriously trying to improve the treatment conditions of patients; because of that, I dared to express my opinion.

The nurse listened to my request attentively; I assumed it was because she rarely had a patient that described what she felt with such admirable eloquence. This was a happier thought than admitting she listened to me because she had no other choice. I kept making questions. I do not recall receiving any concrete response, and I did not understand why I received so many evasive answers. My master's degree is in Public Communications, which means I love to communicate with others. I think I even added a sophisticated tone to my interrogation so that the nurse would know about my education. I assumed I was brilliant and expected an acknowledgement from the nurse that my questions were valuable, and she would discuss my concerns with her superiors.

The nurse kept smiling while she took care of an open wound I had in my belly. That wound consisted of a round hole where a drinking glass could fit in and through it the internal part of my stomach could be seen. This hole had to be kept open, with the help of gauze, so doctors could treat the multiple infections that my abdomen had. Michelle was curing this wound while I continued my conversation. I interpreted her smile as the acknowledgment that my point was well founded, and I added: -I think this is a three way relationship: the doctor, the nurse and the patient. I said and finished my speech with my "punch line:" -you have to listen to all of them, specially the patient because he/she is the one experiencing pain, and I really think that tube down the throat traumatizes the patient too much. Case closed, I thought.

I have no clue on whether my "speech" caused an impression on the nurse or not. At least I got it out of my system. I was exhausted and the tender smile and dedicated care I received from this health worker while she cured my wounds and re-filled the medications that went into my veins, was all I needed to feel safe. Whether she had a response for me or not, regarding what the tube did or did not do, was not revealed at that moment. I understood that even if I had thousands of questions, the answers would be received at a moment not decided by me. Now I had to simply trust those taking care of me and hope their decisions were the right ones. At that moment I just had to be PATIENT.

## 20. Motivate the ill even if they are unconscious, for they can hear you.

Being PATIENT is not easy, in any of the meanings of that word; it entails waiting, a concept that is not appreciated by desperate people like me. The only time when waiting did not exasperate me as much was when I was unconscious. I guess that was the time to test my loved ones;

my husband's test, for example, was when he saw me with the wire in my throat. He was next to me at the intensive care unit and witnessed how I started to fall unconscious. I guess the discomfort with the incident of the "killing nurse" was long gone, since Mario only showed sadness in his face as he saw the bad physical shape I was in.

When he saw me crying, weak and softly complaining of pain, he told me: -you can't go yet; there are people here who love you. I could not bear the pain anymore. -Let me go. I mumbled softly and started to close my eyes, until my husband could only see the whites of them. -You can't go. Mario begged. -You still have to make your films. At that moment I fell unconscious. Mario nervously continued to speak to me; he mentioned the names of three scripts I had written that had not been made yet; he listed them as if they were a list of reasons for me to remain among the living.

Human beings can hear their loved ones, even while unconscious. I discovered that at that moment. Mario must have insisted loud and clear because although I did not remember "giving up" and just wanting to let go, I did have a clear memory of repeating what he had told me while I was in another place.

## Chapter 2:

## How to Optimize the Patient's Experience

### 21. A patient claiming to have been in another dimension could give valuable information.

I MUST CLARIFY THAT those who really know me are aware that I would never dare to talk about something so sacred if I had not experienced it. As a matter of fact, those who believe in a higher spiritual force, regardless of what religion they profess, know that the consequences for anyone who invents something about sacred matters are so terrible that it has been said, in many of them, it would be better for these people if they had never been born. I personally would not even dream about challenging that. I am not telling you this so that you might believe in what I believe. I just hope that knowing how I feel about this matter will convince you on how important it is for me to tell you the truth about my experience on the other side, in the spiritual world that many call heaven.

If a patient ever tells you he/she was there, do not assume he/she is crazy, drugged or lying. The patient in severe condition is more sensitive than other humans. If you insult that person, he/she will refrain from saying what is going on. How can you treat something if you do not even know it exists? Because of that, listen to those patients; you have nothing to lose and a great deal of valuable information to gain. In the worst-case scenario, this information will keep you up to date on what motivates or scares the patient.

This is what I saw in my unconscious state: there was a vast night like space around me but far from making me feel scared, it relaxed me. I am not talking about a sizable space; I am referring to a space so big that it looked infinite. I think there were millions of stars shining in the sky if not more, but I cannot recall clearly since all I cared about was communicating with a light that shined upon me. Do not ask me where I got the idea that I had to communicate with this radiant beam of light that seemed to be coming from the upper part of the sky; I just knew I had to do it.

It felt like I was programmed to react to this light. My spirit, soul or whatever you wish to call our spiritual essence knew how I was supposed to react in this kind of encounter; I also knew who I would be meeting with and how I had to behave. My meeting would be with someone worthy of all reverence. My physical body immediately assumed a praying position; my knees were bend, and I was supporting my arms on a small piece of furniture made of wood, like the ones used for praying by many religious denominations around the world. I immediately put my hands together in praying position. I even knew that I had to lower my head as a sign of respect to the one I wanted to communicate with. I felt like I was the only person in the universe while the light shined upon me. I immediately knew this light was God, even though I could not see a face. I have no clue on how I knew this; I just knew. This meeting would occur at a "holding area" for spirits whose destiny's has not been decided yet; at least that was my interpretation. I knew I was not dead. Once again, I have no idea how I knew. I credit my soul for guiding me on what to do but as far as I knew, I had never been at this place. That is what I thought then. But later on, I remembered this was my second time at this place.

    I was around seven years old the first time I visited this place. Back then; I spoke to the same light in my dreams. Contrary to my actual encounter, when I was 7 years old I did not visit the infinite space that seems nighttime. My meeting during my childhood happened at the backyard of my parent's house; I guess it was because I was a little girl. Darkness scares kids. It was a vivid encounter that I could remember clearly when I awoke. Back then, I opened my eyes widely and woke up with a feeling of urgency.

In my childhood room, I slept next to my twin sister, and she was the first person I saw when I woke up from my dream. To me the encounter had been real. Because of that, I was surprised to see my sister soundly asleep. I thought it was not possible for her to be next to me and not to be awaken by the powerful voice that came from the light and in a very relaxing tone told me: -you are good but in order to be saved, you have to help others get salvation. I knew, even at this early age, the one who had spoken was God, but I did not know how to achieve what I had been ordered.

## 22. If you want to live, do not give up while there is life.

Many years later, I was facing the same powerful light and to tell you the truth, I did not think I had done enough to get salvation for other people. Time to start praying and ask the light to give me another opportunity to remain among the living. Coincidentally, I repeated the same tasks that my husband had told me, as the reasons why I should be allowed to stay in my body and not die yet. Besides the reasons I expressed, so the All powerful would allow me to stay on earth, I let him know I wanted to live not because I was afraid of dying but because I still had unfulfilled goals that I wanted to achieve in this lifetime. -Let it be your will, which is also mine. I said in my prayers and waited with patience, until now uncommon for me, for God's answer.

No response was given from above; I only felt an immense loving force embracing me but as much as I focused nothing else, natural or supernatural, happened that showed me a decision had been made on whether this was my moment to die or not. I had to wait; demanding quick responses does not seem to work in this dimension. I kept praying in my unconscious state, holding onto my life while on the earthly side my husband kept talking as loud as he was allowed, to bring me back to consciousness.

I was at a place without worries, and my husband and my friend Elba were at the chaotic world of life and death in a hospital. I wanted to return to my body, because I was convinced my mission on earth had not been fulfilled yet. At the same time, I felt super comfortable on the other side, not a single bone hurt there. If I came back, my whole body would ache; including parts I did not even know existed. Elba cried sadly, foreseeing her friend would not survive. I did not react but the equipment attached to me assured her I was still alive. My condition was serious; my surgery had revealed my pancreas was severely damaged and my lungs were not working properly.

Since I felt none of these ailments on the other side, I was stubborn enough to keep asking God to let me return to my body. While The Lord decided, my doctors began to remove liquids coming from my pancreas, by placing a tube that would clean my stomach from unwanted spills of damaged organs; two tubes would get the now dangerous pancreatic liquids out of my body and a feeding tube would feed me fortified milk that went straight to my stomach, without going through my mouth. Therefore, I was not going to enjoy the taste of food either. I knew that remaining in my body would represent a painful rehabilitation but it was my intention to live, and I would not give up while I was alive. If death comes quicker to those who wish for it, with me it would have to get in line, for I would not give it any reason to include me in its group.

## 23. A great deal of patients fear that their caretakers will harm them.

I suddenly came out of the holding area where I was in my unconscious state and when I opened my eyes, the first thing I saw were many odd devices attached to my body. I was back at the hospital. God was granting me permission to stay another while on earth. This deserved a celebration. I tried to move but I could not. Celebrating was not possible in this unfortunate body; every part hurt, and I could barely breathe with the help of an uncomfortable oxygen mask I had on.

I assumed it was late at night since I could not hear the noises that characterize hospitals during the day. I looked around, trying to scout the place and spotted a woman sleeping next to me; it was the nurse I had accused of being evil, the killer nurse, the same one that initially put the respirator on my face. Oh God, I just got here from the other side, and you place me next to this woman? Can't you see that she is ahead of me because she can move and I cannot? I panicked. What if this nurse sends me right back to the other side but this time never to return to planet earth? Between the gravity of my condition and the medication I felt so vulnerable that I feared someone would harm me, especially if that someone was the last person I mistreated just before falling unconscious.

A patient's frailty makes her/him fear the caretakers; because of that, when I saw the killer nurse I panicked. I needed my diaper changed, and the employee approached me. Would she kill me with a dirty diaper? The nurse, not knowing about my paranoia, rapidly looked for baby wipes and heated them up in a microwave. She cleaned me up softly with them and the heat of the wipes protected my skin from the cold temperature in the room. I felt so guilty! My fear visualized a possible murderer when in fact she was helping me, even though I was unpleasant to her. She was not mean, as I had called her before; the nurse was just doing her job. The only thing that maybe she could have done differently, was the way she communicated with me; had she warned me sweetly about that horrible respirator, I would not have perceived her as a threat to my life but since she did not say anything and only struggled with me to keep that horrible air hose over my face, I assumed she meant to be mean.

As I saw her changing my diaper, without a single complaint, visual or verbal, I understood she did not mean to harm me. Suddenly, the feeling of anger I had towards her was replaced by a feeling of admiration and gratitude. We tenderly looked at each other, and I dare to say we both understood what it was to be in each other's shoes.

**24. The best recipe for a patient is love and support from his/her loved ones.**

Next day's morning I woke up to a happier reality: my mother and my twin sister had flown in from Puerto Rico and Florida to be with me. My mother's name is Violeta; a tall and beautiful white woman of amber eyes, short blond hair and a loving maternal look. My sister's name is Janet, and she is attractive (if I say otherwise I would be working against me since she is my twin) skinny, short height, dark eyes and short brown hair with some blond highlights. Her executive position molds her confident gaze; however, my presence in such bad shape, at that bed of the intensive care unit, melted her business attitude; there, she was only my tender sister.

Because of my delicate condition, visits were limited to five minutes each hour. If a relative wished to see any of the patients in this unit more than once, they had to wait until next hour when they would get another 5 minutes. Mario, my husband, had already spent three days without sleep because he did not want to miss that brief time he was entitled to per hour.

Violeta and Janet were just beginning this routine and dedicated that first visit to confirm how much they loved me, how they were going to be by my side until I got better and how everyone was praying for my speedy recovery. Neither one called my attention for having climbed the ladder or for the mess I had left at home or for anything else. They dedicated this time to communicate to me how important I was to them, to the world and how necessary was my presence here. Staying among the living is a pleasure with such encouragement; how great it is to be reminded only of the good, without taking into consideration the bad. My relative's supporting and loving words were more effective than any medication.

## 25. A public hospital treats conditions with equal or bigger expertise than a private one.

Just after five minutes, a nurse came to inject me with some medication. My mother and my sister knew they had to leave. They were also exhausted from traveling and said goodbye with the promise of coming back the next day. Everything seemed peaches and cream with the presence of my mother and my twin at the hospital: I was not aware of their worries. However, they had many, even though they never told me. None of them knew my condition was so severe, and they were not happy with my husband's decision to keep them out of the loop for a couple of days, to postpone notifying them about my accident. My mom and my sister felt they had equal right to be involved from the beginning.

Janet was also worried about the hospital's choice. She did not expect me to be at a public one that happened to be so crowded. If the choice had been hers, I would have been at the best room of a private hospital; she would not be sparing off in my care. My point of view was a different one; first of all, a public hospital offered the financial tranquility I needed. It was not my intention to increase my stress with the substantial load of additional expenses incurred in many private hospitals.

But beyond financial reasons, my feeling was that I had more opportunities of survival here. While some friends that are doctors had commented to my relatives they had never heard of a case like mine, this hospital had already treated a similar one. Here they serve so many people with difficult conditions daily that I dare say they have more practice than other luxurious hospitals. Besides, they have more equipment than a private hospital. It was my conviction that this public hospital had as much or more expertise than any of the expensive ones to save me.

## 26. Provide happy faces to patients, sad ones worries or irritates them.

Each member of my family had a different point of view about where and how I should be taken care of. Family ties would be put to the test like never before; there were clashing personalities, cultures and genders (in my immediate family all are women except my husband, the only man.) My relatives had to handle those differences so they would not interfere with my rehabilitation. My mother and sister exhibited a big smile and my interpretation of that was that there were no problems. My husband, however, did not show the super happy face my sister and my mom had. Perhaps it was because he had not slept in several days or because he had to take charge of the mess inherited by my accident; the truth is, he displayed a sad face I did not like in the slightest bit and even irritated me.

I was not aware of the chaos my recklessness had caused. The pain and great discomfort I was experiencing made me focus on my condition; because of that, I did not understand the suffering face of my husband. If the one in bed was his wife, why did my better half looked in worse condition? Usually, Mario is a very funny guy; he is a comedian and always has a joke or funny way to react to everything. That was the husband I wanted next to me, not this impostor that seems to have come out of a tragic novel. It has been said that love shall conquer all; this was a good situation to test that premise. There was plenty of love here; the challenge was to express it so that it would not affect my rehabilitation. Luckily, I felt so happy with my relative's visit that on the next day I woke up with my first improvement since being admitted to the hospital.

### 27. Patients who think about spiritual matters concentrate less on their physical state.

It was barely five thirty in the morning but since I practically had not been able to sleep because I could not breathe properly and felt so bad, it was very late. With great anticipation, I looked at the still foggy sky, eager to see the first rays of the sun and with them begin my day. When they finally showed up and started to warm up the window in front of me, I felt some relief but at the same time, I was very restless; I had the feeling God would show something big to the world through me, and I had no clue of what it was.

I did not know if my anguish, for feeling in such bad physical shape, triggered my mind's need to concentrate on spiritual matters. The truth is that for some unexplainable reason, my need for holding onto the spiritual world was stronger than thinking about my pain; the stronger it got, the more my mind thought about themes like life after death. I concluded that my soul wanted me to get ready, in case I had to leave the physical world to reintegrate into the spiritual one.

The first doctor that saw me that morning was Jeremy.

His kind smile went perfectly with his beautiful physical traits; he was blond, tall and had green eyes, or were they blue? Do they audition these handsome doctors? My health was delicate but that did not stop me from feeling happy to open my eyes to such beautiful visual spectacle. This doctor was the youngest of his group, and he was usually the first one to arrive. He asked me how I felt, with the optimistic tone that identified him, and I answered that I was anxious.

My entire body was trembling, and I did not know why; yet, I had no doubts it was not because of the doctor's presence. I found out what had me so restless after Jeremy formulated another question: -why are you anxious? Then, as if by magic, my mind knew the answer: -because today is God's day. What did I mean by that? I had no clue. The words came out of my lips, but I ignored how they had gotten there. The doctor smiled at me. In California, in the "normal" world, just mentioning the word God could be as dangerous as lighting a fire in a room filled with dynamite. I am not saying people do not believe in God but there are so many religious denominations and spiritual institutions, voicing one's personal view can be the wick that ignites an unpleasant clash.

Fortunately, I was in front of a doctor and that meant in front of me was a person that due to his education and training mastered the art of not showing his personal points of view. Instead, he smiled and my interpretation of this sweet gesture was that he cared about me enough to not contradict me. In my case, I also had many years of education, but I was not even close to the degree of prudence of this doctor. Because of that, it was normal for me to express my spirituality openly. Truth being said, my wish to focus on spiritual matters made me dedicate less time to thinking about my physical pain.

## 28. Every device removed represents a major achievement for the patient.

The time I had been at this hospital had taught me not to focus on spiritual conversations with doctors since none of them participated actively in the chat. Because of that, I opted for talking about my physical condition. I wanted my oxygen tank removed; the plastic hoses bothered my nostrils. The respirator, with the shape of a duck's mouth that gave me the sensation of drowning with air, had been removed already. I had also been liberated from the tube that painfully scraped my throat, courtesy of Snow White, I mean Michelle, the nurse with the sweet voice with not so sweet intentions. What a relief it was to be able to swallow, even if it was just saliva, without that horrible taste of metal in my mouth! My plan, this time around, was to use my feminine tenderness to disarm the masculine armor of the doctor and get him to remove those little hoses from my nose.

With the sweetest voice and the most innocent attitude I could come up with, I told Jeremy: -could you please remove the oxygen? I no longer need it. I spoke sweetly to him but with a hint of the arrogance of a patient who feels healed. -Remove it? The young doctor was not sure he had heard right. —Yes, please, it hurts, and I don't need it anymore. I confirmed with a subtle begging voice and a tender look that moved as much as the cat with boots in the animated feature film Shrek. -Let me see what I can do. The doctor answered while exiting the room.

I felt so happy when a male nurse came and removed my oxygen, a few minutes after I had made the request to the doctor: "ask and you shall receive." There is a lot of wisdom in those words. A mask and a hose would no longer restrict my movements and that meant that I was getting better. Besides, it was a great motivation to be able to show myself to my loved ones without devices on my face; to see the one you love with so much equipment attached, scares anyone. I can barely wait to see their faces.

### 29. Morphine will initially make you feel "happy."

When my relatives came in, big smiles immediately covered their faces. I thought that having the devices removed had been a total success. I did not realize that something else was motivating their smiles. It turns out that after some employees removed my oxygen, they gave me a device to remove the phlegm of my throat; it looked like the instrument dentists use to suction any unwanted liquids from the patient's mouth. Cautiously, I tried it and was glad to find out that using it was not uncomfortable in any way; it removed phlegm coming from my chest and prevented me from choking with them.

I felt so happy using it; the device was long and thin and when I put it in my mouth, it looked like the smoking pipes the stars of old cinema smoked. Yeah right, a Marlene Dietrich with her pipe. I had never smoked, perhaps because of that my relatives laughed when they saw me. I do not think cigarettes are glamorous but just like other people I associate smoking pipes with the famous actresses of the 40's or 50's. To complete the abstract scene of my "glamour smoking," I was high because during the previous night I had been injected with morphine, to help me get rid of the pain. The medication seemed to finally be working and as the morning progressed I felt "happier." I had no clue the morphine was the one responsible for my unexpected "happiness." I had never been so medicated in my life, so it did not cross my mind this was the first sign of a pain killer drug. The truth is I started to behave and talk stranger than usual.

I did not realize that even though I gave these impressive speeches, the moment was not the most adequate one to give them, could it be because at that instant my diaper was being changed? My relatives were smiling, and I was convinced my speech was entertaining and funny. Well, at least they were decent and let me think my wise words were the ones that had them paying attention. Since in my mind I was convinced that my speeches were a total success, I searched for a bigger audience. My first spectator would be the first doctor or nurse that came into my room.

## 30. Drinking a tea of sour herbs might prevent you from getting diabetes.

The doctor came to see me once more. Such is life; he would be the one to enjoy my "recently acquired" wisdom. The doctor had returned because he wanted to show me the results of several tests. He seemed pleased; this patient had responded favorably to the surgery. The first battle against the devastating results of my accident had been won. Besides being alive (the most evident positive outcome) I showed no signs of diabetes, even though my pancreas was fully split in half.

If you do not know how the pancreas and diabetes are related, do not worry; most people, including me, have no idea. If you know what is the relationship between the pancreas and diabetes, congratulations, you can skip the next sentence since you know something I had to learn thanks to an uncomfortable accident. What was explained to me at the hospital, I do not know if it was the doctor, some nurse, or if I looked for it in the Internet, or asked everyone I could find, or the sum of all of the above was that the pancreas produces enzymes and hormones that process everything a person eats. One of those hormones is insulin, which in turn controls diabetes.

Of course, I learned this after the accident; had I been asked before what the pancreas was, the most I could have answered was that it was an organ of the body. Well, it turns out that my precious organ, called pancreas, kept its capacity to create insulin. The doctor that attended me on that occasion got upset at a nurse that had forgotten to inject me with a medication to avoid sudden diabetes. Apparently, human beings can get diabetes with a big scare and my accident qualified as that type of incident. Fortunately, the herb that my friends had given me before we came to the hospital was to avoid sudden diabetes. Its name is Fenugreek, and it is used to lower the glucose levels in the blood without medication. Thanks to my friends, I did not develop this condition. I liked the idea of not having developed diabetes since as a child I had seen my grandmother suffer a great deal with this condition, but I had no clue on how fortunate I was. Doctors performed the diabetes test twice on me; they could not believe I had not developed it. Since my pancreas was now split, it was almost impossible for it to exercise its functions fully. As a matter of fact, when doctors decided to feed me through a tube, they did it because they were convinced the pancreas could not do its job in its present state.

This organ, which relevance was unknown to me, suddenly acquired great importance, even more so when I was notified that contrary to other organs like the liver, the pancreas does not re-generate. Oh Lord, what does that mean? Is there hope for me or not?

### 31. Medications bring concentration and memory problems to patients.

—How are we feeling now? The doctor brought me back to planet earth with that question. —Great. I replied; however, I felt perturbed because I could not concentrate; my thoughts lacked order and this caused me great anxiety. -God bless you Jeremy. I told the doctor while he looked at me with a smile; not even my lack of concentration made me forget to thank him for what they were doing for me. -I feel good. I kept on telling him. —Actually, I was cured since day number two. "God told me." I assured the doctor. How did I come up with that number? I had no clue, but I figured that my mind was trying to remember something The Almighty had revealed to me when I was on the other side. But my memory was a blank, and I had no idea why.

-Really? The doctor replied and his word brought me back to the hospital. He was always so prudent and seemingly interested in what his patient had to say. -Of course. I answered. -But no one believes me. I said this because I had told my family but since none, other than my holy mother, manifested their happiness for such a quick healing time (two days to heal from a split pancreas is a record time) I guessed no one else believed me. Whether they believed me or not, I was certain that while unconscious God had given me a very specific mission to fulfill. Focusing on this mission was the most important thing to do. I could not recall what my mission was, but I was convinced God would clarify to me on that day what I was supposed to do for him in my aching body.

### 32. The mental state test, made by doctors, determines treatment options.

The doctor replied to my discovery with a question. How smart of him. If you do not have an answer, ask another question and perhaps you will find the response you are looking for. Simple but just brilliant! -Where are you? He asked me. These types of questions had already been formulated to me at the hospital. I knew what was coming, a series of questions doctors asked to make sure the patient was conscious and within "reality." At least that was my impression at that moment. I was convinced those silly questions were to find out if the patient was delusional. Because of that, I was proud to know the answers, so they would know I was not crazy.

With a huge smile and the attitude of an informed patient, I responded: -I am at the LAC-USC Medical Center. -Why are you here? The doctor's questioning continued. -I fell while painting a wall. I was quick to answer, and Jeremy was quicker to formulate the next question: -what's today date? -I don't have a calendar but it must be October $3^{rd}$ or $4^{th}$. I replied with the happiness of a girl that has already answered several questions correctly and knows she is going to pass the test. The doctor smiled as well when he recognized in me the confidence of previous patients that celebrate what they interpret to be the first indication of an improvement in their condition.

I did not know then that these questions are to find out the mental state of the patient and to determine if the treatment she is receiving, such as medications, is adequate or if something needs to be changed. But since that information was not available to me at that moment, answering these questions was my way of proving I was not delirious. I did notice something and that was that the doctor changed subjects and took our conversation from a spiritual-religious focus to a medical conversation with his patient. You win some, you lose some; he took away my opportunity to include him in my spiritual salvation of the world and brought me instead to his own way of saving the universe, tending to his patient's health.

The doctor got answers, not only through the questions he asked me but also through my behavior; every movement of mine let him know how much was the medication altering myself.

## 33. Too much pain medication will prevent you from discerning between reality and fantasy.

—I'll be back soon with the team. Jeremy, my doctor, said. He was referring to four other doctors who worked with him on my operation. As he was leaving, I experienced much anxiety, for the pain medication was mixing my thoughts and creating, at the same time, an alternate world; somehow, my confused mind had managed to achieve all of my goals at the same time at this hospital. On the one hand, I had the intention of rewarding the good care doctors and nurses were giving me through a thank you letter I would sent to them, to their superiors and even to the mass communication media of the whole world. Why not? I was strongly medicated and because of that I thought everything was possible; therefore, if I was going to send a thank you letter, the right thing would be that the whole world knew it.

I must admit that under medication I was as ambitious as I am in real life but lacked the limits established by reality. At the same time I wanted the universe to know how well I was being treated at the hospital, I also thought I was capable of achieving all of my professional goals. I thought I could achieve in a single day and with a single event what had taken me an entire lifetime and had not fully fulfilled yet, to produce one of my film scripts with the support of a well-known

Hollywood studio with big Hollywood stars. Isn't that something? My medicated mind dreamed big.

In real life I had been lucky enough to be able to make several independent films with great success. Perhaps because of it, my medicated mind saw as normal that from the intensive care unit I had found great budgets, studios and stars for my next movie. I was convinced that the hospital staff and the celebrities I wanted involved in my film were already working together, in order to make all of my goals come true. How accommodating was my brain! There were no obstacles for my mind. A lot of morphine must have come in through my veins because having doctors and celebrities working side by side, in a hospital and to fulfill the wishes of someone without great fame or fortune, is not a common sight.

The previous day, my pain had been so acute that when I was given one of those hoses with a button to press so that more medicine goes into your blood, I could not stop pressing. Therefore, I was in a "trip" where no passport was needed and as the morning progressed, I felt better and better. As we say in my town: Yeehaw! I was tripping. Can someone please tell the president of the United States I can't see him right now? Could someone tell those pink elephants to leave my room? Don't they know visiting hours are over?

## 34. Even if they seem to understand, medicated patients might interpret something else.

Suddenly, the same doctor who had seen me about an hour earlier returned with a very elegant mature man, dressed in an expensive looking suit. -She's the one. Said Jeremy to the elegant man. They exchanged a few more words while their patient looked at them smiling. -How are we feeling today? Asked Mr. Elegant. —Great. I replied. -I'm glad to hear that. The gentleman answered with a smile. His impeccable fashion sense and his groomed appearance impressed me. I quickly identified him as someone powerful that at the same time was a good person; definitely true that phrase: "the first impression is the last impression."

After that, Mr. elegant and Jeremy left, and I focused my attention on the words said by my doctor: -she's the one. In my mind, however, those words translated into: -she's the chosen one. Chances are the doctors were talking about my operation's success or something like that but my confused mind interpreted something else; I was now convinced that my accident happened because The Almighty had chosen me to convince the world of his existence, my quick healing would be the best proof.

Having medications in my blood did not alter my faith in God, but it did, however, relax me so much that it gave me the sensation that the mission to win followers of the whole world for The Almighty could be achieved from my hospital bed. My mind started to create a situation in which I would address the whole world through a press conference that would take place at the theater of the USC University which, in my mind and for my convenience, happened to be right next to my room and was already filling up with doctoral students, faculty, important personalities and even celebrities such as Mel Gibson, Susan Sarandon, Oprah Winfrey, and the United States President. In other words, not only would I have the mission of proclaiming God's existence, but in the process I would also unite celebrities, politicians, believers and non-believers

    I have to give myself some credit; from a hospital bed I had achieved something practically impossible, unite the rich, the politicians and the famous to serve God. Furthermore, I had managed to bring the actors I wanted involved in one of my films to that auditorium, and I had not invested a single penny. That medicine must have been very good since in one single night it had allowed me to reach the top of entertainment, politics and the spiritual world, and they were all working peacefully together.

    Meanwhile, I kept hearing the doctor's words in my mind: -she's the one. Curiously, it seemed miraculous to me that my pancreas had been healed in two days, but I did not see as extraordinary to be supported by so many famous people that did not even know me, in these difficult times. I considered that as the fair outcome of my professional career and therefore it was not part of the miracle. Since I felt so great, I increased the magnitude of my wishes. My goal was no longer to prove God had healed me; now I wanted to find enough evidence of his existence so that even the most skeptical people would believe in him. Let's face it, if I had already achieved that the president himself came to hear me, converting skeptical people was a "piece of cake."

## 35. Doctors and students will work together to save you.

While my brain continued to find out the way to prove my discovery, around 20 doctors entered my room following doctor Jeremy. When I saw them approaching my bed, I felt super important. They have so many patients to tend to that unless you are in a very delicate condition, you will see them only once a day and during the morning. Because of that, when they came to see me, after hours, to study my case further, it got me really excited.

Most of the doctors that accompanied Dr. Jeremy were in their doctoral residencies. I greeted them happily: -hi everyone. Not even a politician in his/her electoral campaign could have matched my enthusiasm. They all responded kindly and the questioning between them and several of their professors started. They discussed my case and were very pleased to see I was responding well to treatment. The professors would ask the doctors that operated on me what they had done. After that, they asked the doctors in their residencies what other options could have been followed and why they were not chosen. At the end, the doctors that performed the surgery: Dr. James Pierce (surgeon), Dr. Ali Salim (professor), Dr. Hammond (professor), Dr. Hansen, and Dr. Rhee were congratulated for a job well done.

I also used the opportunity to thank them but since I was still under medication, I did it like a hippie from the 60's. With my philosophical tone I told them: -All you need is love, and they've given me plenty of it. I think I sounded just like one of those famous commercials of that time where people coming from all over the world, with their hippie outfit, sang about world brotherhood. Not only did I sound like them, I was probably as "high" as those youngsters of the decade of "peace and love."

The doctors exited with smiles on their faces. I do not know if they were smiling because they liked my words or because they knew I was "high." They were all so prudent that they would have never told me the true reason behind their smiles. Anyways, my brain did not register the fact that I was under the effects of pain medications, so I was convinced they had fallen in love with me instantly. They could not imagine that in my mind they were only a few of the doctors that would attend the great event that had been prepared to talk about my miracle survival.

The archives of my mental data did not include

information regarding the fact that these doctors witness miracles like this one almost every day and although my condition was very special to them, their other cases were equally important. But since in my own story I was the center of attention, I was stubborn enough to think I was unique. The whole world revolved around me; because of that, I was convinced that my accident was the most special. To prove it, I would drink a glass of water to impress the attendees of a press conference on my ability to survive what is lethal to others.

Even though I have never considered getting into politics, my attitude was identical to the one a politician has during campaign when he/she wants to win votes; I listened, thanked and tried to please everyone with my speeches. Move over Mr. President, there is a woman here searching for votes, I mean looking for skeptics to convince.

### 36. Make those who take care of you feel good, and they will make you feel good as well.

I was meditating on my next strategy to win skeptics when a male nurse entered my small room at the intensive care unit. Perfect! I thought. Time to win another "voter" for my "campaign". -Hi Norboll. I told him while reading his nametag. I felt so proud to be able to read the names of those who took care of me before they said mine; it was my way to express how important they were to me. The response I got was a grateful smile and an immediate openness towards me, just for recognizing and appreciating their help by saying their name. It never failed me; I made those who took care of me feel well, and they made me feel good in return.

-Well, hello young lady. Replied the nurse with a tender smile. -Where are you from? I asked Norboll while noticing his Asian features. –Tibet. He responded and my smile became a bigger one. That was a subject I had some knowledge on. Now it was my turn to win that nurse by telling him positive things I knew about his country. -That's where the Dalai Lama is from. I remarked with the enthusiasm of someone who is sure to have found the appropriate subject matter to win his sympathy. -That's right. He asserted with evident joy. Bingo, I had found the appropriate conversation. -Your people are very evolved spiritually. I said, after respectfully letting him know that I believe in Jesus Christ but respected all religions. The nurse's smile grew more. -Even our Bible mentions your people as one of the most spiritually advanced when in the Apocalypse they are mentioned as the men of the shaven heads. I told him and was certain I had won him over. Perhaps he knew that remark is not in the Bible or maybe he was simply aware that medications were altering my perception of things; either way, he seemed to have understood that I just wanted to make him feel included in my salvation plan for the world, and he reacted equally graciously.

As a matter of fact, the nurse was happily surprised to hear this from me. -You are very wise. He said, and we started an amicable conversation while he injected my medication and checked my vital signs. He was such a good nurse that I do not doubt he would have treated me great even if he did not like me, but I was not planning on wasting a chance to win him over and recruit him for my mission. We spoke about spiritual matters, and I was surprised when the Buddhist nurse mentioned Jesus Christ and his mother Mary with the utmost respect and reverence. I had no doubt that this nurse was God sent and would help me prove God's existence to the rest of the world.

## 37. Do not believe everything medicated people say but do not tell them they are lying either.

At that moment, my mom and my twin sister came to visit me. Because of that, I put my conversation with my recently "hired" Buddhist assistant on hold. In my mind, I was already counting on his services as an assistant in the mission to win believers for God. Now I would concentrate on two of my guests of honor to my "press conference." It was my duty to communicate to my relatives about the great event that would take place today, honoring my miraculous healing. Not even in my best health condition could I have made a press conference that had worldwide personalities present, in less than a day. Explain that to a medicated brain!

## JACKIE TORRES

I was about to let my mother and sister know the good news when their faces lit up with the happiness of someone who sees an improvement in the health of their loved one. Their beloved Jackie did not have the tube that went down the throat, nor a respirator in her mouth and even red cheeks on her face. We happily greeted each other with hugs and kisses. Right away, like any good event's producer, I welcomed them and sent them to the place where they could seat to enjoy the show. -I'm glad you came; the ceremony is about to begin. "One of my doctors was talking to the president of the university and told him that I was the chosen one." -I'm the first patient of this hospital to heal from the pancreas in two days.

I said this with such conviction that my holy mother believed it immediately. -That's great. Replied my mother excitedly. -Are you sure it was the president of the university? Inquired my sister, not so easily convinced. I thought her doubt was acceptable and answered with great wisdom: -he looked like it. How unsophisticated was my brain. Regularly, I am a dedicated researcher, thanks to all the professors that demanded that from me at the university but all it took was some medication in my brain to get rid of that need to verify facts. I trusted the person's look as if this offered any proof of his credentials.

The exchange of my "great wisdom" continued. -They are going to have a press conference in a few minutes. -A press conference? My sister asked, still skeptical. -Yes, members of the faculty are going to be there, a lot of doctoral students, my doctors, Oprah Winfrey, Mel Gibson, and Susan Sarandon. I told my sister with great confidence. As soon as she heard those names, she knew something was wrong in my head. I did not notice my sister's disbelief because I was concentrating on organizing the event.

-Go to the auditorium and sit at the front row; we are about to begin. I told my sister Janet and my mother Violeta. Mom believed everything right away and rapidly exited to go to the auditorium. She had come straight from Puerto Rico so celebrities from the United States did not ring a bell for her. Besides, for years her beloved offspring had organized events, press conferences and television shows from one day to the next, so it did not surprise her that her daughter would organize an event like that so quickly. Either she was not surprised or she immediately realized that her daughter was medicated but since she was so prudent, she just stepped out of the room, respecting my request and leaving me with the impression that she had accepted my information as correct.

Janet, however, knew that what her twin had said was not true and was not as eager as my mother to simply do what she was asked for. She had been living in the United States for almost as long as her beloved Jackie; therefore, not only did she know about the people I mentioned but she also knew that getting them together at the same place was not an easy task, not even for her sister, the producer, less so in her health condition. While my sister searched for a way to tell me there would not be a press conference, without breaking my heart, my husband, unaware of the situation, entered the room.

It was my intention to right away tell Mario about the press conference but since I was still upset at the incident with the nurse that he took sides with over me, I just called his attention to it. I scolded him subtly for the incident; it was apparent that my mind had some resentment issues to work with, not even the strong medication had made me forget what had happened with the killer nurse. But Mario was so happy to see me well that he rapidly apologized, definitely a wise decision on his part. Arguing with medicated people is wasting time. Their real world is another so you cannot deal with this patient the same way you would with a person with no chemicals in his/her head. Your entire mind is altered and therefore your reality is not the same as that of the rest of the world. I did not know if Mario was aware of this or if he simply did something few people do and he always does, ask for forgiveness. I have to give him credit for that; he has always been quicker than his wife to ask for forgiveness. I accepted his apology and sent him to the auditorium, to grab a seat for the event. He did not question me and happily went outside.

It was a good thing that no one argued with me. I would not have taken it well. To me, this alternate world created by medication was real. Because of that, I was thankful to my relatives for listening to me with respect. But since medications alter the focus of a person, my mind continued performing multiple tasks without finishing up the previous one. Because of it, I put my role as a producer of the press conference on hold and changed my task; now my new position consisted of being a pollster.

### 38. Hospital employees avoid talking about God to keep a neutral environment.

I wanted to concentrate on my big presentation in front of a worldwide audience but since I did not have a script to prepare with, I decided to make a small survey with all the nurses, doctors, attendants, employees, and anyone who came close to me at the intensive care unit. At least my medication did not alter my desire to present my findings in the most accurate way. I planned to use the answers of those interviewed when my time came to speak at the podium of my imaginary auditorium. -Do you believe in God? I asked each person that came close to me.

Even though I was certain that most of these people believed in God, I did not foresee that most of them preferred to avoid this subject. Talking about the latest robbery, murder, war, drug or crime is acceptable in our society, to prove it, just turn on the news of any TV channel. Violence and excesses do not seem to alarm anyone but mentioning the word God is not acceptable. I was certainly not expecting that reaction.

I was able to ask the question to people of many races, religions and languages. Most were reluctant to answer and those who did respond hesitated. I did not know if it was because they considered the subject a controversial one, or because they wanted to be politically correct by avoiding talking about religion or politics, or if they thought my question was a tricky one that could compromise their jobs, or if they were simply afraid to admit to their spirituality. Truth being said, I asked over twenty people the same question but only three confessed to believe in God; 3 out of 20? Did this mean only 3 believed and the rest were atheist? I was certain that among those 20 there had to be more believers; otherwise, my task was bigger than I had planned.

### 39. Do not drink water if it has been forbidden to you, it could kill you.

That's okay, I thought with the intention of not feeling discouraged; desperate times call for desperate measures. Doctors did not allow me to drink water; apparently any liquid by mouth could kill me in my delicate condition. So I thought that if I drank water and nothing happened in front of an audience, this would convince everyone that I had been healed. I felt so good with the pain medication at that moment that my mind interpreted this as the proof of my full recovery.

Luckily, the hospital employees, who also happened to be

my interviewees, knew that in my condition I could not reason and left every liquid far from my reach. They did the right thing by not trusting me; as thirsty as I was and with my lack of sounding reasoning, courtesy of my medications, I would have drank a gallon of water. My confused brain did not know if my priority should be my thirst, or the poll, or what other thing did I have to do? Oh yes, the press conference.

## 40. Use diplomacy to bring a medicated patient back to reality.

I was thinking about the press conference when my sister entered the room once more. Before coming in, one of the nurses had told her that this patient had said something that was not real, and I should be told the truth. Janet handled the situation smartly; she used diplomacy to bring me back to reality. -We need to go to the auditorium; people are waiting. I told my sister with an urgency tone; I wanted to hurry up, so we would not be late for the event. -There are no more people. She responded. -It is only mom, your husband, the doctor's that already came, and I. My sister was brilliant. She told me who had come, but she did not tell me that there would not be a press conference and since she did not contradict me, I simply assumed that no other people had shown up for the event.

-That's it? I asked, a little disappointed for the little audience that had showed up for the conference. With sweet tenderness she responded: -that's all we need for now, your family. —Okay. I responded, accepting my failure as an event organizer. I felt so tired that I had no energy left to speak at the podium, so it did not bother me to cancel the conference. Besides, my sister's sweet tone of voice was like a lullaby to me.

The chemicals in my head were the reason why the little attendance to such an important event did not bother me at all. Had this happened in my regular professional life, sadness and frustration would have invaded me but since drugs were present in my blood my reasoning was not rational; the news did not bother me in the slightest bit. Now my new focus was a different one; rest was more important than any press conference. At that time, my energy was diminishing, and I needed to rest.

With a brief and loving conversation my sister convinced me that the miracle had already been proven; I was alive, reacting greatly and surrounded by the people I loved. God had chosen to prove his existence that way. My sister was wise! She told me just what I wanted to hear. If God had chosen to show his existence like that; who was I to question him? I do not know if that was Janet's reasoning at that moment but that is how I perceived it; the fact that she did not confront nor contradict me also helped, she did not talk to me harshly or irritated me or told me I was hallucinating.

Her tone of voice was sweet and non-aggressive and my mind interpreted it as her being in agreement with me.

## Chapter 3:

### Patient's concerns

**41. Convey peacefulness to a medicated patient, and he/she will feel safe.**

A PERSON UNDER THE INFLUENCE OF A STRONG DRUG is not in control of her/his senses and basically reacts to stimulus. Do not scold that person because he/she sees everything amplified and will see you as a monster that has to be destroyed. I do not know if my sister knew that or if she simply used common sense; truth being told, she spoke to me with a calm demeanor. My understanding at that moment would not have reasoned; I would have lost it with anyone that got upset or raised the tone of voice or contradicted me. I agreed with my sister's logic and decided to rest after being advised to do so by her. I also asked her to bring my mother inside and after that my husband. I spoke to all of them briefly, and they were happy to see me better.

Once they left, I met another male nurse that would take care of me while at the intensive care unit. He had the same peaceful smile my relatives had and each movement he made was paused, nothing abrupt. His non-verbal language transmitted calmness, and I felt so safe next to him that the pollster in me returned; I could not resist asking him if he believed in God. He responded affirmatively. I was so happy! His enthusiastic response was accompanied by careful care as he healed my open wound; I knew I was in good hands. My exhausted body took a second air, and I began a friendly conversation with the one I expected to be a new member of my mission.

### 42. Medications make you thirsty: if you cannot drink liquids, ask for a lollipop.

Unfortunately, the night was not as pleasant as the day; the effect of the morphine had run out, and I stopped flying in the air to land in a rather unfortunate body. I had difficulty breathing, felt very weak, my heart was beating so fast I thought it was going to pop out and to make things worse, the medications I was given through my IV made me feel terrible and extremely thirsty. My lips resembled those of an old lady, dry and cracked. I desperately wanted to drink some water or eat some ice, but the nurse placed everything far from me; since I could not move, it was not possible for me to satisfy my thirst.

My new ally, the believer nurse, came to flush my feeding tube with soda; he used the liquid to clean it. Hospital staff used soda as a cleaner or a clog dissolver to unclog the tubes that feed patients, the same way plumbers use bleach to unclog the plumbing in a house. That means soda is really bad for a body but since this patient was so thirsty, it seemed like the most precious liquid ever created. That soda would do wonders for my mouth right now. Just to look at it made me salivate. Why do they waste it on cleaning a tube instead of alleviating my thirst with it?

I asked the nurse if I could drink some. He nicely denied it to me; he knew it could be fatal. -But I can give you a lollipop. Said the nice man searching for alternatives. Not exactly what I wanted but it was something so I agreed. The nurse returned with a pastel colored mini sponge, with a stick that looked like a lollipop; definitely not my definition of a lollipop. The sponge was wet but please do not cheat; that is not fair. I sucked the mini sponge but the little water it had did nothing for me. Why are they so greedy? I can see an entire litter of soda close to me; it is a few steps away from my bed.

Did not the doctors know that soda is good for humankind? Had they not seen the commercials that show how happy people around the world are when they have some sort of cola? Why could not I have some of that harmless happiness? The fact of the matter is anything by mouth was not allowed to me, including sodas, healthy juices or water. The little joys of normal living were suspended indefinitely.

### 43. Medications cause insomnia and hallucinations.

The days and nights that followed were very tough; I had constant fever and pneumonia followed. To make things worse, I felt tired because I could not fall asleep. How annoying it is to be really tired and not being able to sleep. I had never suffered from insomnia, except by a few exceptional occasions; because of that, not being able to sleep was new for me. An uninterrupted nap was something I really longed for but that was a luxury I had not been able to enjoy at the hospital. I could not sleep, not only because I could not breathe right but also the pain medication made me hallucinate. On top of it, every time I tried to fall asleep I saw monster-like shadows. When it rains, it pours.

When I thought the quota of calamities had been fulfilled, monsters joined the list. Where did they come from? There are not enough beds for everyone. Can someone please notify them? This is where the "pretty side" of drugs ends; the flying in the air sensation that medications gave me, the quick relief to my pain had come to an end. The time had come to pay the price for that short-lived welfare. Everything in life has a price and the one that corresponds to using drugs is very high. It makes no difference if you plead that you used them legally, like I did when I accepted them as part of my treatment. Drugs do not discern between the legal or illegal user; the side effects are the same for both. This patient had accepted morphine to ease her pain, and it made her feel good for a while but the good sensation vanishes sooner rather than later. Now that its medical effect had ended, it was my turn to experience the other effects it produces, the negative reaction of the mind and body, namely the ugly side of drugs, hallucinations.

## 44. Hallucinations are real for those who experience them.

My hallucinations included seeing monsters that wanted to harm me. To regular people, monsters are only a myth but for those under the influence of a drug, they are as real as any other person. But why were they showing up to me? I concluded that the chemicals in my brain, coupled with my physical frailty, made me the perfect target for any spirit from the other side that wanted to get in touch with a living person. I could not move from my bed and could not control my mind either because of the medications; perhaps those beings knew that and because of it they came to visit me in my dreams. What for? I have no idea. I can theorize they wanted to escape from the place they were trapped at and thought I could help them or that they worked for the dark forces of the universe and wanted to take me with them. Another theory I still have, is that they are human beings that are being tormented in a dimension where torture is constant for them. They seem to not want to be there. I suspect they are spirits trapped in what believers call hell. Poor souls, just thinking that perhaps they did not want to harm me but only wanted to establish some communication, since they needed help to get out of that creepy place, makes me sad. Truth being said, their whining gave me the goose bumps right away. Even the room temperature felt colder. I was freezing!

As soon as I fell asleep, I felt that my spirit relocated to this same hospital room but there were no other humans next to me; I was the only person alive there. Right away my mind recognized this dimension as one the living does not inhabit; I had crossed over to a spooky place. My survival sense alerted me that I had to get out of there quickly. Suddenly, the curtains next to me would come to life and their delicate decorative designs would transform into diabolical beings that seemed to be emerging, germinating, surfacing from the grave; they stretched their hands as if they were trying to come out from underneath the ground as if they had been buried and finally could go free. Their movements were abrupt, and they moved their body parts as if fire was burning them.

They were many and had diverse shapes, each new one scarier than the next. Eerie whining sounds came out of their mouths as if they were experiencing terrible pain and tried to free themselves but could not; it was as though something had them chained, and they barely had the strength to moan. Their whining grew louder as they were able to stretch more, get out of the hole where they seemed to be buried. These moans were accompanied by a sound that resembles the one made by wood when it stretches or shrinks. Sounds similar to a door with a rusty hinge could also be heard.

I was terrified but did not hesitate a second to do what I was certain would keep those spirits far from me, praying with great devotion. Coincidentally, during the prayer, the violet colors of the curtains shined more and seemed to take control of the sinister shadows. It seemed like my prayers ignited that shine in the violet color and at the same time, those areas of the curtain acquired the necessary strength to keep the shadows away from me. Regardless of how much they tried, they could not touch me. Anyways, I had no intention of finding out if the shades could reach me or not; I knew I had to get out of there.

I was asleep but my intelligence was wide-awake and alerting me to exit that place as soon as possible. With a sense of choking and urgency at the same time, I would suddenly wake up. I had less than 5 minutes of sleep but knew that returning to the planet of dreams was still dangerous in my vulnerable condition. The only way to avoid the monsters was not to sleep. That was the price I had to pay for my consumption of medications, my first payment for accepting the drugs that were administered to me for my treatment.

Unfortunately, the monsters were not the only problem the medications had inherited me. My brain created unreal situations, and I was not aware that this world did not exist. Not only was my mind in danger but my body as well; my legs moved by themselves so restlessly that it was impossible to fall asleep. I had only slept a few minutes and was very tired but did not want to face the monsters again.

## 45. Doctors sometimes ignore patient's concerns thinking she/he just fears death.

Both my aches and the scary shades managed to make my first week at the hospital a very unpleasant one. The aches, however, were the ones that concerned me the most. Every time I fell asleep, I felt as though my heart and breathing would stop. Next day, I tried to explain this to a doctor, and she responded I could fall asleep without a worry since my heart was not going to stop beating and my breathing would be enough because my body kept working, even if I went to sleep.

That simple; she sounded just like a teacher talking to a first grader. To me it sounded just like: -go to sleep and stop being a child. If we think about it, her approach was even sillier. I think we all have enough experience going to sleep and knowing that our heart will not stop just because we fall asleep. I was not afraid of dying in my sleep. Why was this so difficult to understand for doctors? Not all of us perceive death as the end of our days.

In my case, I am convinced that death is the transition to the world we were created for, our true home. I am not dying to get there since almost all of us have goals we want to achieve before we leave, but it does not cause me to panic. I simply could not breathe right and that did not let me sleep. It was not dying what concerned me; it was living with that continuous choking sensation.

I guess the doctor had cared for many patients that dreaded death and because of it she assumed that was what concerned me. Obviously her medical explanation did not make me feel better, but she was so polite in her response that I did not have the guts to tell her that the reason behind my insomnia was that something in my body was not allowing me to breathe properly.

### 46. If you feel bad, insist until your problem is examined further.

I insisted so much to the doctor that something was choking me that she ordered another X-ray. That made me feel satisfied; I knew the equipment would reveal the reasons behind my breathing problems. Before she left, the doctor removed a stitch on the right hand side of my shoulder that apparently did not serve any purpose. That detail moved me. If she had noticed something so small, it was clear she was watching over me. I liked the gentle way she removed my stitch with, making sure it did not hurt me.

I was pleased with the doctor, especially when a technician came with his impressive equipment to get the X-rays of my chest. To me that was royalty treatment; only kings and queens can enjoy the luxury of such impressive machinery, transferred to my room in order to avoid me the inconvenience of going to the room where those devices were. I felt so important. Move over kings, dukes and princesses, the new hospital queen was getting personalized X-rays.

### 47. Good care of others encourages the patient to heal.

All were giving their best to help me heal: the X-ray technician, the two nurses that took care of me round the clock, the doctors and my family. That was my biggest incentive, their unselfish dedication to keep me alive. Their effort and enthusiasm pumped up my unfortunate body to continue working despite long nights without proper sleep, continually falling unconscious, unable to drink water or eat food, having fever, throwing up, bearing unbearable pain, experiencing shortness of breath, and many more complications. My body really wanted to quit but since so many people were working so hard to help me, I could not let them down.

Bear with me dear body; we cannot let this people down.

That is how together we achieved what seemed impossible, I survived 10 days at the intensive care unit and was able to be transferred in better health condition to the trauma room. Good-bye and good riddance monsters! You are welcomed to stay in this room to bother the next patient that comes here, but you will not be welcomed in my next room.

### 48. The trauma room has more patients and less staff than the Intensive Care Unit.

They call it the trauma room and that name fits it like a glove, and I do not say it because here is where patients who are still extremely delicate are transferred but because having several people of different nationalities, ethnic origins, languages and religions with all sorts of life and death conditions, in the same room, is simply the perfect recipe to traumatize anyone. Needless to say, I came in oblivious to this reality. As far as I was concerned, this was a 5-star room where I would be treated greatly, and I would be back home in no time.

With that idea I entered the huge room. Since I could not move or walk on my own, I got there lying down on a hospital bed that had wheels and was gently pushed by a nurse assistant. As we progressed, I looked around the large room. The first thing I saw was the restroom; inside, it had a small toilet. I thought it was too narrow but since I could not use it yet because I could not move from my bed, I did not worry about it. The sink was outside and was also very small. The bed kept moving, and I could see the room had around ten single beds, five on each side, each one lined up with the one on the opposite side.

Each patient's space was delineated by curtains that surrounded the bed; next to each one were the necessary devices to treat the patient: IV's, vital signs machine, etc. I was still in delicate shape but seeing my mom, Violeta, my twin sister, Janet, and my husband, Mario, smiling by my side as we explored my new room together, made me feel better. As my bed kept rapidly moving, I saw a Hispanic family. I heard their accent as they spoke and realized they were Peruvian. I know several people from Peru that I like very much, so I could not avoid smiling at them. The mother was the patient at the bed, her husband and their sons and daughters were seating around her. A huge flower arrangement, with beautiful red roses, was next to the mom. Seeing that family, made me feel good. I thought that if the mother was enjoying a better health condition, the same would happen to me and very soon.

-This is your bed. The nurse attendant told me as she suddenly stopped and placed me at the corner of the room. I liked it. It was the best spot of the room, next to two large windows that allowed me to see the city of Los Angeles, from the top of that room on the ninth floor of the hospital. From there, the modern skyscrapers of downtown and the imposing freeway 5, as well as hundreds of vehicles that passed by it, could be seen. The corner was also the most private part of the room and that took away a load off of my shoulders. What a relief! Additional privacy to heal quicker, I thought.

The nurse attendant walked away after training me on how to pull a black cord, placed next to my bed in case I needed to call for help. The cord activated a red light next to my bed, which connected to the lobby where the nurses and attendants were. I thought it was funny since it looked like the alarms used during the 60's and the 70's in the movies, to alert that a spy had infiltrated an ultra-secret place. Interesting way to communicate with nurses, worthy of a patient that loves good stories.

The transfer to the room had concluded with success and without any mishap. It seemed like everything would go smoothly in this place but when my relatives had to leave since visiting hours were over, I realized I would no longer be in my own room being looked after by my "private" nurses. Now I had nine more roommates and this caused me some anxiety perhaps because I remembered how overwhelming it was to be in a bed at the emergency room, next to so many patients in poor condition. But let us be positive; that was there, at the emergency room. This was a new place, and all the patients seemed to be relaxed. At least on that first night no complaints were heard in the room. I guess that being the neighbor of so many patients would not prevent me from resting. Perfect! Now that the monsters stayed at the other room, I will finally fall asleep without interruptions. That thought brought a smile to my face, and I got ready to sleep and have sweet angelic dreams.

### 49. Avoiding morphine eliminates hallucinations, secondary effects and addiction.

It was just 8:00 o'clock in the evening but I was ready for some good sleeping time. An attendant came to take my vital signs while another set up my oxygen. Soon after, a nurse came with two injections, they were something I could live without; both hurt me a great deal because my thin arms were totally bruised due to the fact that some nurses were good injecting and others had the precision of a Parkinson patient. I dreaded those nurses, they could never find a vein when they were getting blood from me and if their only task was to inject, they did it wherever the needle fell, whether it was in an area filled with bruises or not.

When I had received the last injection of the day at 10:00 pm, I thought I was done with my daily dosage of unpleasant situations and got ready to sleep. I closed my eyelids and was so tired that in the blink of an eye landed at the planet of dreams. How joyful! It was as though soft music lulled me to sleep until I started to hear the moans and the creaking of doors and grinding of wood. Please, not again! The monsters returned. You have got to be kidding! Did not we agree you could stay in the other room and bother another patient? Why did you all had to follow me here?

It was obvious I did not want to see those shades; therefore, faster than lightning I opened my eyes and remained awake. -One, two, they are going to get you… That was the song that one of the little girls that had been murdered by the evil character in a horror story sang. I did not think about that song at that moment, but I did realize I was in the same position of those kids; I did not want to go to sleep to avoid dealing with an evil force in my dreams. What a dilemma mine was; I could not sleep during the day due to my aches and at night because of the monsters.

I was convinced that my pain medication produced these hallucinations, so I decided not to take any more morphine even if my whole body hurt. To me it was more important to be able to sleep peacefully at night than to have a brief moment without pain. A decision had been made; first thing in the morning as soon as my doctors came, I would ask them to eliminate the morphine from my treatment, so I could once and for all get rid of the monsters forever.

### 50. Reading the labels of all medications given to you could save your life.

Morphine is not the only medication you should beware of; there is another even more dangerous, the one that has not being prescribed. Precisely on that day, my sister, who always pays attention to details, noticed that a nurse had placed a new medicine on the pole where my medications were placed. She immediately asked what was the medicine for, and the nurse read its label and realized then that the medication was not even for me. She quickly took away the medicine that had mistakenly reached this patient, but I do not want to imagine what would have happened if that medicine would have been given to me. It was a good thing that I always had the company of my family; they never missed those details.

That day I learned you should always read the labels of medications given to you if you want to keep yourself in the planet of the living. For now and since I could not fall asleep, I dedicated some time to look at the patients of the room and discovered that perhaps it was not so bad to not be able to sleep. Apparently, during nighttime, new roommates were admitted and those arrivals were everything but silent.

## 51. Other patient's screams are the most challenging part of the treatment.

My first experience with a patient admitted during nighttime to the trauma room was quite upsetting. A young Caucasian woman that probably was not over 30 years old, screamed in pain while she was brought inside the room. I think I heard the nurses say the young woman had been in a car accident. All of them were treating the patient with great kindness and in an efficient way, but the young woman kept using a language so obscene that it was almost impossible to not be affected by it. She could not stop cursing. She seemed to be in a great deal of pain, so I, who watched from my corner, felt sorry for her. Obviously we were both in pain, even though our ways of expressing it were quite different. But since now, more than ever, I had an idea of how disturbing physical pain can be, I felt empathy for the young woman and really wanted her to feel better.

The woman had a device to keep her neck and back straight. Several nurses and attendants lifted her up from the emergency bed and placed her at her corresponding bed in the trauma section. I tried to briefly pray for her, but her screams were so sharp they took away my concentration; they gave me the chills, just like cats curl when they see something unexpected, every hair of my body was curling with those deafening screams. I did not know whether to pray so that she would be taken to another room to scream or for an elephant hunter to show up and shoot her with a tranquilizer.

What a great set of lungs that girl had, probably her wailing could be heard in the entire floor. Every time the new patient cursed, swore or complained my whole being felt weaker. I guess that is what people mean when they say someone sucked their energy. That girl left me with no energy. I was extremely exhausted with her yelling. An hour or two later, the new patient stopped complaining, at least for a while. She had been given the highest dose of pain medication and had fallen asleep.

Meanwhile, from my corner, I watched the now asleep patient with some concern. People say the first impression is the last impression and the noisy entrance of this girl had left me traumatized. If that was the entrance, how is it going to be when she feels comfortable enough to let her inhibitions go? Oh Lord, let us think about something more positive. What about a kind nurse whose merciful actions make him look like an angel?

### 52. Nurses will try to figure out what bothers you when you feel worse.

My heartbeat was very fast and my vital signs revealed fever. The swearing and cursing of the new patient had left me shaky. To my fortune, a Hispanic nurse came to my rescue; he gave me ice bags to bring down the fever and changed my diaper. With the little voice I had left, I told him about my shortness of breath and about the constant phlegm coming out of my mouth that made me worry about choking. I had already told a doctor but since I did not see the matter examined any further and I kept feeling bad, I thought the nurse could intervene to investigate this more thoroughly.

The nurse looked at me with compassion and helped me by massaging my back, so I would cough up the phlegm and maybe get some sleep. His selfless help moved me, but I felt so bad that not even his massage relieved my choking sensation. When the nurse was about to leave, I hugged him, so he would stay. Poor guy, if we would have been in the open sea and he would have been trying to save me, we both would have drowned. I held onto him as hard as I could. I felt that if he went away, my opportunity of being saved would leave with him.

-What is it? The nurse asked me. I had tears in my eyes. The nurse knew something was wrong but was not sure of what it was. -Should I call the doctor? The nurse told me while my hands held him with a strong grip and did not let go of him, not even by chance. I could not put into words the agony I felt: my abdomen hurt, my chest was also hurting. I was sweating and did not even have the strength to hold my own weight.

The nurse helped me to sit down again, trying to figure out how to help me. With an almost maternal care, he made me feel protected and gave me another massage in my back. He then accommodated me in bed with several pillows, to cushion the discomfort of my tubes and accompanied me until he thought I had relaxed. -If you need me, just pull the cord. He told me with a soft compassionate voice. I tried to behave as civilized as I could. Although my survival instinct wanted to hold onto him once more and not let him escape, I gave up and nodded positively, smiling at him to show him my appreciation.

My common sense had finally recognized that there was

not much more the nurse could do. I agreed to let him go, in order to not delay the help I knew he could give other patients. His selfless help, however, moved my whole being. He did not hesitate to help me with the same devotion given to a loved one. Although pain had control of my body at that moment, my mind admired and recognized this human being as one extremely advanced, spiritually. This nurse, with his shiny white uniform, looked like an angel, performing the deed that would earn him his wings to ascend to heaven.

## 53. A patient's physical frailty will make her/him concentrate on spiritual matters.

Although the room had beds for more patients, at that precise night there were only seven more. I am glad there were no more; if we had another one like the car accident patient, our chances of getting out of there alive diminished and not because she was going to harm us but because it was impossible to concentrate on healing with those screams. Fortunately, the pain medication kept the young car accident woman asleep, and the rest of us did not make any noise, other than a moan here and there. Most, including me, had our curtains closed and all, except me, seemed to be asleep.

It was late at night. I made a brief prayer to thank God I was still alive. I had always been a believer but this time I felt more connected to my spirituality. The frailty of my condition made me realize how unimportant material things are, especially the body. Yes, I know, perhaps I sound a little corny but when you are on the brink of death, your whole perspective changes. Suddenly, you question yourself on things you have not before. Physical appearance, for example, is something women spend a lot of time on. If we just glanced at ourselves in a mirror, we would realize how transient "looking good" is. The hospital staff was smart; there was not even a single mirror in that room.

I did not need to see a reflection in order to know that my weight and shape were not in optimum condition; my belly had huge scars, and I looked so skinny that I resembled a standing noodle. The spiritual world, on the other hand, was more appealing to me. There, nobody competes for a beauty pageant. Every time I prayed, I felt closer to that spiritual world and much further from the physical one. I would have conversations with God and my angels. I did not hear their voices answering back, but I felt I got quick responses. The first thing I asked God was to take my pain away; I explained I could deal with the inconveniences of my condition but requested he took charge of my pain for a while. Of course, after I had messed everything up I wanted help to get out of the problem.

## 54. Concentrated prayers create a tangible protective wall.

I had not had a good night's sleep since I was admitted to the hospital; I wanted to sleep so badly. My body was tired, my eyes felt heavy. I looked at the violet curtains of my room and suddenly fell asleep while my mind saw the violet curtains filling the room with a purple color. I felt at peace in this sudden dream. I was feeling this spiritual lightness when the dark shadows started to form again in the curtains. Go figure, don't they get tired? As soon as I closed my eyes, I had to open them back. I knew God protected me, but I had no strength left to listen to the moans of monsters. I had fulfilled my quota of screams with the car accident patient. Once more, I had no other choice but to remain awake.

Then is when I noticed a see-thru wall that surrounded my corner. Where did that come from? It did not look threatening like the shadows; it had the appearance of a protective wall. The wall was made of ultra-violet light. At least that is what I thought. I cannot recall if I had ever even seen ultra-violet light. Coincidentally, that was the same color I chose to paint the wall that caused my accident. I had chosen it because I had read it is the closest color to the sun. Therefore, it is the closest color to God and it has been credited with providing spiritual peace to those who appreciate it. This wall was just like the one I painted in my house but without the solid structure; you could see thru it.

I must clarify that I was wide-awake and had not taken any pain medication in hours, so I was not hallucinating. A voice, only I seemed to hear, told me the wall was made up of prayers, and it would protect me during the tough times still to come. I then looked outside the window and noticed how that wall, made up of a purple light, grew bigger and bigger from the floor surrounding me until it covered the whole hospital. It must have taken thousands of prayers, maybe even more, to form such a huge wall. Could this be possible? Could so many people be praying for me?

My mom and my husband always told me about the people who sent their prayers for my quick recovery. I remembered all of them, as I looked astonished at the imposing wall. There was my family and friends who prayed daily for me. Many of them formed praying groups where people I did not even know had heard about my accident and decided to pray for me. People from all denominations had included me in their prayers. An evangelical pastor, Mario had just done a movie with, prayed with his congregation. A retired Catholic priest, who was my friend, complemented his prayers by lighting up a Paschal Candle. This is a candle used for very sacred rituals. As he lit it up, its flame extended to an incredible height. He told my relatives this meant a long life yet to come. Surely, the prayers were working. Some people even had praying networks through the Internet.

I always knew prayers were important, but I could have

never imagined that truly concentrated prayer can become a tangible object, a Violet Wall capable of comforting and protecting from evil. As long as people were praying, no evil could get close to me. This was the only time I was able to see the Violet Wall while awake. I would get glimpses of it in my brief dreams when the terrifying shadows wanted to get close to me, but they could not penetrate the wall. I was not able to see the Violet Wall again but now I knew it was there, and I also knew prayers fueled it; so now, more than ever, I prayed.

## 55. Be quick to express your aches to the doctors or you will have to wait until tomorrow.

After a night that felt longer than usual, due to my problems breathing, my doctors came to see me at 5:00 am. I was glad they were early birds because I could communicate my aches to them sooner. Although they only slept few hours, the doctors always had huge smiles and were extremely kind to me, no matter how early or how late it was. -Good morning. -How are we doing today? Doctor Jeremy told me. I knew I had to be quick in explaining what was happening to me since there were many patients waiting for the doctors. -I can't sleep. -I can't breathe right. -I feel like my heart is going to stop every time I try to sleep, and I also see monsters when I begin to dream. -I think it might be the morphine. I said as fast as I could to the doctor. I knew that if I did not speak fast some aches would be left uncovered, so I did not even breathe to be able to say my whole list.

I was convinced that mentioning the word "monsters" would get the doctor's attention. Who would not like to hear the story of someone who claims to have conversations with monsters? I am sure that if I proposed that subject for one of the TV show I had to produce, everyone would have agreed that it would attract great audience. To my surprise, either this doctor is not impressed by monsters, or he had already have patients with the same problem, or the subject matter simply did not call his attention. He was undeterred; did not move a single muscle of his face or his body, did not indicate in any way any interest in the topic.

The only thing he expressed some interest in was for the breathing problem. What a boring doctor this is. Where is his sense of adventure? Does not he know that monsters are the leads of the most incredible stories ever written? There are conventions to follow the feats of famous monsters. Their fans would be curious to find out more about them. Are they from out of space or from this planet? Were they monsters or more like zombies or even werewolves? It seems like this doctor had not been to any of those conventions. His interest for monsters was as big as the one of a child in doing his homework on Christmas day.

Dr. Jeremy concentrated on health issues; he asked me if I needed more oxygen since I was actually getting less through the small plastic device that goes to the nostrils of my nose. I responded that I did not need more oxygen but that something in my chest was not letting me breathe right. My theory was that my problem was in my heart to which Dr. Jeremy responded that it should not be but that he would request another X-ray for me, to see what was going on in my chest. After that, he told me that the rest of the team would come later on, and he left. It was a good thing I made sure to go over everything that concerned me as soon as he came in, since the doctor was only there for a few minutes.

Happy with the possibility that my issue would be addressed, I bid farewell to the doctor. I must admit I was a little discouraged by the fact that my monster story did not cause the same impact on him as it had on me. I wonder if he would have reacted the same if instead of monsters I had told him they were vampires. Coincidentally, vampires also became part of my story in a very unconventional way.

### 56. Get used to blood tests every day.

When doctors departed, the early morning bustle spread all over the room. One of the first employees to arrive was the one in charge of getting blood samples from almost all patients, for the different tests done daily. Oh gosh, if someone terrified us just by showing up it was that woman. Personally, I feared her not because she lacked skill in what she did: as a matter of fact she was quite good, however, every time she did blood tests she would get at least four samples; not even vampires of horror stories are so thirsty.

Some patients referred to her as the "blood sucker" and that name fit her like a glove. Can you see? This patient was not the only one wanting to find some amusement with unpleasant moments. I was not alone in my need to wish that ordinary things became more entertaining, in this not so exciting place; my roommates had the same need. "The blood sucker," now that sounded like the title of an interesting story. Who knows? Perhaps I could get some writers out of these patients; some were quite witty. In fact, one of them nicknamed the nurse that got blood samples "the vampire." Remembering that honorary title, given by that roommate to the nurse while she got my blood samples, made me relax.

The "vampire" was an Asian woman in her 40's or 50's, whose height was around 5 feet 3 inches and had a slender body. She did not look physically intimidating but that changed when we saw her needles, her tubes and her elastic rubber bands that would tightened our arms to draw blood from them. I guess this would be the profession in greater demand if vampires existed. The "vampire" was quite skilled at her task and even though she got several samples of blood, her needles hurt less than most of the injections we received daily. Had she been the only one injecting us, we would have been joyful.

Unfortunately, this nurse was only one of many; when

she left, others came and their injections caused us to panic even more.

### 57. If you are told: -your veins are small, your nurse does not know to inject properly.

Several nurses seemed to have been trained by some ripper, not because they wanted to harm us but because their precision for injections was terrible, and they left our arms filled with bruises. It seemed as though our worst enemies had hired them because those injections hurt us for days. The most common excuses among not so skilled nurses to justify themselves are: "your veins are so little" or "you have difficult veins" or "you have bad veins." I was convinced there was not such a thing because even though my veins were "hard to find" when the nurse was skilled at it she would find them right away. In fact, I was lucky to have one of those employees inject me three days before.

Today, another nurse would be in charge of my IV; I was going to have some tests done, and it had to be replaced. IV's were replaced every 3 to 4 days, to guarantee the flow of the medication. The needle went in my arm a first time; it was quite painful. -Oh, you have very small veins. The nurse claimed. Oh no, not another nurse with Parkinson justifying her lack of stability; announcing her crime as if she was not guilty of the upcoming tragic scene. I knew what that meant; the nurse was bad at injecting, she would justify it by saying the deficient one was the patient, and I would have to submit myself to the torture of at least three more painful tries so that she would achieve placing the IV in its place. Why could not they just say something like: "I really suck at injecting people" or "my IV skills are limited." Us patients would not feel precisely better but at least we would know what is coming our way.

Unfortunately, admitting our weaknesses honestly is very hard for humans. I guess it is because we think that if we admit that we are not good, we would compromise our chances of continuing in our jobs. Therefore, instead of admitting that we cannot do something right we justify our inefficiency, and what is the best way to do it? Blame it on someone else, in this case the patient. If it is the patient's fault, it is by default not the nurse's responsibility. Finally, after the nurse with Parkinson attempted her fate for a third time, the IV was at last in place, and I could rest; two more bruises to my already purple arms. Fortunately, these nurses discovered something that not even the doctors or the tests had revealed; I officially suffered from that incurable disease called "small veins."

## 58. If everyone can eat but you, dinnertime will be very challenging.

As soon as the nurse with Parkinson left, my smell detected breakfast time. At the intensive care unit I had even forgotten what being hungry was. I remember being thirsty but not hungry. In this new room, however, I was not by myself; there were other beds with patients that could eat. When the lady that brought the trays with food entered the room, and I was able to smell the appetizing scent of recently cooked breakfast, my mouth watered. I guess my sense of smell had heightened since my nose sniffed odors just like any little animal that has perceived the smell of its prey. Furthermore, I think I looked as desperate as vampires from youth stories when they smell blood. I became alert, in need of tasting what I smelled. For the first time since my admittance to the hospital, I felt a huge desire to eat.

Almost all of the patients could eat solid food but me. I was being fed through a tube that went through the left side of my stomach to my intestines, which meant that my mouth did not even realize that my body had already eaten cloying milk. As the delicacies my roommates would eat were displayed in front of me: pancakes, eggs, ham, fruit, juice, and coffee I felt a great deal of anxiety, longing to enjoy them too. I felt like Bugs Bunny when enticed by the smell of fresh cooked food flies in the sky, led by the inviting smell to the appealing food. I was aware I could not fly like Bugs Bunny but perhaps I could gain the right to eat by mouth. If a rabbit can fly, then a human that can eat should be an easier task.

That was truly inspiring, to be able to eat like any other person. So when my team of doctors came to see me, I rapidly asked: -when am I going to be able to eat? And adding the personality of a meek and harmless girl I told them: -I see other people eating, and I also have a heart. That innocent face had worked for me in previous occasions, and I was expecting to get the same result this time. Based on the smiles of the doctors, it seemed to be working. -Let's start her on a liquid diet. The professor of the doctors, a handsome and slender African-American man in his 30's that was also my head doctor, Dr. Salim, told Alicia, a friendly young Caucasian woman currently trained by him that took note of everything she was told.

I already liked that doctor and his student as well but now they had my total affection. My mouth watered at the thought of tasting that liquid diet; I did not know what that meant, but I assumed I would be fed with broth or something like that. I love soups, so I felt happy; my smile went from one ear to the next. -Thank you, I love you. I told the doctor satisfied because he had granted my petition. After two weeks without eating anything by mouth, the idea of eating something, even if they were liquids, was super encouraging.

Dr. Salim proceeded then to check my wounds while Alicia, the resident doctor, notified him of the liquids that were coming out of my pancreas. I was so happy with the fact I was going to have lunch, I did not have enough time to remind my doctors about my problems sleeping and breathing. I did, however, make sure to tell my doctors to close the front curtain as they left; I felt weak and wanted to make sure I had enough privacy to concentrate on my healing and on the succulent lunch I would enjoy today and on how relaxing was the unusual silence the room had at that moment.

### 59. Silence in a trauma room is short-lived.

Once the big trauma room was empty of doctors, nurses and attendants I decided to take advantage of the uncommon silence to fall asleep. Call me stubborn but for some reason I always hoped I would be able to take a nice nap. I covered myself with a blanket and closed my eyes when a sudden sound that resembled the one made by chains hitting metal, made me open them abruptly. This already looks like a sinister plot: first the monsters, after that the screaming patient and now, what in the world is causing that sound?

I could not see what was happening in the rest of the room because my curtains were closed; I could only guess. Could it be a broken pipe? What if the room floods, how do I get out? The sound grew louder and louder. Suddenly, the screaming patient started to show off her still healthy lungs; her moans were unbearable. Had there been mirrors in the room, all would have been broken by now. What a high-pitched tone of voice!

I sincerely wanted her to feel better but not at the expense of me feeling worse with her screams. I would have loved to help her, to enjoy a quieter room, but I could not move. The only thing left for me to do was concentrate on my healing, ignore the chaos around me and think I was the only person there. But those screams, goodness gracious! They made it practically impossible for the girl not to be noticed; they could be heard all over the floor.

My new mission was to somehow quiet down that shouting. The tactic I chose was a bit risky; I would advise this patient to help in her healing by concentrating only on herself. I do not know what made me think I would be successful where even the nurses had failed but my theory was that the young woman would rather pay attention to another patient that like her was experiencing pain. I was thinking about how I would communicate "my wise" advice to the patient when she started to accompany her yelling with some begging words: -I'm in pain. The young woman moaned while banging the metal of her bed. -Please! She kept screaming. -I'm in pain!

Right away, a nurse came running to the room. -What's going on? The worriedly nurse asked the patient. -I need pain medication. The young woman was quick to answer with a broken voice. -But you've already had a lot of medication. The nurse replied. -Please, please. The young woman kept begging. -Let me ask your doctor. The nurse answered and quickly left the room while the young woman kept moaning. I said a little prayer for that patient but her screams had left me shaky. The employee returned, in a short period of time, with an injection of morphine that seemed to please her patient right away. She fell asleep and with her rest the peace returned to our room. I assumed that my "intelligent" advices would be given to the young woman when she woke up. Not even by chance would I have dared to disturb her sleep. She looked better asleep and quiet. Awake no one could stand her. But with her sleep peace returned to that room and the rest of us became happy for the silence and for the anticipation of our relative's arrival, whom were allowed to enter starting at 11 in the morning.

### 60. In a room with multiple patients privacy is impossible.

Nothing would make me feel better than my family; their voices were a sweet melody to my ears, contrary to the screams of the patient we will not mention, lest her think of waking up earlier. I felt anxious, in need of seeing my family right away. Their pampering would make me forget the unpleasant moments. It was 11 o'clock in the morning and nothing was more important than seeing them come in. Eleven and one, eleven and two, eleven and three, how come they are not here yet? Every minute waiting in a hospital feels like an eternity to a patient.

I got ready for the occasion by trying to sit down on my bed. Since I could not move my body, mainly because of the tubes I had embedded in my belly, the lever that changes the positions of the bed was my only way to achieve seating down.

After many painful tries, I was able to reach it and just as I sat down, I heard some voices in the hallway. Just in time! I thought. My heart was beating very fast. Could it be my mommy and my husband? Some steps were heard approaching my bed. Suddenly, the right curtain of my "room" opened up. What a pity! It was a nurse assistant that came to get my vital signs. Well, at least that did not hurt. I extended my arm so that she would do her job, but I still heard voices.

The voices belonged to two women making their entrance to the room, an older elegant lady and her granddaughter, who must have been in her 30's. They both came into the big room to check on the young Caucasian woman, which was on the other side of the room. I was happy for the young Caucasian patient. Her family had finally come, and I assumed she was going to be thrilled to see them. Probably, that was why the girl was so distressed, the fact that her family had not come yet. I must admit that my happiness was a bit selfish since I imagined the presence of her family would calm down the patient's screams.

The two pretty ladies of golden hair seemed concerned about this young woman. After checking up on her and realizing she was asleep, they started chatting amongst themselves. -She always does this. The granddaughter, who was also the young woman's sister, told her grandmother. This comment intrigued me. From my corner, I had no other option but to listen to their conversation. There is no privacy in a room divided just by curtains so do not think I like gossiping, it only entertains me; let me pay close attention and listen to what they say.

Grandmother and granddaughter complained about the behavior of the young woman, claiming this was not the first time she did it. She did what? Have a car accident? I had no clue on what they were talking about, but they knew something that this outsider listening to them did not know. They seemed upset at the patient and after a little while the granddaughter went to look for the doctors, to find out more information about her sister's accident. Unaware of the root of their discomfort and like any gossipy neighbor, I made assumptions without having all the information at hand. To me, at that moment, those ruthless villains were behaving badly with the poor accident victim. One thing was that she screamed but another one was not feeling compassion for her in this difficult time.

My brain could not comprehend why were they so harsh and cold with someone that was barely hanging onto life. -No wonder she moans so loudly. I thought. -With that family, I guess I would also sob. I was thinking about this when the granddaughter returned, complaining about the doctors and nurses; it seemed nagging ran in the family. Both, the grandmother and the granddaughter left the hospital infuriated without talking to the young Caucasian woman. This deeply disturbed me. What could the young woman, of the car accident, have done to deserve that her family treated her with such indifference? That was a gossip that deserved further investigation. There would be plenty of time to find out the details of this intriguing family novel during my time at the hospital.

At that moment my beautiful family arrived and the gossip of the car accident girl did not look attractive any more, in comparison to the fond times that awaited me with my pampering family. Young car accident woman whose name I do not know, you keep sleeping at your corner while this patient enjoys her loved ones.

## Chapter 4:

## How to survive a hospital room

### 61. Pampering the patient works wonders for her /his healing.

WHILE THE OTHER PATIENT WAS PRACTICALLY IGNORED by her family, my relatives took care of me in every way. They listened to me carefully as I described my problems breathing and sleeping, and they took care of me. My mom changed my diaper while my twin sister looked for a container to wash my hair; she filled it up with hot water and placed it on the table where the food is served. Mom placed several pillows between the bowl and the bed, to support my head while Janet washed my long hair. This improvised beauty salon made me feel as pampered as if I were at the most luxurious Beverly Hills spa.

My sister even did a sophisticated braid on my hair that made me feel ready for the red carpet. My mother then covered me with blankets so that I could fall asleep and stayed next to me while my sister went outside to buy some things she wanted, to decorate my apartment so that when I got home it looked spectacular. That pampering from my family was an escape to me, a break from the intense work of trying to improve my health while facing a serious condition.

## 62. Phlegm affects breathing and causes choking: getting rid of it will make you feel better.

Just like in a health resort my mother accommodated me with comforting blankets and pillows so that I could reconcile the long awaited sleep, but I continued to have problems breathing and quickly woke up. I asked my mother to massage my back while I bent over a plastic container, to try to cough up the phlegm that was bothering me. The process hurt deeply but we kept doing it for about twenty minutes. Since it hurt me, some tears covered my face. –Sorry. I told my mother to apologize. -Sorry for what? -Don't be silly. My mother replied with a big smile. I barely smiled back; I was very tired but felt much better.

-I'm going to throw this away. My mother commented while taking the plastic container out of the room and returned in a heartbeat to accommodate me in my bed. At that moment my husband came in; he had bought one of those

MP3 devices to listen to music. I got excited with the possibility of falling asleep with the help of that device. -It has a lot of soft and nature music. Mario remarked with enthusiasm as he put the headphones on my ears. My mother then covered me with a blanket. -The music will last for the entire night. Mario assured me with conviction while my mother and him said goodbye; visiting hours were over and both had to leave.

With the amount of phlegm my mother had helped me to expel, it was my intention to give myself into sweet dreams without worrying about choking. The beautiful instrumental music of the device Mario had brought rocked my ears, and I longed that it would give me the long awaited sleep without interruptions.

### 63. Instrumental music and headphones help to isolate from a noisy room.

The music worked! For three hours I was able to sleep. I felt like the music was setting the pace for my heart to beat and for the first time, in days, I fell asleep. My mind was soothed by the soft nature sounds I was hearing, along with instrumental music. My husband did not have time to screen all the music so my sudden dream was invaded by the sounds of a fly, a cow and a dripping faucet. They were all in the nature sounds CD. The fly sound made me wave my hand trying to get it. The dripping water made me want to go to the restroom and the lowing of the cow made me open my eyes suddenly, concerned that this animal was next to me.

I smiled; based on the musical selection, Mario, my husband, certainly did not have a shot at being a disc jockey. The music continued and this time it was Mozart. I fell asleep again. I was happy to be able to isolate myself from the disturbing sounds in my room. But since everything that is good seems to be short-lived, the music lasted for only three hours. The battery was not fully charged, and I soon went back to the reality of my hospital room. -I need pain medication! The young car accident patient screamed from across the room while a nurse attendant argued with her that she had have enough pain medication for that day. Does someone have a muzzle in this room? Give her some medicine to shut her up; with so much noise it is impossible to fall asleep. I thought all of that but did not express it; I did not have the strength to talk.

The more I wished for silence, the more noises emerged from everywhere. On the one side, there was the young woman that screamed, on the other, a talking puppet that had been given to another patient did not stop dancing and singing: -you are my sunshine, my only sunshine. -You make me happy when things are down... Oh Lord, even the puppets talk here. I thought that at least that noise was not unpleasant, annoying perhaps but not disturbing. Either way, it did not help to sleep either.

I was thinking about that when another sound was added to the not so silent night, a woman began to curse. Just what we needed! When I thought this place could not be any more inhospitable, the appealing sound of foul language emerged. I wish my daddy would have been alive and at this hospital with me, on that day, to scold this lady. Foul language was not allowed in my home, so he would have had a feast telling this woman how unacceptable cursing is.

Unfortunately, my dad had passed away the previous year and therefore could not intervene, unless he came as a ghost. That would have been interesting. I do not know if the lady would have been more concerned about the fact that my father was scolding her or about him being a ghost. Come to think of it, with the unpredictable behavior of this woman, perhaps my father would have been the one spooked away.

She was a mature African-American woman, probably in her late 50's or early 60's, who had been admitted to the trauma room on that day. She was arguing with the nurse about the IV; she refused to have one placed in her arm. She argued that she had been there for two days and that she had not received medical attention yet. Because of that, she was refusing the IV. The nurse tried to convince her, but she was not able to get that job done. My goal of being able to sleep was postponed once again. Had all the noisy women in the world conspired to come to my hospital room?

## 64. The care of traveling nurses is the best luxury in a hospital.

It was not long before I had in front of me the break I needed, a woman in her 30's, African American, with a calmed and peaceful demeanor, came to the room to change the dressings covering my wounds. -Hi, I'm Gyolonda, and I'll be your nurse tonight. Said the kind lady with a sweet voice. Her tone of voice was music to my ears, contrary to the scandals of my noisy roommates. The calmed nurse changed my gauze, gathered the liquids that came out of my stomach and even changed my diaper with an unusual commitment to her nursing call. Someone loved me in heaven and sent this angel to my rescue. Her nametag said: traveling nurse. I paid close attention to that.

-What is a traveling nurse? I asked intrigued. -It is a nurse brought from another state. -I, for example, am from Texas. -I'm going to give you an injection now. -Where would you like it, on your arm or on your belly? Said the nurse with a tender tone. –Nowhere. My mind thought. Those injections are quite painful, I quickly remembered, but the nurse was so polite that I gave her an equally kind answer. -What would you recommend? I inquired. -Your belly. Gyolonda replied. -Go ahead. I said, fearing another painful injection. I turned around to look at the curtains of my room. -That's it. Gyolonda said. -What? I remarked. -That's it. She repeated. -Did it hurt? The traveling nurse asked. Hurt me? I did not even feel it.

Thank you dear God for bringing me a nurse that knows how to inject. I did not tell her that last sentence but I did say: -wow, you're very good. With a timid smile, the nurse left. I was amazed. In a few moments I had understood the true meaning of the title "traveling nurse." It meant true perfection in nursing. Why else would a hospital bring a nurse from another state? This skilled woman could inject, change a diaper, cure a wound and even talk in an affectionate way. Just when I thought the chaos at the trauma room did not have a solution, this nurse came along to bring hope and order.

The employee made me feel protected, and I immediately told her about my concern, my breathing and sleeping problem. Her response came right away; in the blink of an eye she called a doctor. This nurse was the solution to my problems. My plan was that the doctor, called by the traveling nurse, would solve my breathing problem; that way, I could sleep no matter how much noise my roommates were making.

### 65. Inactivity weakens muscles: walking will give them their strength back.

By the morning, my team of doctors had studied the X-rays. They told me I should start walking so oxygen would flow better to my body and my muscles got some exercise. It was not the sophisticated solution I expected but if walking some steps helped me to breathe, let the hospital hallways get ready for the new runner of the Los Angeles marathon. I would only wait a bit for my trainers, mom and my husband so that I would have someone to lean on. As soon as both came in, I communicated to them about their new job. They both did what I asked and went along with me in my enthusiasm.

Without wasting time, they helped me to stand up but since I had the pump that fed me attached to my stomach getting ready for the race was a bit complicated, so we called a nurse to remove the device and the pole that held it. Either the nurse had too much to do on that day or she was tired or she was simply lazy; the truth is she told us to take the entire pole with me. Some nerve! Does not she understand that what I have to do is walking; the doctor did not mention a steeplechase. Carrying that pole with me was nuts. Was that nurse taking morphine?

Despite my doubts, I decided to accept the challenge so the staff would realize I was cooperating and would not think I was as problematic as my roommates. So, with a slight smile on my face aimed at the lazy nurse, just like the one given at a job when the boss asks us to do something we do not agree with, I held the pole while my husband and my mother walked next to me, holding me and helping me to carry it. I could barely walk; I felt like I was carrying heavy chains in my derriere.

Taking steps was already hard enough as to add the

weight of the pole that held my feeding pump, the IV and several medications. I wonder if the nurse that suggested it had ever been at the hospital, not as an employee but rather as a patient on a bed. She probably had no idea how difficult it was for someone with an open stomach and thin bruised arms that held 30 pounds of equipment, to walk while carrying such a heavy load when the patient barely weights 98 pounds. I felt exhausted and breathed heavily. I believed I reacted with the same exhaustion of someone that just ran the 26 miles of the Los Angeles Marathon.

My heart was beating super fast. My breathing was desperate; I tried to inhale but could hardly do it. My inactivity had weakened my muscles. After walking a few steps, I felt fatigued and slowly returned to my bed. My mom and my husband helped me to sit down. Their runner had not even begun the race when she had already given up.

### 66. Do not change your healing routine if you want to improve your health.

Later on that day one of my sisters, Miriam, visited me along with one of her sons and her husband. Happy to see them, I did not stop talking. They had driven from San Francisco where Richard, my nephew, was studying. We talked about my surgery and about an operation of my nephew's wife. Suddenly, operations and long stays at the hospital were subjects I had some experience in and was happy to share with others. Using my scarce energies to talk, however, seriously debilitated me. During that day I did not notice it so much since I had more energy then. But during nighttime I suffered a great deal, trying to do basic things such as breathing with the few energy reserves I had left. I learned a lesson: I could not talk much or change my healing routine if I wanted to accelerate my hospital discharge.

## 67. Breathing problems could be caused by liquid in the lungs.

Dr. Sassani, one of my doctors at the trauma room, came excited to my corner. This doctor had physical traits from the Middle East; his skin had that golden tan that characterizes many people from Arab countries. I did not know what his religious beliefs were, but I assumed he was a Muslim, maybe because he seemed to keep some distance with his female patients. With the joy of someone who believes to have found a solution to a big problem, he asked me if I gave him my consent for a procedure he was convinced would help me breathe better. I looked at him enthusiastically. Of course, I said yes. I responded before he finished his question and using the little air I had left.

My husband and my mother were told to wait outside while several resident doctors came to help Dr. Sassani. The doctor explained to me that with a needle he would suction liquid out of my lungs. It was at that moment when I found out I had pneumonia while at the intensive care unit; I had not been previously notified. Now I understood why I had the bothersome phlegm in my chest. Another thing I heard, I cannot recall if it was at that moment or later, was that IV's can fill lungs with water; apparently my poor organs were drowning but no one had notified me. No wonder I felt that I suffocated; it was because my lungs needed a life vest.

Then, why was I told in several occasions to go to sleep at ease when I spoke about my choking sensation? They treated me as if I was a little girl that complains for anything, even though they knew the reason behind my ailment. Fortunately, doctor Sassani seemed confident to have found the solution. It was the first time he would perform this procedure by himself, so he asked for my approval. The doctors with him were not so convinced; they wanted to wait for Dr. Pierce, the surgeon who had operated on me. He had performed this kind of procedure before.

But I desperately needed to breathe, so doctor's Sassani's proposal attracted me more than the one of his co-workers. I really liked Dr. Pierce but Dr. Sassani was in my room at that moment and therefore, he would be the one that would help me. -I trust you. I told Dr. Sassani in a very confident and reassuring way. -God sent you here to help me so go ahead. I told him with great confidence. Dr. Sassani smiled satisfied; his co-workers would no longer object to his intentions since the patient had so eagerly granted permission. That was the green light Dr. Sassani needed to start his procedure.

Without wasting another second, the novice doctor told me to bend forward while sitting on my bed. This was a very painful position for me, due to my open wound and the tubes in the abdomen area, but I desperately wanted to breathe so without thinking about it twice, I bent forward and the procedure began. With my back facing the doctor, he inserted an enormous needle in it, to suction the liquids that had accumulated in my lungs. I did not feel much pain, even though I could see how two big glass containers were filled with liquids; needles aimed at my lungs extracted them. Oh wow, was all that water drowning them? I wonder who will suggest now that I was pretending to be sick!

Despite the inconvenience of the process, I felt like a peacock showing off his beautiful feathers. This was my moment to boast that my complaints had a real and dangerous foundation. When Dr. Sassani finished extracting the liquids, I panicked. My eyes opened wide; I felt desperate for not been able to breathe. I was grasping for air. Dr. Sassani was alarmed as well. Poor thing, I do not know who would have suffered more if I would have died in the process, if him because this was his first time performing this procedure or me because this would have been my last. -Are you okay? The doctor asked me. -I can't breathe. I responded alarmed and with a broken voice. -Bring me the oxygen. I said, trying to inhale some air. The doctors that assisted Dr. Sassani grabbed the tube that came from the oxygen tank and put a mask on my mouth in less than a second. I think they were as alarmed as their patient. This was not a test; it was a life and death situation, perhaps the first several of them had to attend.

After a few tense minutes, I regained control of my body. I breathed on my own again and as soon as I could, I put the doctors at ease. They train for the worse, but I am sure they did not want to see the catastrophe on their first case. I finally felt out of danger. That was reason enough to celebrate. If a patient died today, everything seemed to indicate that someone would not be me. I felt like my lungs were finally able to expand along with other organs, to take their natural form, the one they had before the accident. It was as though those body parts had shrunk for days, trying to avoid the water accumulated in my lungs and now that the liquids were gone they could finally recuperate their original form and position.

Dr. Sassani understood and waited next to me for any other reaction. I am sure he was as relieved as his patient that at least today I would not say goodbye to the world. In seconds I felt much better; my heart seemed to be beating less agitated. -Are you okay? Dr. Sassani asked once more, with his face still pale for the scare. This time, however, I let him know that I could finally breathe. I was talking about myself although I do not know if the doctor took it literally because he breathed deeply and relieved and after him the rest of the doctors. All the doctors left the room satisfied while my mother and my husband returned.

## 68. Due to high-maintenance patients, doctors doubt the real aches of low maintenance ones.

I proudly showed my relatives the containers filled with liquid from my lungs; not even showing an "Oscar" would have made me so proud. I had always thought people who showed their friends and family medical oddities, like the stones they had removed from their kidneys or the scars they have from surgeries, were a little weird but now I totally understood them. They are just so happy to have survived the ordeal that they have to show proof of it, just like an athlete would show off a medal. In my case, I was happy to show off the two big containers with the fluid that was removed from my lungs; it was my trophy. In other circumstances, I would probably have been disgusted to see that but now it was my big prize.

These liquids were the ones responsible for my breathing problems and they were finally gone, trapped inside those two bottles where they could not hurt me or anyone else. I could finally breathe and it felt great, not only physically but mentally as well. The water in my lungs was the proof I needed to give myself more "credibility" with the medical staff. Two doctors had said I could go to sleep because I would keep on breathing. They thought their patient was afraid to die in her sleep. That was not what worried me and this was the way to prove I was not a "crying baby." It feels wonderful when facts confirm your innocence. I would no longer be treated the same way whiny patients were dealt with. This event had placed me in another category, the one of the truly sick patients that look for a reasonable solution to their aches.

Without needing a trial, acquitted of all charges, thanks to the overwhelming evidence of my innocence. The fact is my credibility immediately obtained a better position in that room; cased dismissed in this People's Court.

### 69. If you are requested for an unannounced test, make sure you are the one they want.

Next day, a nurse assistant came to my room with a bed to transport me to a test. None of my doctors had notified me about it. Because of it, when the assistant, very determined to take me with her, was about to transfer me to the other bed, I quickly stopped her and asked what was the test for. She notified me, and I realized that this test had nothing to do with my condition. Right away I let her know that maybe the person she was looking for was not me, and I asked her to tell me the name of the patient needing the test. She then searched in her documents and surely enough found out that the test was for someone else who was not even at the room.

I do not want to imagine what would have happened to any other person, like some I have met that never question anything. They would have gotten a test that would not have helped them and perhaps would have harmed them and on top of it, would have delayed someone who really needed it from getting the test done.

### 70. The liquid diet will not satisfy your hunger nor your palate.

Those who have higher probabilities of successfully overcoming difficulties in a hospital are the ones that take charge of their own welfare. In my case, having asked to be allowed to eat by mouth had led my doctors to grant me this luxury before it was due. That day, I had the pleasure of receiving my first meal in two weeks. For days like this one and paying days, life is worth living. To the beat of my imaginary drums, anticipating the huge banquet I would have after such a long time without eating, I started to open the lid. I opened it with great enthusiasm and did not believe what I saw. This cannot be, is this a practical joke? Where is the hidden camera? I thought this because the employee left the food tray and walked away before I opened it. I guess that employee suspected what my reaction would be. The succulent lunch that would become my first meal by mouth after 20 days at the hospital would be a gelatin, a salty broth, and a juice.

Now that is just being mean, bring me the same food the others have. My brain could not accept my bad fortune. Was this what the doctor meant by a liquid diet? In my hometown, a liquid diet would consist of an incredible chicken broth that would awaken the dead. But this broth has no chicken, no vegetables and it is only a bowl with dirty water. I mean, really? Is this what they call broth here? Such a pity my doctor was not from my hometown! My mind could not stop complaining.

"Don't worry, be happy." The song says. Right next to me was the best remedy to my problem; my mother was from my hometown, and she cooks broths that can awaken anyone. I asked my mom if she could bring a homemade soup the next day, and she said yes. Happiness music was heard in my mind and it filled up the entire hospital. My mouth got watery visualizing myself tasting that peerless chicken soup. Who needs a hospital's liquid diet when your own mother can prepare the best soups in the world?

Of course I ate the gelatin, the salty broth and the juice; "a bird in hand is worth more than two in the bush." They had no flavor, the gelatin and the juice were totally tasteless, and the broth was just salt but at least it was an appetizer after the long wait I had to endure to eat by mouth. The true food would come tomorrow with my mother. If I had waited so long to taste it, one more day was nothing. My happiness would not be interrupted by anything on this day. In fact, since there was no longer liquid in my lungs and after that tasteless banquet I just had, I would probably fall asleep and would be able to complete another mission I had been meaning to fulfill for days, sleep without interruption.

### 71. Use every chance you have to sleep: resting is a luxury in a hospital.

Mom was worth her weight in gold; she covered me with a warm blanket and encouraged me to sleep while watching over me; with such assurance anyone feels safe to fall asleep, choking with phlegm while sleeping would not be a concern anymore. For two hours in a row I slept. No breathing problems, choking or facing monsters; I had a beautiful and energizing nap, like the ones I used to have before the fall and woke up happy to see my mother still there.

I am glad I was able to sleep those two hours because the noisy girl from the room had just awaken and that meant no one else could sleep while she was awake. This time the alarm to wake up were not her screams but a chain sound that rumbled the entire room. Concerned, my mother looked outside the curtains. -It's the new patient. I told her with the arrogance of someone with experience in the field. -She had a car accident. I told her with the enthusiasm of someone tired with the situation. With such noise, there was no possibility to continue sleeping so mom and I had no other choice but to shift our attention towards the car accident patient.

## 72. Patients may fool many but never their doctors.

While we observed the patient's scandal, I went on to tell my mother about the doctors that had come in the morning and asked the young woman what happened before the accident. She answered that she did not remember anything, and they notified her that her tests revealed that she had taken a large dose of amphetamines. Goodness gracious, that sounded like the plot of a novel; huge dosage of amphetamines almost kills the young lady. Why did she take so many pills? Did she attempt to commit suicide? The young woman sustained that she did not even remember the accident. The plot of the novel thickens; the young victim suffers amnesia.

When I heard her from my bed talking to the doctors, I assumed she was telling the truth, but the doctors did not seem so convinced; they obviously knew something that was unknown to me. This story was becoming really interesting.

## 73. Demanding pain medication constantly could indicate a patient's addiction.

-Could you believe her grandmother and her sister came and did not even wait for her to wake up? I made a parenthesis to bring my mother up to date. -She has been sad the whole day, waiting for a relative to come. I notified the author of my days. We both felt sad for the young woman, especially my mother; she could not understand how a mother could not be by her daughter's side in such a difficult time. Mom and I did not know what was going on at that home and our point of reference was ours, where family is always first.

When we heard the patient screaming again, to demand her pain medication although she had been given the maximum dosage recently, I realized that perhaps her family was not the villain in this story. The evil character of this movie could be her. The treatment for her wounds did not seem to matter as much as her constant dosage of pain medication. That seemed to be her real illness; she was addicted to drugs, whether they were amphetamines or morphine. Realizing this alarmed me and since I felt rested because I had slept for two hours, my body felt energized enough to help thy neighbor.

I decided that it was my duty to help the young woman and at the same time lend a helping hand to the rest of the patients in the room, including me. I would teach this girl the rules of conduct and survival in a hospital. Since I already had some experience in the matter, I thought that my knowledge would educate this rookie patient. My task would be to get out of my bed and walk to hers, which was by itself a huge project. Once there, I would let the young woman know that she was not alone and that she can help herself.

Move over motivational speakers, the new life coach had begun her task. With the enthusiasm of those starting a new job, I asked my mother to help me walk once again around the room. I guess mom thought my advices would help the girl somehow; either that or she did not contradict me because she knew I needed to walk. Anyway, it was a great relief that my mother backed me up; otherwise, I would not have dared to walk around the room with the pole that held my IV and medications.

With my mother holding me and helping me to carry the pole, I walked towards the young woman and told her, with the little voice that came out of my mouth: -God loves you, but you have to love yourself. -Just talk to God and concentrate on your healing. The young woman seemed pleased to hear these words. She smiled tenderly, and I assumed my brief but hefty speech had moved her or the fact that the message came from another patient that could barely walk and looked so ill.

-Come here please. The patient asked me. Just shoot me! I certainly was not expecting that reaction. What is my emergency plan? My mind thought; I panicked and did not know whether to do what I was asked or just do like this patient, fake amnesia when asked uncomfortable questions. Were not you so prepared to give speeches? What is your back up plan if your audience gets violent? My brain kept searching for alternatives. She looked quite big and intimidating.

Although her body was lying on a bed and it was hard to tell her height, she looked tall and strong. If I did not cover my bases, this big woman could toss me around like a simple piece of paper.

My little body was substantially smaller; she was an extra large size Yankee, versus a pocket size Hispanic; there was no need for her to stand up so I could find out. She was not overweight; actually, she was rather slim with a big bone structure. My skeleton was small from top to bottom and greatly under my ideal weight so the thought of risking my already delicate anatomy, to try to help this big looking woman, did not make much sense.

I hesitated for a few seconds but finally decided to be a Good Samaritan and approached the young woman cautiously. Please God take care of me, otherwise you will have to welcome me very beaten up there. My mother was behind me, and she is quite big so if anything went wrong, I am sure she would defend me. -Give me your hand. The young woman said. My sixth sense, if that is the one for survival, told me this was not a brilliant idea. But after hesitating once more, I convinced myself I had enough protection, in case something went wrong. I gave the patient my hand. -Thank you. -You're an angel. Said the young woman, and I felt super sorry for a few moments, until I looked carefully at her eyes; they did not look focused, her gaze looked totally gone. Her face was facing me but her eyes seemed far. It was the same glance of people I have met under the influence of drugs.

I truly wished my message motivated a positive change in her but seeing her eyes, I knew my words went nowhere. -God loves you. I repeated once more; trying to get my message across that young woman's brain, now filled with medications. -Now you have to love yourself. I assured her. The young woman replied: -thank you. But my whole being felt there was nobody there listening to me and that every answer coming from her lips was an act rehearsed multiple times and destined to obtain what she wanted by faking vulnerability.

Needless to say, I was not successful in teaching co-existing rules to the car accident patient. My hope was that her family visited her so that she would be so busy that she would not even think about medications. For now, she was tame after I had spoken to her. I crossed my fingers while I walked towards my bed, hoping that meekness would last some hours.

## 74. If you barely have the strength to walk, a walker can be provided to support yourself.

During the small walk to my bed, I felt I would not have enough strength to reach it. My legs were as heavy as lead, the pole with my medications certainly made every step harder. It was then when Amin, a slender African nurse in her 30's and with a 5 feet 5 inches height, saw me making a big effort to walk and asked me with a sweet tone of voice if I preferred a walker. At last, someone with common sense spoke. Excited, I said yes and Amin quickly requested it. I was starting to get used to the idea that for every person that behaved irrationally at the hospital, there were at least 3 others that behaved in a compassionate and considerate way.

I developed special affection for this nurse; she spoke softly and strived to care for each patient. When my mom asked for clean sheets, she would bring extra ones. When a patient missed her meal for any reason, she would look for something to feed her. She was the mold of an unselfish nurse. I would have been so happy if all the nurses were equally good but since not everything can be peaches and cream at the nursing department, there had to be an evil one. Anyone who thinks villains only exist in novels or stories surely has not met the "Unhappy Nurse Attendant."

### 75. While many nurses and assistants help the patient, others help themselves.

The one whose name shall not be repeated, to avoid any probability of duplicating the formula and increasing the chances of other patients suffering the torment of her cares, worked during the night shift at the trauma room. At least the name of the room fit the cold woman like a glove since it was traumatic to be treated by her. She was a big overweight woman, African-American, in her late 30's or early 40's. I met her the second time I had been fed by mouth during the day; it was a few hours after visiting hours were over. I was barely able to move and was not able to go to the restroom, so I still wore diapers.

I pulled the black cord, the one used to call the nurses, to let the attendant know my diaper needed to be changed. The intimidating nurse attendant did not hide her disgust while changing my diaper. I felt so ashamed witnessing the revulsion she displayed as she did her task. I felt extremely vulnerable and would have given anything to be able to change the diaper myself or even better, to be able to go to the restroom. -You know, you have to work with me. -You should be going to the restroom. The nurse attendant told me quite upset.

Wait a minute, did I hear right? Did she just ask me to help her do her job? I did not tell her this, but I thought about it; it was not even possible for me to move. Cannot she see that? I must admit that if this would have happened to me in my regular self, chances were my reaction would have been as confrontational as hers was. Luckily, in those days my personality was eager to understand thy neighbor. I am not sure if it was because I felt close to death or if my religious beliefs had finally made a better human being out of me or if the medications just had me stoned but some or all of the above, were responsible for my uncommon and peaceful way of behaving.

-But I can't bend yet. I sweetly told the nurse attendant

with a very soft and low voice, trying to make her come to her senses. -Well, you have to start doing it. This was the assistant's answer to my remark. Her words had a cold and pounding beat tone; she sounded just like the villain from kid's stories, Cruella de Vil. I did not tell the lady anything. Did I just say lady? Did I have medications last night? Nope, at least not the kind that makes you feel drugged. Well, I guess I must be becoming someone more civilized.

The truth is that I did not tell the assistant how much I disapproved of her response, verbally or physically; I did not frown my forehead or respond right away with a "smart" remark. I just let her talk and remained quiet; I just simply did not know how to react. For some reason, I now analyzed what I thought and said carefully, to make sure the answer was the appropriate one from someone who believed in God. That did not stop me from feeling afraid of the assistant. Suddenly, I felt really afraid to announce my diaper's changing time.

Hours later, even though I was really afraid to do so, I had to pull the black cord again. Some steps approached. Fearing it would be the unhappy assistant I squeezed my sheet, just like someone who accepts a tragic fate. The curtains of my corner were quickly opened and luckily, the one who peeked was another assistant. I relaxed immensely and told her that my diaper needed to be changed. -I'll call your nurse. The attendant said and quickly left before I could say anything else.

I then felt terror, my knees trembled and even my teeth

clenched. What if she asks the unhappy assistant? At that moment I felt that if my condition did not kill me, the assistant would. For the first time, since I started my stay in this hospital, I did not feel safe. -Oh no, not again. -I'm not going to change her again. Said the nurse attendant loudly and with an aggressive tone from the hallway where these health employees were located. Everyone heard her; I felt so ashamed. I heard her and started to feel great anguish. I waited for her perturbing presence but seconds and minutes passed, and she did not come. I do not know what worried me more if the fact that my skin was getting greatly irritated for the need of a diaper change or the desperation of not knowing if the one that would help me would be this woman that loathed doing it so much.

After half hour, I got an answer. A new assistant that was very polite did the deed in a quick and adequate way. I must admit I relaxed when I saw that the one that came to help me was not the unhappy assistant but now I dreaded even eating, for fear of needing a diaper change. Luckily, the morning shift had come. The evil assistant, who like vampires spread her evil ways during night shifts, had to leave as soon as the sun came out, to allow some happier employees take care of patients. The only shift where other employees seemed as miserable as the unhappy nurse assistant was the one on Sunday nights.

## 76. Sunday nights are the worse shifts in a hospital.

At sunset and nightfall on Sundays, patients could anticipate a hard evening. At that time, the staff taking care of us was very limited and not necessarily the happiest one. For some of them, this was their second working shift, and they were very tired. I cannot blame them for not being so thrilled about working so many extra hours. Many of them did not even want to stay for a second shift but had to accept it; this triggered the sleepy and unhappy state of many employees. I accept that if I had to work 16-hour shifts in a hospital, where tasks are so exhausting and involve life and death situations, I would not be happy either. Sometimes, other than regular vital check ups, these employees were gone for longer periods of time than the patients would have wanted. On several occasions, we had to wait too long to get pain medication. On one of those occasions the young car accident woman, whose addiction earned her the nickname of "the junkie," complained for a long time; listening to her screaming that way worsen the condition of the rest of the patients. Why did not anyone from the hospital come to help her or shut her up?

The girl started hitting the frame of her bed once again; she woke up all of us patients in the room, but no one from the nursing staff came, even though the noise was insanely high. There was only one nurse available but since she had other rooms to take care of, it seems she did not notice the chaos in ours. On top of it, when someone finally responded to the screams, it was because one of the beds had to be made to welcome a new patient. The responder, unfortunately for me, was the unhappy assistant. I must admit that the confrontation between two highly complicated people, such as the unhappy assistant and the junkie, was interesting. The patient gave a show that included screams, hitting the frame of her bed and complaining loudly and the assistant fully ignored her; she went in and out of the room as if she had not heard a thing and the junkie, who was used to getting her way screaming, kept yelling to find out if someone paid attention.

### 77. Bringing a TV will entertain you but it will also attract unwanted patients.

Not only did we have to deal with the unhappy assistant that hated her job, but we also had to put up with the tantrums of the junkie. Why was this young patient in our room and not in a rehabilitation place for addicts? As the young woman demanded her medication, the older woman who had been recently admitted started to talk to herself. For a conversation at least two people are needed, right? Apparently this dame did not know that since she could have long conversations with herself. -I want to watch television. -How come we have no television? -I hear a television. -Where's that music coming from?  Said the restless lady loudly.

The music was a car commercial that could be heard from my television set. At a corner of the room, my husband had left the TV on with low volume, so I could have a light on at night. The mature woman seemed to have perfect hearing since she was able to hear it. Like a bloodhound smelling his pray, this lady followed the sound to spot the TV. She started searching behind every curtain of the room; without permission she opened each one, to see if she could watch TV. I felt great paranoia; the last thing I wanted was an unstable woman in my room, especially after hearing her cursing at the nurses earlier that day.

As the woman searched every curtain, getting dangerously close to mine, panic possessed me, just like fear takes over possible victims of a serial killer. I felt like the next one to be sacrificed and wished to be able to move, so I could hide or turn off the TV. When the old woman was about to open my curtain, I held my breath as if expecting my sure death. Then, out of nowhere, a saving voice was heard. Another patient told the woman to stop her search; she warned her in a firm and sentencing voice that the television was mine, not the hospital's property. The warning made the woman stop in her tracks.

I could not believe my good fortune. God bless that anonymous hero that saved my life when I needed it the most. I could breathe again as I heard the voice of my rescuer calling the attention of the mature woman whose meek response seem to indicate she felt ashamed of her behavior. With the remote control, as quick as my aching body allowed me to, I turned off the TV. I could hear the discouraged steps of the old woman, slowly walking away from my corner and despite feeling sorry for her, for she could not get the entertainment she was looking for, I did not feel guilty. My health was far more important that this lady's whims. If I truly wanted to get better, I had to put my health first, even if this felt a little selfish.

I guess there are moments when we should put our own health ahead of things that are not so important. I felt great relief with every step the mature woman made to get away from my corner. If someone had to deal with her tantrums today, at least it would not be me; I felt sorry for the nurse that had to do it a couple of minutes later.

## 78. Ignoring roommates with mental problems could be the healthy thing to do.

The nurse came to the bed of the mature woman with an IV; apparently, she needed a surgical procedure that required it. Yet, the patient refused it. The employees had insisted since last night, but the lady did not allow it; she claimed that she was also a nurse, and she knew they were doing a bad job. From the first moment I laid eyes on her, I knew something was not right in her head, but I did not understand why the nurses did not notice or did not care about the fact that this woman seemed to be crazy. She behaved exactly like other insane people I had come across in my life.

This woman made no sense in almost anything she said, including the reasons for avoiding the IV; she alleged to have been in the hospital for a week when she had been admitted the day before. She claimed to be a nurse but did not have a basic understanding of it. She insisted she had health insurance with a health plan of great reputation but was on Medicaid, the state's free health coverage. She boasted about being a talent agent of Hollywood stars when that was obviously not the case. I must admit when she said that, my ears paid great attention. What if she was not crazy? This might as well be my opportunity at stardom. Now, that would be wishful thinking!

I was weak, in a hospital bed but my brain kept working just fine. I knew this woman was not in her senses and although human beings often cherish the idea of making our dreams come true instantly and magically, like when we play a lottery ticket, it was evident that patient had as many connections in Hollywood as plain Jane had in Wichita. The woman had so many careers that it was almost impossible to not realize that her mind was not completely there.

Many of her behaviors were obsessive, such as cleaning; she tried to sterilize the restroom with paper towels. If being echo-friendly and protecting the planet rests on people like her, this world is in serious trouble. I think she used half a roll of paper to clean an already clean restroom. But none of the obsessive behaviors compared to the bad attitude she gave the nurses. When one of them tried to put her IV on, the woman's complaints increased.

The nurse finally gave up; the mature woman's cursing was the last thing she was willing to accept. The nurse left after turning off the lights of the room. The mature woman complained for a while; she alleged it was too early to go to sleep and wanted to know who had turned off the light. After a while, she got tired of complaining and finally fell asleep. Let us all go to sleep, lest the insane woman awake or even worse, the junkie!

### 79. If a nurse assistant panics, the patient will worry even more.

The morning came rather quickly and with it a new shift. Another nurse attendant checked my vitals and seemed very nice. She changed my diaper without a single complaint, and I felt relieved. The nurse attendant then started to empty the tubes that channeled the pancreatic liquids, from inside my stomach into two small plastic balls placed outside it. When the attendant emptied one of those balls, she opened her eyes wide in disbelief. -Did you see that? The nurse attendant said alarmed. I looked at the ball that had just been emptied; it filled up quickly with liquid from my pancreas, in the blink of an eye. -I have never seen anything like it. Remarked surprised the nurse assistant as she emptied the now again filled up ball.

I got concerned; how could I not if these nurses and assistants rarely seem surprised with anything. If this nurse was so surprised, it could only mean I was in really bad shape, I thought. Because of it, when my mother and my husband came that day, I told them about the incident and asked mom to call my other sisters, so they would come to see me, in case I was in worse condition and did not survive.

Such petition made my mother extremely sad; this was the first time I saw tears in her eyes. She had constantly shown her best smile, so I would not get discouraged. But the possibility of her daughter departing before she did, broke my mother's heart. I tried to cheer her up. -I feel better mom. I told her. -It is just in case. -You know they would not forgive us if something happened, and they did not get to come. I said with a tender smile, trying to encourage the author of my days.

Mom tried to refrain from crying, took her phone and exit the room to call her daughters; she did not want me to see her crying. Even in her darkest hour, she was more concerned about her daughter than about herself. If one day I get to be half the good human being my mother is, I would consider myself extremely blessed. Her prudence moved and motivated me. In a few days, we all realized my health was improving; my condition was not as grave as the nurse assistant had led me to believe. After this, I learned to not give so much importance to assistant's comments since they do not have the preparation of a doctor; their diagnosis is just guesses.

## 80. Ignoring some things can be the best decision in a hospital.

The tranquil afternoon became chaos when the insane patient, whose bed was next to the junkie, started to complain loudly that someone had stolen her credit cards. The two big complainers had their beds next to each other, coincidence or punishment? The fact is the nurse tried to explain with great patience that nobody had been in that corner, but the crazy woman replied with insults and demands. How uncomfortable is when someone closed by insinuates a robbery; it makes all of us feel pointed at.

Seeing the uncontrollable behavior of the angry woman, mom told me about a time when my father shared a hospital room with an Alzheimer's patient. Back then, my father was the one sleeping when some me shoes landed abruptly on him. He barely had the strength to cover himself a little with his blanket. Poor dad, I identify with him now more than ever; the blanket did for him what the closed curtains did for me, keep unwanted patients away.

Therefore, although the insane woman was speaking loudly, I decided to ignore her and let the nurses and assistants deal with her. I did not feel proud to do it but life at the hospital was teaching me that sometimes ignoring some things is the prudent thing to do. If you do not join the show, with luck it might be shorter, and we can all rest sooner. And yes, as a matter of fact, the show concluded quickly because nobody, other than the nurse, paid attention to the insane patient. But when it rains it pours, silence did not last long. A few instants later, the roommate whose bed was next to the mature woman and held the title of the noisiest of the room, the junkie, had visitors.

## Chapter 5:

## The art of co-existing in a hospital

### 81. Do not help those who do not want to be helped, use your energy in your own healing.

FINALLY SOMEONE WAS VISITING the young car accident woman: their voices and laughter penetrated my curtains. How great! Mom and I thought. Maybe her family would obtain what my motivational skills were not able to achieve. We hoped a family reunion would help this patient to be less whiny. From our corner, mom and I could see another young blond woman who we assumed was the junkie's younger sister. Their conversation, however, was not a family oriented one, unless her relatives happened to be the ones of Don Corleone's family in the movie "The Godfather". They were talking about drugs. One of the visitors was telling the patient that she had to take care of herself. -No more dope. He told her. Soon, he mentioned other drugs that supposedly the junkie was taking before the accident.

From my corner, I thought about how sad it is that many patients lie to their doctors about drugs they have taken or cigarettes they have smoked, as if doctors would not find out everything that concerned their patient's health with their multiple body tests. I knew it was a matter of hours before doctors found out about the many drugs the young patient had in her blood. It was not my responsibility to tell them, not because I did not want to help but because when my doctors came I barely had time to tell them what was wrong with me. Anyways, this young woman did not seem to use the help offered to her in a positive way; therefore, my energies were put to better use by taking care of my own well being.

Now that my mother was with me, I would walk a little. This time I had a walker that was brought in by an attendant of the physical therapy department, whom taught me to use it. Another nurse had disconnected my tubes, so I could walk without obstacles. I could now concentrate on walking and not on figuring out how to hold the IV with the little energy I had left.

As I passed by the young woman's bed, I was able to glance at some of her visitors. What a disappointment, they were not relatives but friends; that is not to say that being visited by friends is worth less than being visited by relatives.

The point is those friends were not precisely the positive influence needed by the girl. One of them was also a patient; his hospital pajama gave him away. He got treatment at floor number 11, the one designated to drug addicts. All of the other friends also looked like people slaved by drugs; their faces had the same lost look the young woman had.

I was a bit discouraged. I really had hoped the wicked witches were this young woman's relatives, and she was the princess, but her relatives were not the evil characters in this story. She was the rotten apple, not the good princess who got poisoned when she bit the apple. Confirming the sad reality only made me feel worse. I kept walking slowly out of the room, beaten, defeated, like someone who loses a battle. I guess that is how the young woman's relatives felt; chances were they left as soon as they found out the accident of their relative was triggered by drugs.

I kept walking out of the room, leaving behind the voices and laughter of the girl's visitors and trying to concentrate on my own healing so that the young woman's situation would not affect me. Walking away physically, however, did not make my worries go away. Just like when you have a problem, walking away does not make it go away. But this time, I had no other choice but to walk away and let that woman solve her own situation. She had created this chaos and it was her duty to get out of it. The rest of us could only observe and hope the hurricane caused by the young woman's consumption of drugs would not get unleashed again.

## 82. The patient that refuses treatment is discharged.

Moments later I returned to my bed; I was as exhausted as if I had climbed Mount Everest. Trying to get healthier in a place where other people's well being occupies your mind, is truly challenging. Mom helped me to lie down. -How come you are refusing the IV? Both, mom and I heard a doctor as he addressed the mature patient at the other corner of the room. Patience Jackie! I had not finished thinking about the junkie when the insane lady took the spotlight once more, too many divas to deal with.

-I'm not refusing it. Said the mature woman. -See, I have been here for days, weeks even and I have not gotten attention. The insane woman reassured but the doctor, as well as everyone there, knew she was not telling the truth. -Then, let me set your IV so we can prep you for your procedure. The doctor said, trying to go along with the patient. God bless this doctor's patience. In normal life, anyone would have responded with some insults to this woman to make her come to her senses but not the doctor.

Totally unaware of her good fortune of being treated with so much respect by the hospital's employees, even though she was behaving worse than a crying baby, the mature woman continued with her tantrums. She refused once again the IV while complaining about how late it was for that already. -Then, you are refusing treatment. Said the doctor, this time growing a little impatient. -I'm not. The patient declared and started to cry. Her tears looked just like the ones kids show when they want to convince you of something they know is a lie.

The doctor obviously did not buy it. Probably, just like many parents with weeping children, he had seen these "dry tears show" too many times to be impressed. Because of that, he told the nurse: -write down that she refuses treatment. -I don't. The patient said, clearly forgetting about the theatrics of the tears, which would have demanded a broken voice, so she would still seem to be crying and suffering.

The doctor armed himself with the patience that only someone so educated can exhibit. -Then we can go ahead and place the IV? He said with a very proper tone but with a hint of impatience. –No. She answered, still pretending to be crying. -Write it down. -We can't help you like this. Said the doctor first to the nurse and later to the patient, obviously fed up with the old woman's intransigence, before leaving the room. The nurse kept walking behind him, and the patient remained in the room crying or pretending to be, probably convinced that her show had been successful.

## 83. If you allow darkness in your life, get ready for disaster.

After a few minutes, I got an unexpected visit. -Jackie, are you there? A sweet voice was heard outside the curtains. —Yes. I replied intrigued. -It's Madeleine, Christopher and David; may we come in? Continued saying the sweet voice and I was able to confirm that the one talking was my fellow actress Madeleine. -Of course. I happily replied. These were the actors I had been working with in a film that had been finished just a week before my accident. The presence of those friends made me feel super happy; somehow, they made me feel closer to recovery. For half an hour we all dreamed together about the positive things this film would bring us and for the first time since my accident, I dared to plan for the future.

It was not until much later that I thought about the idea that my participation in that movie could have had something to do with my accident. As crazy as it sounded, I could not stop thinking about the fact that I had acted in a horror film and perhaps that had attracted my adversity. The tragedies that for years have surrounded actors who have participated in such films, have received widespread publicity around the world, and I now wondered if that had brought me to this hospital. I had never acted in a horror film but when a director I had worked with requested it, I auto-convinced myself I should participate; otherwise, I believed in superstitions.

# SAVE ME FIRST

With that thought in mind I went to Mexico, along with my fellow actors to make the movie. As we entered the luxurious mansion of four floors where we would stay and that would also be used as one of the locations for the film, I felt some coldness in the air. I had goose bumps, and we all felt that someone we could not see positioned him or herself in front of us. -There're ghosts in here. I pointed out a little concerned to the young owner of the house, who was also the producer of the movie. -Nobody told me there would be ghosts. I told the guy with certain humor but also with some preoccupation of confirming my hunch.

Surprised, he replied: -how do you know? His response caught me off guard; I was expecting him to say any other thing but not to confirm the presence we all had perceived. -I sense someone. I told the young man, a little worried for the decision I had made of participating in this movie. What if my concerns were not superstitions? What if horror films do attract dark forces? —It is my grandmother. -She lived here for many years, but she is a good spirit. The young man said; his response made me land once again in that place.

The light-heartedness of this young man replaced that first impression with excitement when he showed us the beautiful mansion that would be our home for a whole week; it had its own library, its private theater with elegant movie chairs and incredible spacious rooms. The house was so big it had its own elevator. I would sleep in a huge room on the second floor. I did not feel there were ghosts there. That was a relief. I was not afraid of ghosts, at least I wanted to pretend that but pretending or not, I preferred not to deal with them.

As the shooting progressed, we discovered there were other spirits in the other house we were filming at and these ones did not seem to be positive; they made eerie sounds in the middle of the night, and we could feel their presence, even during midday. But the film was finished on time and nothing bad seemed to have happened. Perhaps my doubts about making horror films were unfounded after all, a simple superstition like one of my acquaintances had suggested.

It would have been so easy to pay attention to my hunch, but us human beings tend to want to experiment things first hand, even though in our heart we know it is not right. Just a week after we finished the horror film, my destiny changed dramatically. I had this accident that had brought me to this hospital and that keeps me struggling between life and death. Who says playing with demonic subjects does not harm anyone? Whoever tells me that should get ready for a heated argument.

I did not link my participation in this horror movie to my tragic accident until much later when I realized that indeed many negative things had happened to the people involved with the film. For starters, I experienced this accident. To continue, another actor died immediately after a sudden illness. Curiously enough, the director called that actor to do another horror film but he could not participate in that film or in any other; he died rather quickly. To complete the tragedies, the other actors faced big problems in their marriages and their finances and as much as the director tried to finish editing the film for its release, it never saw the light of day.

In my mind, there was no doubt that God did not want this film to be released. I did not feel punished but rather guided to a more positive realm. Had I not experienced this accident, chances were I would have kept doing films like this one, thinking there is no harm in them: but after my stay at the hospital, I had a more complete picture of what these kind of movies do to people who watch them. For the past weeks, negative spirits that make eerie sounds have haunted me.

Many times, when I prayed to God for protection, I remembered how many horror films I had watched in my childhood; now, I was sorry I had watched them. If my recent film had been shown, many other people would have been haunted by eerie sounds and images that would also include my face. That would be terrible, the fact that my face would provoke panic in a kid or an adult. I hope the director and the producer of the film forgive me but somehow I am happy if this film is never released.

## 84. Traveling nurses inspire confidence in the patient.

As exciting as the world of cinema felt, I now had to forget about the fantasy of films and focus on more important things, like keeping myself alive. A new nurse came to check up on me; she was a tall and beautiful African-American woman in her 40's. She inspired so much respect that for a moment I assumed she was a doctor. –I'm Lillian. -I will be your nurse tonight. She said with a confident and sweet tone of voice. She was so sweet that my spirit quickly perked and with great anticipation I looked at her badge. She was another traveling nurse! My entire being knew what that meant, pure perfection in my care. Every time a traveling nurse took care of me, she would do it with the same dedication my mother put into taking care of me; I knew I could put my life in her hands with total confidence.

Not even the high maintenance girls, with their complaints, would make me feel bad tonight. This nurse will take care of me just like the angels would. As soon as my husband returned, I told my mother: -you can go and rest. As a matter of fact, mom was really tired, but she did not show it or complain. She only wanted her daughter to get better. –Are you sure? Mom asked, noticing my sudden enthusiasm. –Yes. I responded. Both, my mom and my husband, left to take a much-needed rest after making sure everything was in its right place, in case their dear Jackie needed something but this time none of those precautions were needed. The best of the best of the nursing world would take care of me that night and that gave me peace of mind.

## 85. Your gases may decrease by changing the milk you are fed with.

Lillian, last night's traveling nurse, came to change the dressings that covered my wounds and to pour more milk inside the device that fed me. She seemed a little upset while curing my wounds. -It's not fair, you know. -You've been through so much. The imposing nurse told me with a very compassionate tone. This comment moved me. Lillian took care of me with the tenderness and devotion of someone who takes care of a dearly loved relative. Not even the continuous burps coming out of my mouth, which were caused by the medications and the milk I was given through the tubes that went to my intestines, seemed to bother her.

I felt so ashamed for not being able to control those disgusting burps, but Lillian did not seem to mind. -If you need anything, just pull the cord. Said the nurse with the sweet tone of a consenting mother. She behaved just like moms when after feeding their babies they smile satisfied because the kid has gotten rid of gases. I felt safe and loved; this was going to be a good night.

The next day, when I woke up, I felt rested for the first time since being admitted to the hospital. The relaxing sleep time fueled my energy, and I woke up with a greater desire to speed up my rehabilitation. My doctors came early to check on me. I told them about concerns, such as the phlegm that still made me feel like I would choke and my inability to control any bowel movement and my constant chest gases, which I believed could be relieved by changing the milk formula I was fed through my feeding pump.

I then asked for my milk to be changed. The nurses provided me one that had less sugar and I accepted it gladly; anyways, my mouth would never find out if the milk was sweet or sour. The change of milk proved to be the perfect recipe to diminish my gases.

### 86. Do not try to help troubled people, let the professionals take care of them.

The goal was to accelerate my healing as much as possible; the arrival of new patients was an obstacle. That day a woman from El Salvador was admitted, her accent gave her away, even though she did not speak much; she was rather screaming as if being stabbed to death while she was placed on her bed. From my corner, I was able to see her. She did not have any medical equipment attached to her body, neither did she have wounds that looked painful; she did not even have an oxygen mask on or at least an IV, yet she could not stop screaming; her tone of voice was harsh and loud.

The patient scowled at everyone, and I assumed it was

because she could not bear the pain, so I decided to make her feel better: -don't cry. I told her with a compassionate tone and trying to "save the world" with my intervention. -They will take good care of you here. I added, assuming those words would calm her anxiety. The woman looked at me and her stare did not conceal her surprise when she saw the tubes embedded to my body. She did not respond, but I thought it was because her pain was so strong that it did not let her think, or she was too tired to answer, or she felt ashamed for her screams since she looked in better physical condition than me.

Suddenly, the new patient started to scream again, this time way louder. She scared me; the last thing I expected was that violent reaction. No tears came out of her eyes but if pain was measured by screams, this patient was dying. I decided to intervene again convinced I could make this woman relax with a few inspirational words. I guess that inasmuch as I felt so rested after the previous night, the motivational speaker in me flourished once more. -You'll be okay. -I've been here for almost three weeks, and they have been great. I commented with great confidence and enthusiasm. -Three weeks? The new patient yielded and then started to scream even louder.

Did an animal just bite her? She is going to leave us deaf! Perhaps my motivational skills were a little rusty. A nurse that was nearby made a signal, and I understood I had to stop my conversation with the new patient. That was as far as my intention to help that woman went. She obviously did not want my help. I did not address her anymore. I felt sorry for not being able to help, but I learned every patient handles illnesses, pain and hospitals differently and only trained staff, like nurses and doctors, is prepared to deal with them.

### 87. Surrounding yourself with positive people will recharge the energy lost with negative ones.

This screaming concert so early in the morning had left me without strength; I guess what people say about some persons draining your positive energy, with their negative one, is true. Luckily, my family always came to recharge my batteries. That day my mom, my twin and my husband came with my other two sisters. I was so happy to see them! They started to pamper me right away; their good vibe made me feel better.

My sister Carmen asked for time off at her job in Puerto Rico and left her husband and her two young daughters to take care of me in Los Angeles, California. My youngest sister, Omayra, had to put up a big fight with her bosses but came anyway. The presence of my family made me feel like the luckiest woman alive. Right away, my sisters divided tasks to help me, not only at the hospital but also in all of my responsibilities out of it. Once their tasks were distributed, my sisters and my husband left while my mother remained by my side. The nurses were happy to see the great help mom gave them. They did not have to worry about me as long as Violeta was there. In case they were needed, they came happily and rapidly, seeing the support they were getting from this mother, something that perhaps they wished happened with other patients like the junkie, whom never received the visit of her family with the exception of the first day when she was asleep. Perhaps because of that, as time went by, she exhibited a reprehensible conduct.

## 88. The hospital does not tolerate patients that come only to get drugged.

That day my mother had to witness the show given by the junkie. The girl demanded her medication with screams as usual but since the nurse tending to her denied it because the girl had already gotten the maximum dosage, she became hysterical; she threw her food and everything she could reach at the employee and afterwards at an assistant that came to help her. Right away, reinforces came to tie the uncontrollable young woman to her bed. All the patients of the room were nervous. My mother also watched the incident in disbelief. We were even more amazed at the patience and self-control of nurses and doctors in disturbing moments such as this one.

But everybody's patience had reached its limit. People who come to the hospital after morphine are not considered patients and their selfish behavior, that affects the possibilities of other people getting prompt attention, is considered unacceptable. The junkie had fallen into that category; she cared more for the drugs she was receiving than for the treatment for her accident. She should have warned the doctors of her addiction, so she could be treated in rehabilitating places, like the one they had on another floor in the hospital. She would be transferred there, in order to free the bed and assign it to a real patient who wants to be cured, not doped.

That night the atmosphere was still tense because of the violent confrontation between the young woman and the nurse. The patients, including me, could not understand why the girl was still in the room. Lillian, the visiting nurse, looked quite upset for the first time. She was tender and loving to all but seemed upset at the junkie. -I need pain medication. The young woman dared to scream from her corner once more but this time Lillian responded with authority: -there's no more medicine for you, and I don't want to hear anything else from you. The young woman did not dare to answer. Even addicts recognize whom not to challenge. I guess there was some sanity left in this patient as to recognize that this nurse had the height and the physical strength to cause serious damage if Lillian had opted to do that.

Obviously the nurse would have never dared to do that in the hospital but perhaps the patient ventured to think about what would happen to her outside. Whatever motives she had, the young woman seemed to finally have come to her senses and understand that her best option was not to mess with the intimidating nurse. The junkie only complained once more when security agents and several attendants finally took her out of the room.

## 89. The first thing patients and relatives lose in a hospital is control.

If on the one hand high maintenance patients make rehabilitation in a hospital a titanic task, on the other, there are other distractions that make the recovery a slower one; one of them is the sudden loss of control patients and relatives experience. No matter how hard we try, no one can control the situation; therefore, the situation controls everyone. In my case, I could not control my body or my noisy roommates, so I tried to control my family. Mario, my husband, could not control his house now filled with my relatives, so he tried to control the situation by rebelling. He disagreed with practically everything proposed by my relatives and by me.

The funny thing was that during my stay at the hospital he looked like the most famous rebel in modern history: Che Guevara. He had hair all over his face because he was going to portray the famous character as an actor for a documentary of TV's History Channel. Everything seemed like one of those movie parodies from Hollywood. On the one hand, there was the living image of Che Guevara represented by my other half and on the other, the opposing regime now represented by my relatives and me. My appearance was not precisely the one of an invincible enemy because my tubes and my oxygen took luster out of my so-called leadership.

One thing was certain though, my little mouth was worse than an atomic bomb; its words could hurt more than any weapon, especially if the other combatant was someone whose weak points I knew so well, like my husband's. As a leader, it was my duty to stop this "rebellion." Everyone had to agree with me in my territory so in order to achieve it, what did I do? I looked for a history character that had more power than Che Guevara, now represented by my husband. Since that day I had morphine in my veins, the chemicals in my body made me make an odd choice. So when my husband confronted me as Che Guevara, I said I was Hitler.

The little room, filled by my sisters, my mother, and my husband made a brief silence; Hitler was a bad choice. On top of it, since this patient had lost so much hair, thanks to the medications, I had the hairdo of this German character, with the parting of my hair on my left side and the scarce straight hair covering up the slight baldness that started to show on my right side; I only needed a mustache to complete the totally abstract visual. Had this control fight gone too far? Judging by the strong laughs that followed that was precisely the case. No one could stop laughing; Hitler vs. Che Guevara, now that would have been an interesting sight, too tragic and too comedic at the same time.

Good thing everyone, including me, understood that I was not precisely the "leader" to follow as long as I had morphine in my blood; neither was my husband's Che Guevara's spirit the appropriate one to follow in this battle. We all had to deal with the fact that the only one in control, in a situation like this one, was and always will be God so the sooner we all let go of our need to control our destiny, the faster everything will fall back into place.

## 90. The patient's attitude and his/her family's involvement influence the healing process.

Most of the patients just wanted some order in our chaotic room so the arrival of a silent roommate gave us some relief. Her name was Francisca, a middle-aged Mexican woman with a very advanced cancer. Fortunately for us, she was totally different from the noisy patients; even though she was in delicate condition, she never screamed, not even once. She constantly prayed in silence and did not start any argument with anyone; she had simply come to be healed.

Hospital cares aside, two factors are key in a patient's healing: attitude and family involvement. Positive patients, like Francisca, always heal faster than the negative ones. By the same token, the patients who can count on the support of their families, as long as their relatives are equally positive, heal even faster. I did not read this in any book; I witnessed it continually in my long stay at the hospital. Another thing I witnessed was that Hispanic patients had better odds at healing than the Caucasian or African-American ones, simply because their families were there to take care of them. Because of it, they do not get lost in the system.

Caucasian and African-American patients are more independent and rarely, if ever, are they visited by their relatives; at least that was the case in my room. The mature African-American woman, who refused to get her IV, did not receive the support of her family and her attitude was anything but positive; she constantly cursed, refused almost every treatment and even the sweet nurses were losing their patience. If they turned off the lights in the room, the crazy patient turned them on again. If they requested silence, she made more noise. If they came to take her vitals, she treated the employees disrespectfully. Needless to say, they all got tired of her and the next morning the inevitable happened.

## 91. Some patients get violent when they are discharged: keep your distance.

-You have been discharged. The nurse said kindly to the deranged woman. -Why? Asked the mature African-American woman, visibly surprised and unable to understand the reason for her discharge. The nurse, without any animosity in her voice or traces of confrontation, manifested to her that the hospital could not take care of a patient who refused treatment. The mature woman lost her temper and cursed the employees for hours. I do not know why she was allowed to be there after her discharge, but the woman took a long time to pack her things while crying.

The rest of the patients in the room were glad to know she would leave; her screams and cursing made us all nervous, and we all hoped her departure would occur quickly. I did not even go for my walk around the hospital, to comply with my doctor's recommendation for exercise, not only because I felt weak but also because I did not want to face the now violent patient.

### 92. If physically you cannot do something, do not do it, you may worsen your condition.

That cold night, the nurse assistant that seemed to hate her job and had refused to change my diaper two days before, came back. As soon as I saw her, I was in total distress. -What am I going to do? I panicked. This meant I would not have anyone to change my diaper. I did not want to have to face the unhappy nurse attendant once again, so I decided to go to the restroom by myself.

As soon as I walked a few steps, I knew I was doing the wrong thing. I could barely walk; the feeding pump and the pole that held it felt like 500 pounds to me. I was weak, breathing with great difficulty and did not have the physical strength to go to the restroom, let alone by myself. Yet, I was determined to reach my goal. Anything was better than submitting to the humiliation of that nurse.

After slowly and painfully walking across the room, I finally made it to the restroom with incredible effort. Once there, I had no clue on how I was going to sit down; I had an open wound, four tubes embedded to my stomach and inside it was a split pancreas that made bending practically impossible. The nurse attendant knew this, yet she demanded I help her "do her job." The minute I tried to bend, the pain I felt tripled; it was as though I had broken something inside of me. Why did I pay attention to a lazy nurse? I started to use the toilet but felt so weak that I almost fainted. Minutes later, I tried to stand up but the pain did not allow me to. Then, a sudden loud knock hit the restroom door. -Open up! A woman screamed, and I was able to verify it was the deranged woman. I went through so much trouble to hide from her, and she found me at the restroom. What a nice place to hear demands, at the least honorable position and feeling really bad and on top of it, I could not respond to her; I felt I was dying.

-There're other patients here. The screams of the woman kept on going, accompanied by her florid curses. I wanted to reply but no sound came out of my vocal cords; I could not even alert the nurse so that someone came to help me stand up. Up to a certain degree, not having a voice to answer back was a positive thing; I would have told some harsh truths to the derange patient. I guess in that case, "every cloud has a silver lining." Since the uncontrollable woman did not get a response from me, she left, or she was taken out of the hospital. The truth of the matter is that when I finally was able to stand up and open the door, the mature woman was no longer there. I was glad because I felt in worse condition than when I entered that restroom and was not physically ready for that encounter.

### 93. Never compromise your health for anyone that does not want to do her/his job.

Bending down to use the toilet had probably caused an internal hemorrhage, at least that is how I felt; boiling liquids flowed uncontrollably inside my belly. As soon as I opened the door, I tried to ask for help but my voice was not loud enough to call anyone's attention. It was not until I almost fell down that the new nurse saw me, ran to me and caught me, just in time before hitting the floor. The nurse was a loving Korean woman, in her 40's or 50's with a height of around 5 feet and 4 inches. Holding me, she helped me to reach my bed.

-Oh my God, what happened? The Korean nurse asked me visibly concerned. I mumbled with the little voice I had left that I was not supposed to go to the restroom, but a nurse attendant had asked me to do it. While the employee listened to my story, she started to cure my wounds and changed the dressings covering them; they were wet and cold and were freezing me. For the first time, during that shift, I was as dry as I was supposed to be and this brought me great relief.

My tubes leaked on the sides; because of it, my dressings had to be changed at least four times a day. Sometimes they leaked more; this was one of those occasions. Bending to use the restroom made my internal liquids go crazy. Thankfully, the Korean nurse did not begrudge on the amount of dressings she used to cover up the tubes; otherwise, I would have felt just like a baby who pees many times in the same diaper.

The nurse also requested a commode so that whenever I needed to go to the restroom, I could do so right next to my bed, without the danger of fainting while on my way. But as much as that polite employee helped me that night, the damage caused by the visit to the restroom was already made. Complying with what I had been asked for by someone from the staff, created a setback in my rehabilitation; I could not move from my bed for three days and if I tried, I felt excruciating pain.

### 94. A massage is worth gold in a hospital.

The next day, during visiting hours, my mother, husband and two of my friends noticed the bad shape I was in. My friend Elba was especially upset to hear about the nurse attendant who refused to change my diaper and made me go to the restroom. She told me that if the nurse attendant came again, I had to call the staff supervisor to request that nurse attendant removed from my care. Her advice sounded appealing and well founded since she was the friend that had worked at this hospital for 33 years and had brought me here but since I was in my "love thy neighbor" mood while at the hospital, I thought requesting the removal of someone from my care could compromise her job. I did not want to harm anyone but was greatly upset at this assistant.

Luckily, that shift was already gone and now people that loved me surrounded me. One of the friends that was there was an expert in lymphatic massages; her name is Amparo, which coincidentally means "protection" in Spanish. As soon as she came in, she honored her name and gave me real protection. After praying with me, she gave a soft massage to my feet. I closed my eyes and immediately felt as though a current of energy came from Amparo's hand into my feet and burst rapidly into my damaged organs, giving them an incredible feeling of healing warmth. She did this by touching specific places on my feet and later on, on my hands and head. Every time she touched a new body part, she said a prayer.

We felt great faith in this procedure, and I instantly experienced great relief. When the massage was over, everyone in the room was so relaxed that even my husband had fallen asleep; the peace in that tiny "room" was incredible.

## 95. If you do not feel safe with a nurse or assistant, ask to be taken care of by another one.

Peace does not last long in a hospital. -Can you stand? I heard a woman say when none of the allies from my family and friends were in the room. -You need to take a shower. The cold voice continued, almost side-by-side to my curtain. -Just shoot me! I thought, is the unhappy assistant's voice. She was talking to a new patient placed at the bed next to mine that was apparently covered in blood. The voice of the assistant gave me the goose bumps.

Knowing that a patient next to my bed was covered in blood, probably because she was the victim of a crime or the perpetrator of it, did not scare me at all. The voice of the unhappy nurse attendant, however, almost paralyzed me. Right away, I became very anxious. I remembered my friend's words: -call the staff supervisor. After thinking about it, for a few moments, that was exactly what I did.

My heart was beating extremely fast; I panicked. I pulled the black cord for emergencies and to my dismay the one who answered was the nurse attendant that seemed to hate me. -What do you want? She asked in a mortified way. Trying to hide how terrified I felt, I behaved like an actress and spoke with the security of an executive. -I want to see the staff supervisor. I said this without hesitation but with my mumbling voice. The nurse attendant looked at me briefly; my heart seemed to stop in expectation. Rapidly, she closed the curtains, and I could finally breathe again.

Moments later, the supervisor came. She was a timid Caucasian woman in her 30's or 40's, with a height of about 5 feet and 2 inches. I explained to her, in a peaceful way, I did not want to be taken care of by the nurse attendant. -Why? The supervisor inquired. I told her about the incident, and the supervisor understood; nevertheless, she tried to convince me to accept the care of the nurse attendant. -At night we don't have many nurse attendants. Today, we only have two for the whole floor. Said the supervisor, trying to convince me. -Then leave me without an attendant. I was quick to answer, even though I barely had the strength to talk. -Don't worry; we'll manage. The supervisor pointed out, understanding she would not change my mind.

From that day on, the unhappy nurse attendant was not allowed to treat me. I felt so relieved. I could care less if I had to wait a long time before being taken care of. To me feeling safe was more important than being quickly taken care of by the same person who would make me feel worse.

### 96. Better to wait for a traveling nurse than to rapidly be taken care of by a mediocre nurse.

That same night I saw in the distance, at the end of the room, a nurse in a red uniform. Could it be possible? I could not give credit to this sudden and drastic change of luck. In my first difficult nights at the hospital, a nurse that wore a red uniform had taken care of me with great devotion. My heart started to beat faster, anticipating the probable encounter. I watched from my corner, waiting to catch a glimpse of the nurse's face. She turned around. It was her! The same nurse that had helped me at the intensive care unit was now at the trauma room. Blessed be God. My night would be, after all, fabulous.

The beautiful woman in the red uniform was a traveling nurse. It took a while for her to treat me since she took plenty of time with each of her patients but when she finally reached my corner, I felt incredibly blessed to have her there. Right away, my wounds were cured, my diaper changed, my liquids removed, my wet gown changed. I felt so protected that I started to whisper a song I had heard from a puppet that one of the patients of the room had received as a gift: -you are my sunshine, my only sunshine. -You make me happy when things are down... -Please don't take my sunshine away. I sang to her with a mumbling voice but with great appreciation.

The nurse with the red uniform seemed pleased to hear her patient singing her this tune. It was as though these moments were the reward she got for her long hours of taking care of the sick. The beautiful Caucasian nurse, with blue eyes and golden hair, certainly seemed like an angel as she lovingly wrapped me in a warm sheet. Feeling like a little kid, pampered by her mother, I thanked her and feeling loved and safe closed my eyes and fell soundly asleep.

## 97. Inept employees destroy the work of good ones.

If all employees that take care of patients were as prepared as the nurse in the red uniform, rehabilitation would be considerably faster; unfortunately, inept employees also abound in a hospital. That morning an assistant came to pick me up for a CAT Scan test, which consists of some powerful X-rays that take 360-degree pictures of the internal organs, the spinal cord and the vertebrae. The young woman taking me to the test came by herself and instead of asking for help to move me to her bed, she pulled me by the arm; either she was not given the information about my delicate condition, or she decided to not read my record. It was a miracle she did not dislocate my arm. The truth of the matter is that she pulled me as if I was in perfect condition and the sudden movement made my delicate abdomen get worse. I did not want to be thought of as a "crying baby" by the hospital staff, so I bared the pain and did not say a word.

I had waited quite some time for this test and now that it would finally be made, I would not add any obstacles. Waiting for another test meant drinking a horrible tasting medicine called "the contrast." It also meant no being able to eat, not even the liquid diet I had fought so hard to get. On top of all this, waiting for another test meant another IV on my arm, to receive any additional medication during the test. That was equivalent to being "pinched" with several needles until someone found my vein. Needless to say, I did not want to experiment this process again, so I bared the pain of being pulled and we went straight to the CAT Scan room.

### 98. With so many tests and employees, not knowing a patient's needs is the norm.

Once at the room of the tests, the staff requested I lay down on my stomach. Did I hear right? Don't they see the tubes embedded and the huge open hole with several infections in my belly? I wanted to comply with what I was asked, so they would know I was cooperating, but I could not move, less so lay down on my abdomen. My instinct told me that trying was madness. Nevertheless, I tried to be an obedient patient. After all, they are the professionals, I reasoned. But the task was impossible, the pain excruciating and I had to let them know I just could not lie on my belly.

The most experienced technician understood right away but another one that was with him and seemed inexperienced, insisted that I had to do it. Fools rush in where angels fear to tread. Luckily, the experienced technician stood firm on his decision that the test could be done without having me laying on my belly. Instead, I lie down on my back. Unfortunately, the damage had been done; I simply could not move. I had to lie flat on my back on the test's bed and this, in turn, seemed to upset my already split pancreas even more.

I learned a big lesson that day: I discovered that being a

good patient also consists on warning caregivers about the seriousness of our condition. With so many patients and even more caregivers, many of those who take care of us have no clue of our severe condition. I also learned that if something looks terribly wrong, it probably is. I knew I could not lie down on my abdomen; yet, I thought all the people at that room would not force me to something that would work against me. Wrong again, these people do so many tests and bring in so many patients daily that overlooking special necessities of any patient is the norm, rather than the exception.

### 99. The secondary effects of medications are many and none are good.

I wished I had a manual to know these things before hand but since that was not the case, I learned the hard way to always be the first one to warn any caregivers about anything that concerned my own health. The infections in my abdomen increased as well as the dosages of medication. I felt extremely weak with the medications. Since I rarely took medicines in my daily life, their side effects felt stronger. I had strong cramps all over my body and felt like a drunken person that did not even enjoy the taste of alcohol and went directly to suffer the hangover. I also felt nausea and sometimes felt depressed without reason. Also, my skin was so dry that it cracked and fell off my heels in thin layers. My hair was also falling dramatically. No beauty contest would have considered me acceptable at that time.

Next morning, when the doctors came, I begged them to reduce the amount of medication I was receiving through the IV at least for a day and see what happened. If I got worse, I would gladly take them again. My head doctor, Dr. Salim, did not give a conclusive answer at that moment; he always analyzed his options carefully. Next day, however, once the medication bags from the IV were empty, I did not receive any more of those antibiotics. Yes! This doctor is a dream come true; I would put my life in his hands a thousand times.

The removal of those medicines made the secondary effects go away and once again I had more control of my body. Let's get ready to rumble, I no longer have those medications that make me feel stupid; now I'm ready for battle.

### 100. Patients long for free will: getting it motivates them to work in their rehabilitation.

I was convinced that more food through my mouth, as opposed to that feeding tube that fed me that cloying milk through my stomach, would make me feel better. I was not very hungry; a few spoons of homemade soup would motivate me to continue the strenuous rehabilitation. It was not the quantity of food I missed, it was the opportunity to be able to eat like any other regular person; because of it, I asked my doctors for a solid food diet. -What do you want? Asked one of the female doctors. -A strawberry. I replied excited because they had paid attention. The power of advertising! The previous night I had seen a commercial on television that showed an appetizing strawberry, and I craved for it. -A strawberry? The doctor asked while looking at the head doctor who in turn asked another doctor: -are they even in season? -Let us see what we can do. The female doctor said and I got happy since in previous occasions when I had been given ambivalent answers such as this one, the outcome turned out to be in my favor.

At that moment, I did not know that my team of doctors had gone through several arguments with the doctors from the gastroenterology department, whom did not want their patient to eat anything by mouth, not even liquids. They were convinced that the feeding pump was all Jackie needed and this was safer because the tube that fed me went directly to my small intestines and did not go through my damaged pancreas; but what about my opinion? What is the use of living if you feel like you are in jail? My whole being longed for free will and eating a strawberry sounded like my bail. In medical terms it did not make sense to give me that strawberry but in human terms I desperately needed it for what that fruit represented.

My doctors agreed to feed me by mouth since they were convinced this would do more good than harm. The fact that I felt so weak and was so skinny was crucial in their determination. To my luck, on that same day, I received a plate filled with fruit; it looked so appealing that I did not know where to start. How consenting were my doctors. I only had a few bites and although there was not even a single strawberry because they were not in season, the few bites I had made me feel liberated, owner of my own palate. How fresh, juicy and ripe were those fruits! Of course, "after the binge comes the hangover;" painful gases accompanied by shortness of breath came to visit me sharply; this was a price I was more than willing to pay in order to accelerate my rehabilitation. I knew that if I could handle some solid food without fever or diarrhea, I would "graduate" to a higher "level" and be allowed to eat diverse solid foods. That was my new goal, not having to settle with being part of the audience that simply watches and smells the delicious plates that her roommates ate.

## Chapter 6:

## What to avoid, accept and find in a hospital

### 101. Sadness feeds illnesses.

BEING ABLE TO EAT THE HOSPITAL'S FOOD was a dream come true for me but for a new patient at the room it seemed to be a nightmare. Her name was Camilla, a Mexican woman in her late 50's with cancer. She was assigned to the bed next to Francisca, the other patient with cancer. Camilla got colorful food that looked appetizing, yet she did not want to eat it. We both started a conversation when one of the attendants, who did not speak Spanish, was placing the device for vitals on her arm. Camilla was trying to explain to her that the right arm was hurting a great deal because it was the one used the most for IV's and was quite bruised. The nurse attendant did not understand, so I translated what Camilla was saying from my corner. This would be the beginning of a beautiful friendship between the two of us.

Day after day we witnessed each other's ups and downs. Camilla also became very friendly with my mother and offered her hospital food to my mom because she really disliked it, and her daughter always brought her food from outside. Camilla was a great roommate; she did not complain and accepted the medications she was given. But her recovery was slow because she did not want to be in the hospital. Most of us patients did not want to be there, but Camilla's case went even further; she was extremely homesick, she wanted to go back to her small town in Mexico where she had the happiest times of her life.

Her sadness and nostalgia was killing her more than the cancer in her blood. Camilla was certain that moving back to Mexico, to her little hometown, would make her feel better, but her sons did not want her to leave: they wanted their mom here, receiving what they thought was the best care for her illness. Unfortunately, the sadness she felt made her feel worse by the second. She cried constantly and all the patients felt sorry for her.

One day, Camilla was listening to Christian music and praying while crying. She looked so sad that I stood up, with the little strength I had, and went to her bed. -Don't cry.

-Everything is going to be all right. I told her, the motivator in me could not resist the temptation to influence this woman to be happy. Tears kept rolling down Camilla's face, so I proposed to make a prayer between Camilla, Francisca, the other patient next to her, and me. I prayed so that Camilla would see her illness not as a punishment but as an event only the strong survive and if she was going through it, God must be convinced that she would endure it and obtain something very positive from this, in the long run. A nice motivating speech wrapped in a prayer; I thought it would be a big hit.

That seemed to be the case; Camilla seemed calmed after the prayer. A few moments later, however, she started to cry again. Go figure! Either my prayer was not good enough or my speech lacked impact. Plan B: Francisca, the other patient, held Camilla's hand and told her to be strong and positive and she would get better. Okay, it sounded like my little speech but the speaker was someone that had cancer as well and Francisca was at an advanced level, almost terminal. How much more credibility could the speech get? Right? Camilla would surely be touched by the words of this patient that not only shared her condition but also managed to get better every day, thanks to her positivism.

Francisca did not have a single ounce of self-pity. There she was, in worse condition than Camilla, with a definitely more advanced cancer and yet she was the one trying to cheer her up. Seeing that Camilla was still sad, I dared to unleash

Plan C: I started to talk about the beautiful small towns I had visited in Mexico. Camilla's face immediately lit up. Bingo! I had found the way to cheer her up. Talking about her beloved Mexico proved to be the medicine she needed. Camilla rapidly shared stories about her small town with a huge smile on her face and for a magical moment her worries seemed to vanish, and her memories took the three of us to a happier world.

### 102. As a precaution, visitors should not help other patients.

Language was not the only factor that united Camilla, Francisca and I; we also enjoyed sharing our good or bad fortune during our treatment. Other patients did not have the same need to socialize. They were lonely people and did not socialize with other patients or received the visit of their relatives. Mom and I felt sorry for a woman that had not been visited by anyone. She wanted someone to fix her pillows since she had a car accident and could barely move. The patient asked someone to help her, and my mom, without thinking about it twice, went to her rescue. I felt so proud to be able to share my mother's help.

In her super-hero role, Violeta hurried to help the woman when a nurse intercepted her and warned her not to help the patient. Both of us were in shock. What were the motives behind denying help to his woman? We did not get a response at that moment, but we learned soon enough that it was a preventive measure. We found out that many people get extremely complicated when they are in a hospital; they sue for anything, even if someone is just trying to help them. Many factors could be responsible for this, among them, lawyers on TV commercials; they promise to give anyone fair compensation for practically anything. In Los Angeles suing is an everyday sight. If your doctor was not able to revive someone destined to die, just sue him or her and get your rightful compensation, whatever that means.

Our society is constantly looking for culprits. Is because of this that only relatives and friends are allowed near a patient in a hospital, to avoid any situation that could potentially become negative; in other words, to avoid being sued. For example, if my mom would have done something as simple as placing the pillow where the patient wanted it and in doing so hurt the patient in some way, the consequences could have been devastating to the hospital, the patient and even my mom. Mother and daughter would have to watch, pretend we did not see a thing, wait and pray that those lonely patients would get the gift of receiving the visit of their loved ones.

### 103. Patients who do not follow protocol are released early.

Maria del Carmen and Omayra, two of my sisters, entered the room at that point to bid me goodbye and to give me some presents before leaving, since both were returning home on the next day. I will always remember the days we spent together at that hospital as the most meaningful of our lifelong relationships. Other patients were not so lucky; the occasional volunteers that visit hospitals only visited them, but the sick surely prefers to be frequented by our loved ones.

Unfortunately, many patients do not receive that long awaited visit; such was the case of a woman who had come to the hospital covered in blood two nights before. She had no visitors, not that she would have noticed since she was always asleep. After two days of being delivered into the arms of Morpheus and waking up just to request pain medication and some food, a doctor came to talk to her: -why haven't you been to the health clinic to follow up on your appointments? The doctor inquired. He seemed upset since the patient had advanced diabetes she was not taking care of, even though the county's health system provided her with medicine and free care.

The patient, an obese African-American middle-aged woman, did not seem to come up with an acceptable answer. -Do you know your diabetes is at a very advanced stage? -We cannot help you if you don't help yourself. The doctor said, visibly upset. Perhaps she did not know what those words meant but the witness in me had some experience in the subject matter; the patient had made two of the mistakes doctors do not accept from patients: not following up on treatment and using the hospital as a hotel, restaurant and a way to get drugged. The result came rather quickly.

-The patient is discharged. Announced the doctor to the nurse, which after filling-up some paperwork returned to wake up the current ex-patient. -Ma'am, you are discharged; you can go home. Said the nurse to the still sleepy woman. —Ah. The patient replied, still trying to wake up. -Do you have an address? Asked the nurse. —No. The woman responded, barely being able to open her tired eyelids. She was homeless and therefore did not want to leave the hospital. -Why? The patient asked the nurse. -You have been sleeping all the time and taking pain medication. The nurse replied as if letting the patient know she had been busted.

The woman understood perfectly. -Can I have more medication to take with me? The lady dared to ask, obviously more concerned about getting drugged than about getting treatment for her diabetes. -Let me see what the doctor says. The nurse replied and returned a while later with two Tylenols. -No more medication for you ma'am. -Do you have someone to pick you up? The nurse asked her. —No. The patient replied. The nurse left and returned with some spare change: -this is for your bus. She told her and officially discharged her.

From my corner I watched the incident and had mixed feelings. On the one hand, I felt sorry for this patient who was still obviously sick, with advanced diabetes and taking the bus to go to sleep in the streets. That was a very scary reality.

On the other hand, I understood the doctor's reaction. Someone who really wanted to get better, a person who followed up on his/her treatment could have used that hospital bed. Yet, the thought of that old woman sleeping in the streets that night when the night before she was the roommate in the bed next to me, was quite disturbing.

As sorry as I felt, I knew that the irresponsible behavior of the woman was what got her discharged, not her homeless condition. Actually, the hospital staff treated her with great respect. There was no disgust in the faces of the employees for the bad condition of the woman's skin. Neither did they make a wry face to react to how she smelled when she came in or acted surprised when they admitted her covered in blood. They treated her just as they would any other patient with health insurance, but she did not seem to value her life enough to follow the steps she had been given by her doctors and there was a price to pay for it.

## 104. Nurses in training want to practice with the patient: allowing them will benefit both.

As the homeless woman slowly walked towards the room's exit, I noticed the presence of a group of people that, contrary to her, followed directions easily, the nurses in training. A beautiful female nursing professor, Caucasian, thin with fair skin and long brown hair in her late 30's, supervised the students. With a sweet tone of voice she asked patients if her students could perform nursing activities such as checking vitals, wound care and injections.

At first, the obvious reaction of many patients is: -no student will treat me. But when people see the devotion of these students, how incredibly fast they come when they are requested and even before they are called and how eager they are to make the patient feel better; then, it is the patient who eagerly awaits them. All the future nurses wanted to practice with me since I was the only patient, at that time, at the trauma room with an open wound.

I found that funny and weird at the same time. I felt like the frog kids get to cut open at biology in school. Fortunately, the goal of these students was not to cut my body in pieces like the school's frog; they just wanted to practice with me and were actually excited about it. Go figure! Truth being told, these students' cares made my mornings more pleasurable.

## 105. A mistake in your hospital's paperwork could be the difference between life and death.

An Asian nurse that belonged to the group of nurses in training was among the ones that collected the liquids that came out of my tubes. He did most of his nursing work greatly: checked vitals, placed IV's, injected me, etc. But apparently he made a mistake by writing down an erroneous amount of dangerous liquids coming from my pancreas. One of the doctors scolded him harshly. For the first time, since my admission to the hospital, I saw one of my doctors really upset.

The young Asian male nurse, in training, rapidly corrected the mistake in the paperwork. I felt sorry for him; he had been shamed in front of his classmates. Nevertheless, I understood why the doctor called the attention of that student with such a strict approach; a mistake in a patient's paperwork could mean the difference between life and death, especially in this case. The liquids had to be measured in a precise way, to know exactly the medication needed to dry them up; recording a smaller amount or a higher one would affect my health considerably. One thing was certain, that soon to be nurse never made that mistake again and all of his paperwork was flawless from then on.

### 106. Nursing students give undivided attention because they have few patients.

Each nursing student was in charge of two patients; this worked in favor of the ill because we were helped instantly. Many of the apprentices had extraordinary gifts. One of the nurses in training was a young Hispanic woman that had so much talent to inject that I rapidly bonded with her. I am not saying that being injected is reason to celebrate but having the task done right is. Counting on someone that had precision to inject when my arms and thighs were as purple as Barney the TV character was a good reason to celebrate. That being said, I was so sore due to the previous injections that my enthusiasm was not as apparent, but I will be eternally grateful to this student for polishing her skills so quickly in that area.

Another thing these trainees did was to change the dressings of my open wound and the dressings of the leaks around the tubes in my stomach. For some strange reason, these nurses in training actually thought it was exciting. Had they come from another planet? I am not complaining but it was weird that someone enjoyed that. I guess they were excited to be able to practice what they had learned with someone that had so many body parts in bad shape. I guess auto mechanics feel the same excitement when they get to fix a rare car. I was a rare subject and somehow that was a positive thing.

The first time the students did the procedure, their professor asked me for approval to allow several of her students witness the "great" occasion while one of the students performed it. Having so many individuals watching, as another student cleaned my open wound, did not sound glamorous at all. But the teacher was so sweet, and I felt in so much debt with the hospital that I could not say no. To my surprise, the students were extremely cautious; they rigorously made sure the equipment and gloves were 100% sterilized. Not even a single germ could enter those gloves to cut the gauze.

Their professor was guiding them to put the sterilized

gloves on, in such a way that no exterior part of them would get infected by anything, not even their hands. At first the process was slow; they had to put the gloves on almost without touching them but once they repeated it several times, and I was a good subject for this since my dressings needed to be changed at least four times a day, they became quite skilled at it. Sometimes the students were better help than some of the nurses, whom frequently had too many patients. Therefore, their time was too limited to be so cautious about germs; of course, these students still had a long way to go before reaching the perfection of employees such as Gyolonda, my favorite traveling nurse. She did the same "ritual" of placing the sterilized gloves on a flat surface and later on placing them on, but she did it in a blink of an eye and never touched the exterior part of the gloves since this would be the one that would touch my body; definitely nursing perfection and what the trainees would one day become, with hard work and great dedication.

When these students left, we missed them since they provided us with enthusiastic personalized attention all morning long. We also benefited from the indirect care of the professor, who supervised the students so they would perform the best possible work.

## 107. If it is not in your record, you are doing it under your own responsibility.

That day I eagerly awaited my mother's arrival; she was going to bring me a succulent homemade soup. Just to visualize myself indulging in that exquisite dish made me salivate. I already had the doctor's permission to eat it but my record only stated that I could have a liquid diet. I was not planning on clarifying my record's mistake at that moment; my stomach came first and it was roaring. After so many days without being able to taste real food, my hunger needed to be urgently sated. Whoever came to me with gelatins was not welcomed anymore.

Since my doctor was not around, to prove this patient had permission to eat, I had to put a plan in motion to avoid being discovered by the nurses: "operation soup," a risky mission to rescue my hungry stomach. My husband would stay outside the "entrance" of the small "room," which consisted of curtains instead of walls, to alert me in case the enemy, represented by the nurse of that shift, came. Mario would watch the maximum-security halls of this dangerous hospital where any nurse or assistant could intercept our exchange of infiltrated flavors.

My mother belonged to the secret squad; she would bring in the bowl with the soup. Her task was to circumvent controls by hiding the precious broth under her purse. Mario was looking nervously at the nurse's regime; the smell of the unique food had put them on alert. Those odors clearly did not come from the hospital's food; they were more intense because the soup had classified ingredients that belonged to a secret family recipe and therefore cannot be disclosed. The delicious odor made us vulnerable of being discovered, but Mario served as a shield for Violeta, and she was able to reach my secret hiding place with the liquid I longed for.

Agent mom would feed me right next to the curtain, to make sure she could see or listen to the signal of Commander Mario. My mission was the hardest of them all; I was in charge of feeding my hungry appetite and that was a dangerous mission that required the skill of slowing down, even if I wanted to swallow that entire plate in one bite. Exercising great auto-control, I ate only a small portion of the soup; I could not eat much in order to allow the pancreas to heal. I was a responsible spy after all.

I guess I felt as happy as the archeologists feel when they find the historic piece they have been searching for all their lives. This was my great finding, a survival elixir that tasted just like the prophecies had announced; it was the most delicious food I had ever tasted. My combat comrades immediately hid all the evidence of the crime but my face showed the satisfaction of the great achievement; finally I had gone back to eating food, and I was in heaven!

The following day I reminded my doctors to put a note on my record saying that I was allowed to eat. Unfortunately, when the nurse came, I found out that the correction had not been added. That was indeed a big problem. Obviously, these people did not know the risks of being a spy. I had no other option but to use the same "hiding" technique with my mother's help. Our other comrade, Commander Mario, was not with us on this occasion. Needless to say, that reduction in staff led us to our failure this time around. That shift's nurse discovered us. I explained to her that I had the doctor's permission. -It is not in your chart. The nurse replied with the same attitude of a spy from a hostile country. -You are eating that under your own responsibility. She expressed with the strict tone of the cliché Russian or German spies while leaving, visibly upset.

### 108. If you have permission, make sure it is written on your record.

Oh no, she did not just say that! Was she suggesting I was lying and did not have permission to eat that soup? Now we are talking about a major accusation here. Yes, major, I am the drama queen here, not her. The doctor had given me permission to eat that soup. My new mission was to clean up my name. Why do they always assume the convalescent is the one lying? Well, perhaps it was the fact that the car accident patient lied about the drugs she took or maybe because the crazy lady lied about how long she had been in the hospital or it could have been because I preferred not to tell the doctors in training everything about me when they interviewed me to practice their interrogation skills with patients. With so many people treating me and knowing everything about me, this was the only way for me to limit the information obtained by people who did not treat me directly. That is not lying. ¿Is it?

Okay, I admit it; perhaps us patients lie from time to time, but I was not lying this time. My honor could not be tainted just like that. Yeah, I know, honor is not a word we use much in Los Angeles but it sounds good so that is precisely what I did: defend my honor. I stood up, like warriors do, well maybe less threatening looking due to my tubes, but I had the same spirit and was going to fight until my honor had been cleared. With the help of my mother and my walker, we walked slowly to the nurse's lobby next to my room. I could almost hear the music of warriors accompanying us while we reached the lobby.

Very determined, I asked to see my chart. Of course, I was sweet to the nurse at the lobby, a good warrior always knows whom to fight. As I read my chart, I discovered that indeed I had permission to eat, courtesy of my head doctors. But after it, there was a signature of another doctor granting me only the liquids diet. Who invited this intruder to this dance? I silently asked myself and to my fortune, the doctor was right there at that moment and the warrior in me went to face him right away. -Why are you demoting me to a liquid diet? The doctor, a handsome Hispanic gastroenterologist in his 30's, slightly jumped at the sound of my voice. Poor man, what a way to introduce myself, but I had my reasons, he had signed a document a nurse had written without making sure it was right. He told me he had only signed what the nurse had given him. In my mind I thought many things, none of them positive, about how casual the doctor had taken signing a paper with information unknown to him. Excuse me. I beg your pardon. Did I hear right? What if it was your wife giving you the divorce papers and asking for all of your money? Would you sign them "just because someone gave them to you"?

Well, that was what my mind thought. I knew the doctor had power, so I would have never told him that. Instead, I used my best manners to explain to him how long it had taken me to get a solid diet approved. I must admit I did show "some" of my impatience. Well, I admit it; I showed a great deal of impatience. I think even the doctor felt a little intimidated by me, and he should be thankful I was not showing the 100% Puerto Rican girl temper I usually possess. However, I was not rude, I only showed my passion for what I believed to be fair. I checked the documents in my chart and showed how my head doctor had approved, in writing, a solid diet. The gastroenterologist apologized and signed another document that cleared the problem. Poor man, he was so peaceful, and this patient had the spirit of a revolutionary. I hope he has forgiven me, and I also hope he understood a hungry person has the potential of becoming anyone's worst enemy. Needless to say, the one who won this combat was this stubborn patient. Finally, I was allowed to eat a solid diet. My honor had been cleared. I even gave the doctor a huge smile. I do not know if he smiled back at me because he liked me or because he just thought it was best not to contradict me. I prefer to think he liked me. But doctor, if you ever read this, I want to apologize. When I'm hungry, I don't know anyone.

### 109. Fear is a bad advisor in a hospital: do not let it decide for you.

Every battle won made me feel better and I wished new dear friends, such as Camilla, also moved forward in their rehabilitation. Yet, far from improving, this cancer patient seemed to be getting worse. Her sadness constantly fueled the bad state of her cancer and chemotherapy had to begin sooner than expected; this made her feel worse. She wanted to leave as soon as possible; staying to receive treatment meant extending her stay indefinitely. It was a no win situation. If she stayed, sadness would keep worsening her health and if she left the already advanced illness would worsen. Being able to leave the hospital and return only for her follow up appointments would surely bring her happiness and that feeling is a better advisor than sadness in a hospital.

That night, after seeing the bad results Camilla's grief

provoked, all of the patients witnessed the havoc caused by allowing fear take control of one's self in a hospital. The event occurred a few moments after the lights had been turned off. Some nurse assistants brought a new patient to the room. From my bed I could not see her because my curtains were closed, but I clearly heard an old Hispanic woman. Her moans gave away the panic she felt. The nurse assistant asked her something but since the elderly woman did not speak English, she did not respond.

Immediately, I wanted to help. Listening to someone nearby so frightened made me overlook what I had learned in previous instances, with out of control patients. Without second thoughts, the super hero in me came "to the rescue." -Don't worry ma'am. I told the new patient in Spanish. -They are going to take good care of you. I told the lady, forgetting those same words had unleashed Troy with another patient, in that same room. Fortunately, that was not the case with this lady. She did not speak English so listening to someone speaking in her own language, Spanish, must have felt like being saved while drowning in open sea. At least I wanted to see it like that, in order to not quit helping her.

The elderly lady was quick to tell me what she wanted to convey to the doctors; she commented alarmed: -tell them I can't breathe. I immediately communicated the staff what the lady had said. Come to think of it, that was my super power; I could help this woman with my knowledge of English. It was not a sophisticated super power or supernatural, like the ones on cartoons but it was the skill needed at that moment and to me it had as much value as a super power.

The attendants seemed glad of having someone to translate since there were no bilingual nurses around at that moment. A doctor quickly told me through the curtain: -tell her we have two options: we can put a tube down her throat, so she can breathe, or we can make an incision on her throat, so she can breathe. I rapidly translated. The elderly woman was even faster to answer. -Open up my throat, I can't breathe. She said desperately. I repeated her words in English and the doctor, in a matter of seconds, put the whole place in motion. Panic had made a choice for this patient and that is the worst advisor anyone can have in a hospital. Had she not been so afraid, she would have opted for the tube in the throat and would have avoided great problems but changing her mind was not an option anymore, the assistants and nurses were running all over the room.

## 110. Sometimes, delicate procedures will be performed in rooms filled with patients.

You have got to be kidding, are they going to operate this lady right here next to my curtain? I heard someone say the emergency room was too crowded and there was no time to waste, so they were going to operate the woman at the same room where 9 other patients slept. The old lady asked me to pray for her. She kept repeating that she did not want to die. When I was in the same position as this woman, I was lucky the doctor made the decision for me since I was unconscious, and I say I was lucky because my doctor chose to keep my throat intact and used the tube which although painful would spare me health problems for the rest of my existence. Had the option been mine, perhaps I would have allowed fear decide for me, just as this woman's panic had made the choice for her. Doctors respected such decision and prepared the patient for surgery. They brought some equipment from another room and while they got ready, I did as I was asked: I started to pray.

    I concentrated very hard on my prayer. I asked God to help the new patient relax and not to be afraid so the procedure would be a success. At one point, I opened my arms and pointed them towards the direction of the new patient's bed, in order to give her some healing energy; this made me feel worse. It was as though this woman had taken all the energy I had left. As crazy as this might sound, I felt that while I prayed with the palms of my hands opened towards the desperate woman's bed, she sucked the energy I was offering and left me with nothing. At the same time the other patient's throat was cut open, I felt as if I had been drenched of all energy left in my body; I could clearly feel the other woman's pain. As incredible as this could sound, it was as if at that precise moment we had exchanged positions.

## 111. The suffering of other patients will make you feel worse.

I cried silently with mixed emotions. How could I get better if every night I was exposed to the suffering of new patients? With tears in my eyes and great sorrow in my heart I listened as the doctors performed the procedure, still praying so the elderly lady would not die, at least not there, not next to my bed. And I say this in the most selfish possible way; praying for that woman in this occasion had nothing to do with my love to thy neighbor. Rather, I felt I could not bear witnessing the death of someone so afraid to die. Had she died, all of us patients would have felt traumatized. That would add another reason to call this place the trauma room. Please God do not take that lady with you yet!

By the time the procedure ended and the new patient was safely asleep, the rest of the patients of the room were quite shaken, including me. The incident had created a commotion in me. My muscles became knots in my back and the pain became truly unbearable. So much for my super powers! I quit!

For the first time, in my lengthy stay at the hospital, I moaned in pain; I tried to hold it, but I could not. By then, doctors were already gone and there was not a single nurse in the room since they were taking the new patient to another floor. My pain moans lasted over three hours. It was then that two nurses finally came to my rescue. -Please put me out of my misery. I told them, barely able to utter some words. The nurses did not know what to do, and I was in so much pain at that moment I did not realize how funny that remark must have sounded: -put me out of my misery. Is not that the phrase that cowboys use when they are about to die because someone just shot them, and they beg their killer to give them an "honorable" death? Either I hurry up to explain the nurses what I meant, or I will have to settle for their puzzled look as if I were talking in a dialect from another planet.

 -Give me something strong, morphine, whatever, just put me out. I told them, and I assumed that would make them understand but almost instantly I realized the implications of what I had said. -Put me out. What a dumb choice of words. Is not that the phrase used by pet owners who ask veterinarians to inject their suffering pet so that they may die without pain? Can you recall Doctor Kevorkian, the one who became famous in the United States for supervising the death of his patients with medications? What if some of those nurses had worked for him? To my fortune that was not the case, the nurses understood and went to seek a doctor's approval.

 By the time I finally got my morphine shot more than 5 hours had gone by since my pain began. What a bad timing to get so delicate. Before falling asleep, I made sure to ask two of the patients to forgive me since they tried to help me when no one answered my call. Chances are they were as worried for me as I had been for the old lady's surgery. How difficult it was for all of us to get better when the stress of witnessing another roommate's suffering was always present.

### 112. Someone who gives you a massage will be more effective than a muscle relaxer.

Once the nurses injected me, I was finally able to sleep. -Call my husband please. I told one of the patients before I fell asleep. She had offered to call my relatives with her cell phone. We suspected that my muscles had big knots due to a sudden movement. A massage on my back would fix the problem right away but the hospital did not have employees in this area and if a patient had knots in his/her muscles, they were given a muscle-relaxer. Please forgive me manufacturers of that liquid but it did nothing for me. The treacherous morphine fared better because it, at the very least, allowed me to fall asleep.

Nonetheless, as soon as I woke up the pain of the knots was still there. I counted every minute until 11:00 am arrived, and my husband was allowed to enter the hospital. He would be a much better remedy than the relaxer or the morphine, since he could give me a massage that would break the muscle knots on my back. The few techniques my husband had learned with our mutual friend, Manuel, ended my pain. My husband solved the problem with a simple yet effective massage, but I could not help wonder: what happens with patients who do not have family support like I did?

My head doctor, of that week, explained to me there were two people who performed such tasks but their service hours were few and only for certain cases. As soon as I heard the explanation, I said with sorrow: -that's sad you know, imagine how many patients would be pain free with the right massage. The doctor meditated about my words but did not say anything else about the subject; I do not know if it was because she thought I had formulated a metaphorical question or because she really did not have an answer or because her attention should be targeting more urgent matters; the truth is I was not able to obtain an answer. I thought that together, the doctor and this patient, could help "save the world" with my opinion and experience. But what could the doctor do? Just like the technicians with limited hours, she was merely another employee.

Truth being told, natural remedies have not found their way into conventional hospitals in the United States; how beneficial would it be for patients if this changed. For now, I had the joy of being one of the few with the fortune of having someone helping me in that sense. There is too much burden on patients with severe trauma as to add simple but extremely painful muscle knots, therefore, having friends and family that could help in this area means a great deal.

### 113. Experiencing pain motivates many patients to share their human frailty with others.

Thanks to my husband's massage I slept like a baby that night. Next day, when I woke up, I noticed a new patient; a young African-American woman, apparently in her 20's, was assigned to the bed in front of me. Wow, that was not normal in this room if that is a word that describes this place at any moment; a patient had come in without screaming her heart out. This girl was so quiet I did not realize her presence, just a few steps from me. How cool, a low maintenance roommate. Now we are talking. I do not even know her, and I like her already.

She looked rather healthy. At first glance, she could do everything "normal" people do: walk, breathe, eat solid food and go to the restroom. The only thing that called attention to her was a belly that seemed to be carrying an 8-months-old unborn baby. -Why would they have a future mother in the severe trauma section? I wondered.

One morning the answer came straight from the lips of the young African-American woman: -I have AIDS, it is a tumor. She said, in a casual way. Let it be known that those of us in the room were not looking weirdly at her or asking. Her straightforwardness left us patients in shock. A tumor that size and AIDS at such a young age? Her announcement did not feed major curiosity on our behalf, even though in our daily lives a testimony such as this one would have ignited a series of questions, to satisfy the curiosity of those present. But those of us who were there were patients as well. Pain had forced us to see things differently. Instead of focusing on gossip, our attention focused on how this roommate faced her tragedy in such a courageous way.

How could this woman be so brave, despite the fact that she is facing an incurable condition that causes her excruciating pain and that will soon be the cause of her death, leaving two little orphan kids when she passes away? She was facing the end of her world, yet she did it with such class. Long gone were the days when someone announced they had AIDS and all we thought about was to keep our distance, at all cost, from that person.

Only once did I hear her sobbing and softly moaning at nighttime of pain. Otherwise, she faced her situation with such dignity that those of us who saw her could not avoid feeling admiration for her. No one had asked her what her condition was and yet it was normal, not only for her but for most patients, to share misfortunes with other convalescent people. Somehow, being close to death or being in pain frees many and they are more open to share their human frailty with others.

## 114. Making fun of our tragedies can be an excellent prescription.

Not only were most patients willing to share their misfortunes but the bigger their "tragedy," the more "celebrated" they were by others for having endured it. We joked about our calamities. It was joyful to make fun of someone really ill, as long as that someone was you. That way, no one could blame us for making a mockery of other people's pain. Our favorite self-mockery moment was when we made fun of how we would evacuate the hospital, in case of an emergency.

This was Camilla's evacuation plan: since she could still walk, she would push my bed because I could not move. Francisca would lead us while limping with her cane. The three of us laughed about how slow the evacuation process of this large group of women, that could barely move, would be in case of an earthquake or fire. I declare myself guilty of mocking all the patients, whom like me walked around the hallways of the hospital. We moved so slow that I could not resist nicknaming that place, "the zombies hallway." And the name fit us to perfection; we all looked too skinny and those who were not, looked very unhealthy. We walked slowly due to our conditions and our faces did not hide the pain. So the only thing needed was the music of one of those television series of zombies, and we were perfect to star in it.

I do not know why but I had this sensation that at some point one of those "zombies" was going to start dancing like the ones in Michael Jackson's "Thriller" video. Now that would have been a very entertaining sight. I do not think anyone in those hallways had the strength or was physically able of performing any of those fancy dances but just imagining a scene like that made tragedy lose its rigidity.

When Robert and Cheryl Zapién, two of my friends, came to visit me and I told them to be careful because the "zombies" were coming, they reacted confused; they thought they had heard wrong. Since most people come to a hospital with a rather solemn attitude, feeling sorry for the patient, the last thing they expect is the patient to make fun of her. Once they realized it was a joke, they could not stop laughing. I guess the zombies they visualized following us were as funny as the ones I envisioned.

## 115. Relationships change after a hospital stay: they either break or bind more.

Aside from making fun of our "tragedies," us patients sometimes found the energy to talk about more relevant subject matters. To all of us being in a hospital, so close to death, gave us the unique opportunity of self-assessment and analysis of our relationships. To really heal, physically and mentally, we recognized the need to modify our behavior as well as the conduct of those we live with. We could modify our behaviors but changing other people's conduct was a whole different ballgame. It must be because of this that when someone comes out of a hospital many relationships change, they break or bind more but there is always a transformation; you never come out the same.

The young woman with AIDS, for example, had two kids and it seems the hospital stay had made their ties even stronger. She had not seen them during that time and this separation had made her appreciate even more the value of her offspring; not even her painful tumor diminished her desire to go back home, to take her kids out on an upcoming holiday. It was highly unlikely doctors would grant her wish since her condition was quite delicate. But that young woman longed to reunite with her kids so much that she never complained, took her medications and followed all of the doctor's recommendations. The night before the celebration, the doctor of the young woman had not given her permission to leave the hospital. Her health had gotten worse on that day; she complained with pain all night.

Next day, however, a miracle happened. It seemed like the young African-American woman wanted to see her kids so much that she woke up, fixed her hair nicely and even went to the first floor of the hospital, dressed as a civilian, to get coffee for her and other patients. Her doctors had not discharged her, and she was quite impatient. But at around six o'clock the good news came: the young woman had been discharged. She had not done anything extraordinary to achieve it, the only thing she had done was to put great effort in improving her health, follow doctor's orders and keep herself positive on getting what she was asking for and apparently this had given her great results. I suppose doctors weighed the advantages of letting her go versus the disadvantages and considered that her departure would benefit her, more than staying here longing for her kids.

All of us roommates were so happy to see this young woman go; her kids would enjoy the presence of their mother. We were happy but nostalgic at the same time since we all had to remain at the hospital. Far from allowing me to go home, like this young woman, my doctors said that if liquids kept coming out of my pancreas I would probably need another surgery, which meant that not only would I not leave soon but also that my stay in this hospital would last longer. Then is when I got desperate. I had already been in the hospital for a month and staying for a longer time gave me the goose bumps. Because of it, without thinking about it twice, I immediately designed a plan to convince my allies I was ready to leave the hospital. If it had worked for the young woman that was going home today, chances are it would work for me as well.

## 116. In a hospital, there is always someone who has suffered more than us.

That night I found someone to put my motivational skills to the test. My first subject would be one of my favorite traveling nurses, Gyolonda. While she changed the dressings that covered my wounds, I commented to her, as casual as possible trying to sound without an agenda, how eager I was to go home. –Is not that I don't like you. I clarified. -I do. I told her, so she would not misinterpret and then I continued. -I am just ready to go home. -I've been here for a long time. -I'm the only one who remains at the room. -Everyone else comes for a few days and leaves. I told her with a "poor me" attitude. The only thing missing were the violins, in order to appeal to my caretaker's compassion.

When I thought I had proven I was the patient that had suffered the most in this room, I presented my last argument in my defense: -I guess I am the patient who has been here the longest or has there been anyone who has been here longer than me? Gylonda's response came rather quickly. -Oh yeah. She told me casually while she kept cleaning my open wound. She did not even blink or made any gesture; to her, this seemed like an every day subject without great relevance. Gyolonda did not notice how discouraged I was to discover that someone else had been in this room longer than me. Could it be possible that someone was a bigger victim than my precious self? How could that be if the drama queen was the girl on the bed right now? How could there be someone with a greater feat than mine? There had to be a mistake, I probably had heard wrong.

I looked at Gyolonda wanting her to tell me it was a joke, wanting her to confirm I was the titan, the only survivor for more than a month in this room. She wasted no time in clarifying to me: -we had a patient here for a year. -A year? I said to her without being able to hide my surprise. Had someone already stolen the survivor crown from me in this room? Lord have mercy; that is stamina, a year of listening to the screams of other patients? That person should be declared a martyr. When he dies, he should be canonized.

-Where did that leave me? I had suddenly become an ordinary patient with an every day survival story. —Yes. Gyolonda said as if she could have heard my thought and then continued talking: -and he could not move from his bed in all that time. I looked at her disillusioned, almost wanting to tell her: -do not continue, do not rub on my face my lack of glory. Everyone kicks you when you are down. Wait a minute, who is the one down? The one who had it worse was that person, not me. There were still eleven months left. I was certain that if I tried, a month would not go by without going home a winner.

Thanks unknown patient. What a great lesson you have given me today; you left me without excuses to complain.

Why would I complain if some patients have a heavier load than mine?

## 117. Beware of lazy nurses; run away from health's politicians.

The ones that benefited the most, from the hospital's practice of bringing nurses from other countries, were the patients. The nurses from Africa did not elude demeaning work such as changing diapers, dressings or curing wounds. Nonetheless, several local nurses were extremely lazy to perform these tasks and almost always found a way to get someone else to do that work. I remember a male nurse from Los Angeles that would always ask an assistant to perform those jobs; I never saw him do any of the tasks nurses do. The only thing he did was talk to patients as if he were a doctor or a motivational speaker, but the ill are more motivated by deeds than words. We needed a nurse to look after us, not one that talked to us as if he were going to run for a political position. Needless to say, I would have never voted for him. Thanks to this lazy male nurse my roommates suffered mediocre care. Luckily, I never had to be taken care of by him. That was good for both of us since I would not have been as resigned as the other inhabitants of the room. My goal was to heal as soon as possible and this required real cares and not speeches from motivational speakers wannabes.

I guess the administrative staff of the hospital was aware

of the existence of these lazy nurses and because of it they resorted to nurses from other countries. That thought is more positive than thinking they hired the foreigners because they were cheaper. I must clarify there were local nurses that worked hard and that not all imported nurses were hard workers. In fact, some of the imported nurses had already being "infected" by the lazy nurses and assistants already working at the hospital. In many occasions, I witnessed how some male assistants, among them a young African man, always eluded hard tasks; I never saw him change a diaper or heal a wound. But, in general, most of the nurses and female assistants from Africa were hard workers.

### 118. The best way to deal with careless patients is ignoring them.

Many times the English language skills of some of the assistants was still very basic, such was the case of a happy Chinese woman. She could not understand many phrases in English, but she always did her job diligently; she checked vitals and changed patient's diapers. One day a Chinese woman was admitted to the room. The assistant was very happy; finally she could speak her own language and thanks to her this new patient, her family, the doctors and nurses were able to adequately communicate.

Of course, not everything was "peaches and cream" for the happy Chinese attendant. From time to time, she had to care for patients who did not want to listen to the many languages spoken at the trauma room. One of them was a Caucasian woman in her late 30's or early 40's that had been brought into the room recently, with several devices to keep her still after a car accident. This patient seemed to enjoy mocking the Chinese nurse's accent and demanded that the nurse spoke English, even though that is what the attendant was speaking as best as she could.

Had I felt better, I would have told her a thing or two, none of them nice, to this un-welcomed roommate. It is not fair to make fun of someone who is helping. Fortunately, nurses and attendants know this kind of patients too well to get stuck on them for long and even though the nurse assistant got sad one day because the same woman seemed upset for not understanding her, she soon learned that those people will need more than a hospital stay to heal their souls. The best way to deal with them is simply to ignore them, ignore their "tantrums" and tend to them only when true physical healing is needed.

### 119. Demanding constant attention from the staff will get you the opposite.

The new patient, whom we will call Miss Selfish, deserves that title because the only thing she cared about was fulfilling her needs, without any regard for the negative consequences this would bring to the rest of the people living, working or visiting this trauma room. Miss Selfish had a very perturbing way of becoming the center of attention; she screamed her lungs out for everything. Either having a car accident is the most painful thing in the world or we just got the noisiest accident patients in the planet. This woman demanded service to the staff as if she were in a 5 star hotel. Even though most of the nurses were cool and accommodating, it was evident how hard it was for them to keep up a smile when the car accident patient, Miss Selfish, demanded anything. When we all thought the witches had abandoned the story, another one, even more evil, emerged.

My guess is that this patient has no significant other. Who could stand someone so demanding? She was making life miserable for everyone. As soon as a nurse came to inject me, she screamed, so she would get seen first. Thankfully, my head doctor noticed how Miss Selfish always loved to be the center of attention. In one occasion, he came with several doctors in their residence to see me. The doctors were in the middle of a discussion about my condition, and Miss Selfish decided to join the conversation and demand something. My doctor rapidly replied: -looks like we have a high maintenance patient here. He said this raising his tone of voice a bit while his face looked towards the patient's bed, so she would hear it and understand he was referring to her. The rest of us knew what the concept meant, a high maintenance patient is someone that complains for everything, creates problems and does not follow hospital rules. All, except that patient, laughed; we were glad the doctor put that annoying woman in her rightful place.

At least the intellect of that conflictive patient had not perished with her accident, and she seemed to understand she would not get away with her tantrums with everyone. I smiled from ear to ear. As we say in my hometown: "suck this one while I get the next one ready," which means "if this tasted sour, next one will be even worse," so you are better off not doing it again. Nagging to our caretakers has repercussions; no one wanted to take care of this patient that demanded so much attention.

### 120. A patient taken care of by a nurse with a true calling has a better chance of survival.

As soon as my doctors left, after the epic reality check to the annoying roommate, a nurse with a gift to give high maintenance patients a clearer perspective on things, came in to inject me. Gloria is a Hispanic woman around her 20's or early 30's, probably 5'4" to 5'6" tall, with dark hair wrapped in a ponytail. Besides her craft of not beating around the bush, she has an admirable gift to inject medication without causing pain. My hard and dry arms were thankful for that since needles could barely penetrate my skin; this was tough because of the many injections I had been given. This nurse was very precise with IV's and never needed helpers to find my veins.

The thing that characterized Gloria the most, nonetheless,

was her conviction that a patient's healing demanded the help of his/her relatives. She told my mother and I that she had seen how dozens of patients went from being very ill to miraculously heal, thanks to the support of their family. By the same token, she had witnessed patients who were rather okay become gravely ill, for the lack of involvement of their family. One time, she personally called the sons and daughters of a patient who kept calling them and crying because they had not come to see her. Gloria took her chances and appealed to the common sense of these relatives, telling them how much their mother missed them and how their absence was making her get worse.

At first, the relatives were quite upset; they were offended by the fact that a nurse was telling them what they had to do. But that phone call saved that mother's life when they finally showed up and with them the mother's will to live again. Gloria risked her position a great deal. In this country, people are prone to complain or even sue those who work in public positions. Luckily, Gloria did not care much for formalities. Her goal was to save a patient at a time, even if this meant putting her own position at risk. This was something that also characterized several of the employees in the trauma room, the life of their patients had a more important place than their own; they were nurses with a true calling, not just nurses with a title, and their dedication increased the chances of survival of their patients.

## Chapter 7:

### What Every Patient Should Know

**121. If the medical staff is trying to help you, pay attention: they know what is good for you.**

There was a young patient from Bangladesh who complained to the staff supervisor. She claimed that Gloria, the nurse, was demanding too much from her. The patient was about 5'3" to 5'5" tall and was probably around 27 years old; her hair went down to her shoulders and her skin had a light dark tone but she looked extremely pale. A tumor had been removed from her stomach, and she was loosing too much weight because she threw up everything she ate. She did not do this intentionally; her digestive system simply did not tolerate any food.

Gloria knew this young woman was fighting a race against

time and to keep her alive it was necessary that she ate and walked. The nurse did not seem to be bothered by the fact that the girl from Bangladesh reported her and far from getting discouraged, she demanded more from her. None of the other nurses dedicated so much time to this new patient, perhaps because she did not follow up on instructions during her firsts days. Gloria did not give up and soon the patient understood that this nurse was actually the one that cared the most for her. The employee became the best friend of this young woman and almost a surrogate mother to her, since her real mother was not given a humanitarian visa to come from Bangladesh to Los Angeles.

### 122. Pulling the black cord is the acceptable way to communicate with nurses.

I cannot tell if it was for cultural reasons or for the immaturity of her young age, but the girl from Bangladesh took longer than expected to learn basic behavioral rules in a hospital room. During her firsts days she preferred to call out the nurses, instead of pulling the black cord. This was uncomfortable to most of the patients since silence is crucial for healing. Those of us who inhabited the room had not gotten used to the yelling and demands of Miss Selfish when the girl from Bangladesh joined her in an unpleasant choir. Both of them had chose to scream: -nurse, nurse. One screamed first and the other one after, as if it were an echo.

When these women screamed those two little words, every time they wanted to be taken care of, their high-pitched tones hurt the hearing of the other patients. We could not understand why the girl from Bangladesh had to call out our caretakers. The other one, Miss Selfish, did it because she seemed to enjoy being the center of attention but the girl from Bangladesh did not seem to be so selfish. The rest of us, convalescent patients, felt sadness for her delicate condition but not for her screams, and we hoped that with a little bit of guidance the nurses would modify her behavior. –Nurse, nurse. The girl from Bangladesh repeated with her soft voice when to our surprise Miss Selfish joined her with an extremely high-pitched tone: -nurse… nurse. Screamed this woman way louder than the girl from Bangladesh. -This new patient needs your help, someone… The demanding female kept screaming: -this young woman needs a nurse.

The screams of Miss Selfish scared the patient from Bangladesh so much that she opted for staying quiet; I guess it was then when she realized how terrible those screams sounded. Even though the young woman from Bangladesh became silent, Miss Selfish continued with her tantrum. Her way of helping thy neighbor was unusual; she did not stop screaming until a nurse showed up. After a while, the employees also got tired; both patients were told to call the nurses using the black cord.

A short while after, the wish of the nurses and the rest of

us patients became a reality, at least with one of the members of the choir, the young woman from Bangladesh. She decreased the use of her voice to call the employees and started to use the most acceptable way of communication, pulling the black cord. Miss Selfish, however, did not seem to reason and screamed for everything; soon enough, all of us, the inhabitants of the room and the staff working in it, started to get tired of her.

### 123. Let doctors know what you want, and they will try to help you.

Fortunately, not all patients were noisy. Francisca, the cancer patient sleeping at the bed next to Camilla, was very quiet but she had been discharged in the morning. Her good attitude towards life, as well as her supportive family and the great treatment she received at the hospital, made her cancer go into remission. While her family packed her belongings happily, Camilla, the other patient with cancer, watched them with teary eyes. -You're going to be okay soon; just have faith. Said Francisca to her roommate while she departed.

By then, all of us patients knew Camilla wanted to leave the hospital. We had seen her crying at her bed or with her daughter next to the hospital's elevator. Many of us prayed that Camilla would get better so that she would soon go home, but doctors had not given her permission to leave.

They said her condition had worsened, and she needed to stay for a longer time. That morning I decided to intervene; blame the super hero spirit in me. I told Camilla's doctor that she wanted to go home and that in my opinion she would get better if she did. Us human beings think that medicine is learned by osmosis. I had only been a few weeks at the hospital and already thought I could give my professional opinion to the doctor. But the doctor gave me a quick reality check. Without offending me, he ruled out that option. Better luck next time Camilla! At least I tried. My friend did not give up and asked the doctor if they could allow her to go home and return only for appointments and tests. The doctors said no.

Discouraged, Camilla and I returned to our respective beds; she was walking with her head down feeling defeated while my walker helped me to not fall down. An hour later Camilla's doctor returned. -This is the time of your next appointment; make sure you keep it. Her head doctor told her while giving her a document. Two other doctors accompanied him. -You can go home. The doctor reaffirmed while Camilla remained in shock; she did not know if she had understood him right.

But the rest of us roommates understood clearly and burst into a huge applause; we were extremely thrilled. Camilla's miracle happened right before our eyes, and we all reacted with immense joy. Those who could jump, jumped, those of us who were at our beds applauded and cried with joy. Even doctors were surprised to see all patients and their relatives celebrating, happy to see Camilla's wish granted. We could not stop applauding and cheering. —Wow. The doctor exclaimed surprised. -People really love you here. Said the doctor with evident happiness, due to the contagious enthusiasm in the entire room.

Camilla was as happy as a kid with a new toy. -I can go? She asked without being able to believe her luck. -Provided that you keep up with your appointments, yes. Reaffirmed the pleased doctor. Camilla wanted to leave, and she did not stop trying until doctors found a way to please her. "Those who persevere conquer," says an old saying in Spanish. -Call your daughter. My mother excited told Camilla while giving her a cell phone.

I think all of us patients were crying; there was a waterfall of happy tears. We knew we would miss Camilla, but we were happy to see her go. This glorious moment alone must have improved her health considerably. Von voyage my dear Camilla!

## 124. You must be infection free before certain tests can be performed.

With the departure of Camilla and Francisca, it was only a matter of hours before new patients filled those empty beds. Hopefully, those new roommates will not be high maintenance. How can nurses put up with so many problematic patients? After only one month of being here, I felt my tolerance levels had been exceeded.

As soon as I saw my doctors next day, I asked them when would they discharge me. If it had worked for Camilla, perhaps it would work for me too. My doctors did not give me a concrete answer. -I'm requesting a test made with a small camera. My main doctor told me. The camera would see my internal organs and fix the pancreas with a laser beam. -After that test, we will see. The doctor assured me. Even though his answer was ambivalent, I focused on the fact that it was not a negative one. I was also notified that in order for some tests to be made, I needed to be infection free.

If the requisite to accelerate my hospital's departure was getting rid of my infections, I was going to fulfill it right away. Diligently, I endured cold ice bags under my armpits, on my forehead and behind my neck to bring that fever down. I also forced myself to cough up the pneumonia's phlegm. I kept myself alert; spotting anything that could trigger an infection. I made sure no one turned on the air conditioner, so I would not get the flu. But Miss Selfish loved to send people to turn it on, even during wintertime. I do not know if she really felt hot or if she simply enjoyed making our lives miserable. Our efforts to avoid getting infections were in vain. Leaving my cold feet uncovered at night, to avoid getting fever or reducing the amount of food I ate by mouth so the pancreas would heal, was of no use if the air conditioner provoked a cold. Days would go by before I had the test done so my mission was too keep the air conditioner off, to avoid getting sick. With great zeal, I intercepted anyone that got close to the air conditioner, which happened to be right next to my bed. If Miss Selfish wanted to be cold, it would be over my dead corpse.

## 125. Being bilingual helps a great deal in a hospital.

Unfortunately, with new patients coming to the trauma room, I had to increase my guard. The first patient admitted was a short and thin elderly Hispanic woman who apparently suffered from Alzheimer's. She was wandering disoriented in the hallways, without IV, with blood coming out of her arm and with her gown showing her derriere. None of the nude stars show their assets so casually; she was baring it all, but she did not even notice.

A nurse in the hallway, the same one that helped me when I was about to fall on the floor, spotted the patient; how timely was this employee. Avoiding bigger problems, she brought the new patient back to the trauma room and explained to her that she could not walk around the hospital half naked and that she should not remove her IV. The new patient only smiled; apparently she did not understand a word of what the nurse had said.

At that moment, from my corner, I decided to help using my "super power": being bilingual. -Señora, no se puede quitar el suero. (Ma'am you cannot remove your IV.) I told the elderly woman. The nurse felt relieved. -Good, you speak Spanish. -Can you tell me what she wants? The nurse asked. The employee asked worried. I listened attentively to the patient, but she was not even speaking Spanish, her native tongue; in fact, she was just mumbling; no complete words came out of her mouth. I let the nurse know this, and she felt relieved. I was so proud to be able to help. Being bilingual is a real treasure in a hospital and can help save lives. The nurse discovered that her patient did not have any special need and proceeded to cover her up with a blanket while telling her with signals, as if she were a little kid, not to remove her IV. The elderly woman smiled, like a baby who thinks it is playtime; it was a tender picture of human compassion.

## 126. Unless you are seriously ill, you will wait for a long time for your tests.

The employees that would perform my test did not show up on the day set. My female doctors told me it was because there were too many people on waiting list and the ones with more severe conditions had priority. On the one hand, it was a relief to find out I was in better shape than those patients but on the other, I felt frustrated. I waited for several days for this test and endured great inconveniences but the test was not done as scheduled. Were those people making last minute cancellations aware of how difficult it is for a patient to stay away from infections at a hospital, or how painful the needles for IV's are, or how eagerly the patient awaits to complete these tests to get out of the hospital, or the hunger the ill feels because they are not allowed to eat since the previous night? I did not tell them that, but I thought about it. Either way, it's all in a days work in a hospital, and I had to wait until next day.

The next morning came and after it, the afternoon; I waited and waited, but no one from the gastroenterology department came and feeling desperate I went with my mother to the nurses lobby, to find out if the test could still be done on that day. Come to think of it, my mother and I were like "peaceful revolutionaries," we did not remain still waiting for a dreadful end. If we saw catastrophe coming, we made a plan to face the enemy. In this case, those unknown patients were my rivals since they also needed my same exam. That sounded cruel but it was the truth. Good thing I did not analyze it that way then. I guess someone has to lose in a battle and, as selfish as it sounds, I was determined to not be that someone. Yet, despite the fact I asked a nurse to make the phone calls, the test was not made on that day. Nevertheless, the war was not over, and I intended to win it. For now, I would eat and rest. I was starving!

That afternoon a doctor from the gastroenterology

department came. He apologized for the test's delay and explained to me what it would consist of; the laser ray would fix the pancreas as long as it was only partially broken. If it was fully split in half, this procedure would not work for me. He confused me, I did not know if those were good or bad news. The only thing left was to wait.

5 days later I repeated the bothersome preparation process; nothing to eat or drink after midnight and another painful IV but the only one who came was the same gastroenterologist doctor and not to perform the test but to talk. I did not feel like talking; what I wanted was the test to be made, so I could go home. I listened to him attentively but discouraged. He said he did not want to make mistakes and since my condition was so delicate, he would request a "road map" of my internal organs. That meant that in order to do the test they had to do another one first, an MRI, which means Magnetic Resonance Imaging. To me, those terms were as though they were talking in an ancient language, but I found out later it is a technique that uses magnetic fields and radio waves to produce a detailed image of bones and the soft tissues of the body. In other words, this test would reveal the precise location of each organ and their condition.

Next morning, my new head doctors tried to cheer me up: -they want to make sure there are no mistakes. Assured Leah, a beautiful Asian doctor in her late 20's and my new head doctor. What war would be complete without the pep talk of the general? I was given an appointment two days later and just when I had lost all hope of them coming to pick me up, a young and handsome African-American man in his late 30's came with a bed to take me to the exam.

I was so happy that to me he had the same gallantry of a knight rescuing the maiden in a white stallion. He did not come galloping, but he moved so smoothly that he had nothing to envy from a gallant knight from medieval times. His white horse was my means of transportation; that shiny bed with white sheets had the same romantic appeal. I was so happy, I would have jumped right onto the bed if I could have but since my movements were still very limited, the noble gentleman, along with my mother, and my husband covered me in blankets and my journey to freedom began. Finally, I had come out of the waiting list to have the test done.

### 127. Not all tests can be performed on all patients.

I was indeed a lucky woman; otherwise, I would not be on the verge of having an MRI test after 7:00 pm when most tests are done during daytime. As my bed kept moving towards the office where the test would be done, I greeted everyone; I waved my hand at every person I saw. I was not a politician seeking votes, but I certainly felt like I had won an election. Blow the horns general! I have won this battle!

My smile was so huge I could have done a toothpaste

commercial. I was so sure this would be my last time experiencing this type of test that I could not hide my joy. It was my last time at the battlefield; I would not smell death anymore. The fragrance of roses and violets awaited me back home, and I would get the welcome heroes get, once they have won the war.

As soon as the results were ready, the same gastroenterologist who previously explained the test talked to me. The small camera, to heal with a laser beam, could not be used on me. My world fell apart. There has to be a mistake here. My sad face communicated to the doctor, without saying a single word. The gastroenterologist understood my discouragement and explained to me he had hoped that my pancreas was only partially cut but it was fully split. This meant that the laser beam, of the camera test, would not be able to fix my pancreas. Therefore, I needed another surgery to contain the fluids coming from this damaged organ.

When I had already taken for granted that I was a beauty queen who had just won Miss Universe, I found out I had not even made it to the finalists. This was not, after all, my last parade down the catwalk of this hospital. I had not won my ticket to any exotic place of the world; I was not even going to my tranquil home. The only prize I had won was to continue my splendid stay at this luxurious hospital that even though it did not have beauty queens from around the world, it did have plenty of drama queens, with all sorts of traumas, representing many nations of the world.

### 128. Keeping your mind busy will make you feel better.

My mother and my husband took the news of the test rather well; they knew showing any sign of sadness would make me feel worse. Their strength gave me the positive attitude I needed. That day, my husband brought a laptop, loaned by a friend, so I could read e-mails to feel closer to home. Keeping my mind busy reading them made me feel better. I had more than nine hundred messages. Most were junk mail but I wanted to feel special, so to me those were 900 e-mails from friends and family. I could only read a few per day, since I was still weak and could only concentrate on tasks for short periods of time.

### 129. Accept the help offered to you when you are sick.

Cultural shock is inevitable between couples from different countries. If you add living in a foreign country, there is a vast cultural diversity. My husband is a Mexican, I am a Puerto Rican and our home, for almost two decades, has been Los Angeles, California. We are constantly learning what is acceptable and what is not for each other. In my homeland, it is acceptable to receive financial help from relatives when you are in a hospital, whereas this did not seem to be acceptable in my husband's country.

At first, my husband did not want to accept any help; it was not the right thing to do in his culture. He yet had to understand that we must accept the help offered by others, especially when we are sick. This is how people show how much they care for you. They know you have been in a hospital and have no way of earning a living there. They know this because they have probably experienced it first hand, and they will not take no for an answer.

My husband understood the saying "pay it forward" and admitted that later on he would do the same for anyone who got sick or faced a tough situation. But for now, it was his wife's turn. Glorita, a cousin, for example, took care of several bills and also sent me books, magazines and candies, something worthy of praise since this cousin was in another hospital undergoing surgery. How big is the heart of someone who helps someone else in a hospital while she is also in another hospital?

I tried to make a mental list of people that helped me during these difficult times and realized it was longer than anticipated. Over 40 relatives and friends and over 40 doctors, nurses, attendants, technicians, and volunteers were taking care of me; accepting their help was a wise decision.

## 130. Accept the help of positive volunteers.

Even people unknown to me were eager to make this painful moment a bearable one. Some adolescents that came to each room, looking for any patient that wanted to go to religious services, called my attention. Accepting the help of these positive volunteers was a pleasure to me. They brought their own wheelchairs and carefully covered the patients to take them to the first floor where there was a chapel that offered religious celebrations from different denominations.

This hour of prayer, music and blessings was very often the most awaited moment of the week for many of the patients. During that instant, pain seemed to take a break. Everyone in that chapel wanted us to get better. They were mainly volunteers, more than thirty adolescents who came to take care of the sick and accompanied us during the religious celebration, to make sure we were all right.

If a patient had to exit the chapel, like I did once when I had to be seen by my doctors, the volunteers were quick to take us wherever we needed to be. One day, during the ceremony, a choir of volunteers that had come from Long Beach, California, sang. Their music moved me a great deal; I felt angels were the ones cheering me up and overwhelmed I cried. The ceremony was a bilingual one, English and Spanish; and I understood both languages, so I felt double blessed. An hour in that chapel, next to those positive volunteers, gave me the strength needed to face the tough times.

An adolescent Hispanic female that took me to the celebration on that day, apparently had problems with her mom. On our way back to my room, the young woman got a call from her mom, who was arguing with her on the phone that she should be home studying and not at the hospital. I felt so sad. That mother did not see greatness in her own daughter. Her daughter could have been outside drinking and using drugs; instead, she was helping thy neighbor unselfishly. The mother was so focused on her own agenda that she did not even notice that her daughter's was perhaps more admirable. I felt honored to be taken care of by this volunteer, who assisted me even though this caused her problems at home.

Another volunteer that moved me was a Catholic priest named Robert. The day I met him, I expected him to behave priest-like; I thought he would insist on giving me a confession or something like that. Nothing farther from the truth, he came as a friend. In one occasion, chatting with him, I told him about how upset I was with one patient's behavior, I cannot recall if it was Miss Selfish or the crazy patient; the fact is I spoke about her. We are so used to gossiping that I did not realize that was exactly what I was doing; I was gossiping about thy neighbor. But I did not notice until Robert, the priest, wisely changed the subject of the conversation. The interesting thing was that he did not scold me or accuse me of my devilish behavior; he simply did not join me in my game of blames and by doing so, he taught me that if you do not have anything good to say about someone, it is best to not say anything at all.

### 131. Ignore negative volunteers.

I guess, with a lot of practice, some day I will learn to be like the discreet Father Robert but today a volunteer that came deserves that I gossip about her. It turns out she came to my bed and told me that my condition was a punishment from God. In an instant she brought out the worse feelings in me. How dare she judge me if we did not know each other? What made her think someone in a bed, in such bad health condition, would receive her comment positively? This lady would have been great if her goal would have been to make thy neighbor feel depressed enough to commit suicide. I guess that was not her goal. In some weird way, I believe the volunteer thought she was serving God by telling me my accident was a punishment.

Following the reasoning of this volunteer if each person in delicate condition in a hospital is there because of divine punishment, then, ill sinners overpopulate the world. Of course, we would have to be quite ignorant to give any credibility to such an absurd declaration. In fact, to me, being at this hospital meant totally the opposite. This was a priceless learning gift, given by my creator to people he deems capable of resisting it.

Nothing of what I thought I would tell this volunteer was positive, so I decided not to tell her anything. My energy was not enough to waste it on someone that had not come to help but to condemn. It was my intention to avoid falling into the same trap the woman, now judging me, had fallen into. She was convinced her point of view was the right one, and everyone else was wrong, unless they believed the same thing she did. Anger was taking over me so I preferred to fake falling asleep so the volunteer would leave; to my luck, it worked.

The woman felt offended and exited furiously. She was so immersed in her micro-world; she did not realize that by ignoring her this patient was being kind to her. Not communicating to her the bad feelings she provoked in me, with her irresponsible and uninformed comment, was really kind and compassionate. Ignoring her served me more than getting into an argument with her. Negative volunteers think they are serving thy neighbor but the truth is they are only trying to impose their own agendas and beliefs. If someone's goal is getting something in return, she or he is not giving it for free; therefore, that person is not a volunteer.

## 132. Do not watch TV news or commercials while in a hospital.

When the executioner left, I mean the volunteer; I wanted to forget the bad experience watching some television. Ironically, I did not feel better. While I changed channels, I saw images of murders, robberies and rapes. Those were the themes presented on the news. With such motivating images, who would want to return to that society? For someone on a hospital bed, going through so much pain, seeing those images only gets you more depressed; because of it, I opted for not watching TV news while at the hospital.

They made me feel so sad that I decided to see something happier: commercials. But commercials confused me even more. With so much spare time, you can analyze things you never even think of. On the one hand, there were a great deal of commercials inviting consumers to taste many foods and on the other, several adds promoted losing weight as a way to be accepted by society. What is the deal here, you guys want me to eat or to lose weight? I felt like an alien, incapable of understanding why human beings are so contradictory.

This was a good time to come out of that bubble society traps us in, time to rebel against so much vanity. After being on the verge of death, watching on television or reading in a magazine about the dress, make-up or jewel that would get me accepted by others, seemed so insignificant. Four tubes and an open wound pierced my stomach; no jewels would decorate my scars enough to make them look attractive.

The award shows on television also seemed bland to me, without value. Everyone hosting those events spoke about dressing well and with expensive name brands as if human beings really needed that to live. Being in a hospital, however, had taught me that health is far more important than clothing or accessories to decorate the body. What are brand name high heels good for if I barely have the balance to walk? Why would I buy a fine dress if the liquids from the pancreas would stain it immediately? What would a designer purse be good for at this hospital? Not only would I not find anyone to show it off to but also the only attention I might get could be from someone wanting to steal it. I did not need anything of what was offered in those commercials or in the award shows. It was obvious I would not be on the red carpet with a glamour dress any time soon and yet this did not bother me in the slightest bit.

This hospital stay offered me a wider and wiser perspective: the importance of material things is not as big as TV news, award shows, commercials and the media in general describes; physical and spiritual health, however, are priceless.

### 133. Be active, not passive.

I did not know if this was positive or not but what happened around me, in this trauma room, was far more entertaining than any television show. Among the new patients admitted to the room was Maria, a middle-aged Hispanic woman with a hole in her heart. She was very shy, seemed to be scared all the time. She went hungry on her first day because she did not dare to ask if she could eat.

When I notified the nurse that the new patient had not had food in 24 hours, she was surprised, apologized to her, placed her on the dinner list, and quickly brought her a sandwich, which was hers, so the patient could eat something right away. Any of the high maintenance patients would have caused a tremendous commotion, had they not been fed for so long. Contrary to them, Maria behaved like someone who accepted her luck with resignation. This is mortal in a hospital; the patient must get involved in everything concerning his or her care. If you just sit and wait, nothing will happen or if it does, it could be too late.

Had I not intervened so that this woman would eat, she would have kept going hungry, thinking that was part of the treatment. Had this woman not heard the saying, "God helps those who help themselves?" Contrary to Maria, I did not let circumstances dictate my destiny; because of it, I decided to infuse some common sense into this resigned lady. I explained to her that she had to talk when something did not seem right. She thanked me for supporting her but seemed afraid to talk. Since the new patient did not speak English, I also offered her to serve as a translator whenever she needed to communicate with the hospital staff.

Something that called my attention was that Maria had not eaten anything even though her husband was with her during the entire day. Why did he not ask for food for her or ask the doctors why his wife could not be fed?

**134. Do not allow anyone to cry, unless you are dead.**

It turned out Maria's husband was twice as timid as her and seemed so overwhelmed by her condition that he did not help much. In fact, Maria would be in a great mood the whole day until her husband came, grabbed her hand and started to cry. Lord have mercy! Just when I thought I had seen it all, a crying man emerges. That was definitely not my favorite sight, but I admit that when I first saw him I thought it was moving. As the days went by, however, that man's tears started to annoy me. If she is the one in pain, why is he the one crying?

This addiction to pain, on the husband's side, seemed to cause great discomfort to Maria, but she did not do anything to stop him. One day, with tears in his eyes, he told his wife that their kids missed her and needed her home. He wanted her to leave the hospital, even with her delicate condition, to take care of their little kids. No wonder he cried so much, he was not sad for her, what worried him was having to take care of his kids. That is a low punch!

I felt really annoyed when I heard Maria confirming her

husband's petition. How could a woman, with a hole in her heart, expect to heal if instead of going home to rest, she had to take care of five little kids? To me, the husband's attitude seemed to be extremely selfish. If he did not realize how severe his wife's condition was, my goal was to open her eyes before it was too late. My motivation was not to cause division in someone's matrimony but to help improve this woman's health. Now that I knew the importance of being healthy, I was determined to make Maria understand that being healthy cannot be compromised for anyone, even if tears fell like rain with the same abundance of the Niagara Falls.

### 135. Getting treatment is not an option, it is your duty; fulfill it!

Maria's husband told me that she had been in the hospital a few months before. At that time, she was kept under observation and her heart surgery did not happen; maybe that was the reason why he wanted Maria to go back home. My sixth sense, if that is the one for the common sense, told me this was not the case but aside from his motives, the super hero in me was determined to make my roommate's health the one that won in this situation. Five doctors had decided to operate on Maria and call me crazy but if 5 medical doctors say they have to urgently fix your heart, do not think about it; do it and get it over with.

The doctors only needed her approval. As I translated

what doctors were saying, so Maria would approve the surgery, she seemed undecided; something made her hesitate. I behaved like a mother scolding her daughter; I gave her a strict look like saying: -you better say yes. I did it on the sly, so doctors would not realize I was trying to influence Maria's decision, but she opted for staying quiet. The doctors told her to think about it and consult it with whomever she had to, and they left with the promise of coming back later on that day for her answer.

I advised Maria to accept the offer. I explained to her that it was not prudent to put her health on hold any longer: -these doctors do not approve this kind of surgery so frequently. I told her, trying to infuse common sense in her brain. I used every convincing method I could think of, to convince this woman to accept free medical treatment that would save her life. How can anyone even think about that? She needed an urgent operation, and she was going to get it for free at this hospital; she had everything to win and nothing to lose. But Maria did not feel her health was a priority or maybe she was concern that her husband would not approve the procedure because he preferred her to go back home to take care of the kids.

-You cannot help them if you are sick. I told her, trying to make her understand the seriousness of her condition. -He has to understand and if he does not, he still has to manage anyways. I added, determined with all my being to convince her to accept something as basic as medical care in an emergency; getting treatment is not an option; it is a duty. So when Maria's husband came, I took command of the situation. A general knows when a soldier might freak out when the time to make tough decisions comes.

-The doctors came. I told Maria's husband and added: -your prayers were answered. -They are going to finally fix your wife's heart. -They have to operate next Monday. -See, finally the surgery you had been waiting for so long is going to happen. I said with the confidence of a judge dictating sentence. Maria looked at me with a sense of relief. It was as though a big weight had been lifted off her shoulders. Her husband, however, looked discouraged. He had come to the hospital on that day perhaps with the idea of taking his wife home, so he did not have to baby-sit their children anymore.

I kept my serious business face. I guess being an actress has its perks in moments like this one. The husband had no other alternative but to accept what had "already being decided by the doctors." The "enemy" had lost his battle and this had contributed to a new ally winning hers. Next time the doctors came, Maria agreed to surgery and signed the documents authorizing it while across the room and from my bed I had to translate the instructions given by the doctors. I was so satisfied to see that Maria doing the right thing. She had taken the first step to get better by accepting the doctors' help.

Maria's husband cried once more on that day, perhaps to convince her to cancel the surgery. He was sobbing! But my thoughts this time around were not the ones I originally had of him; his selfishness was upsetting to me. His crocodile tears did not move anyone. This man used drama blatantly to manipulate his wife. It was clear he had gotten away with it many times, because Maria was on the verge of canceling the surgery. Fortunately, and I do not mean to brag about my acting abilities but I am definitely a better performer than Maria's husband. I am definitely a better actor than he is. My scene was so credible that he did not question the veracity of it, and Maria would finally have her surgery.

### 136. Always choose humor over drama.

At the same time Maria was admitted to our room, another patient also named Maria and that we will call Maria 2 was admitted to the room. Contrary to Maria, Maria 2 was not a woman resigned to her luck. She was opinionated, funny and she became, during her stay at the room, my super hero partner. With her super powers, light-heartedness and happiness, she helped me to convince the first Maria to accept the surgery. That night, after the husband of the first Maria had left, Maria 2 and I approached her to find out how she felt. Maria number one responded in a solemn way: -I'm going up. While she spoke, she was pointing towards the ceiling with her index finger. Maria 2 quickly responded: -don't say that; you are going to be fine. To which Maria 1 debated: -but I'm going up. -I'm going to the 10$^{th}$ floor. She asserted, laughing at her joke.

The three of us cracked up. I had to contain my laughter after a brief beat: laughing hurt my incisions. Good thing Maria had chosen humor, instead of behaving like her husband that cried and suffered for everything. What a sense of freedom it was to make fun of "tragedy." All of a sudden, we could laugh and realize that nothing is as bad as it seems. There is always a lighter side to everything and if we hold onto it long enough, nothing will ever bring us down.

If being in good spirits was the goal, Maria 2 fulfilled her mission; she always found the funny side of everything. She had a baby recently, but her husband had not come to visit her yet. I never knew how she felt about that because she kept herself happy and making jokes. It was so refreshing to see a patient that took her ailments with humor. One day we were all tired of the car accident patient, namely Miss Selfish, and Maria imitated her voice: -nurse, nurse. She did it with such incredible resemblance that I had to tell her to stop because I really wanted to laugh, and I could not. My abdomen hurt from cracking up; laughter was our best weapon to stop the negativity of others from affecting our health.

### 137. Do not allow bullying in your room.

With so many convalescents living under the same roof, there is always someone who wants to be the boss, claiming to be the leader. At that specific moment, the self-proclaimed boss of the room was Miss Selfish. Maria 2 disliked the way this troubled woman demanded the other roommates to speak English when they were not addressing her, so she could understand what they were saying. The nerve! She wanted us to stop speaking Spanish amongst ourselves because she did not understand. We were across the room, many feet away from her, yet this woman wanted to participate in our conversation. None of the two Marias spoke English, so we did not communicate in that language, but Miss Selfish could care less; the only thing she cared about was being on the spotlight and knowing what everyone said. If we spoke Spanish, she mocked us, imitating our language.

Maria 2 did not like this and mocked Miss Selfish back in a funny way. Maria 1 and I found this really funny. The rest of the patients also shared the same discomfort with the need of Miss Selfish to be the center of attention, but Maria 2 was one of the few patients with enough strength to "fight back." When Miss Selfish asked an employee to turn the air conditioner on, even though it was not hot, Maria 2 turned it off; something the rest of us appreciated, especially the girl from Bangladesh since her condition had worsened and she felt very cold.

Maria 2 was like those big kids that not even the bullies dare to mess with. As long as she was here, the rest of us were protected from high maintenance patients that wanted to make our stay in the room chaos; she did not allow bullying. I do not think she was taller than 5'6" or 5'7" but that did not stop her from speaking her mind and doing something about it. Fortunately, she was on our side, on the side of those who only want to survive another day. Therefore, when Miss Selfish mocked any of the patients or the employees, Maria 2 rapidly scolded or mocked her. The result was that Miss Selfish, the queen of bullying, had to stay quiet at least for a while and when she was silent the rest of us could rest.

### 138. If the problem is big, put it in God's hand.

The only day Maria 2 was not as upbeat as usual was the day she finally found out what her condition was. That day, an Asian male doctor came to speak to her and since her English was not so great she asked me to translate. The doctor said Maria had cancer. I was in shock. Oh Lord, how do I tell her? I had to pretend to be as casual as possible but felt extremely nervous to give her the news. I translated quickly as if talking faster would diminish the pain Maria 2 would feel. She was surprised, did not expect those news. She interrupted the doctor to ask something else but with a gesture

I pointed out to her to wait until he finished and proceeded to translate the rest of the message.

Soon, the doctor left us alone. I wanted to cheer my roommate up but did not know how to do it. Maria 2, despite feeling very sad, tried to pretend that she would deal with the illness the same way she had dealt with her life. But I knew better; this was a very sad night for Maria, and she had no relatives to share it with. Instead, she thanked me for translating everything. I felt sorry for her and after she went back to her bed I remained in mine and did the only thing I could do now for my new friend: pray, place such big problem in the hands of the only one that could solve it, God.

### 139. Wounds left by tubes, placed by doctors, heal instantly.

I wanted to go home; there, I would not have to suffer watching my friends battle for their lives. But how could I achieve it if I still had four tubes piercing my body and an open wound? As I wondered about this, my feeding pump started to beep. I really disliked that sound; to patients it meant proximate death. Nurses are used to this sound; they hear it all the time. Patients, on the other hand, never get used to it so the sooner an employee turned it off, the better we felt. When the device was silenced, I felt relieved for not hearing it and also because I saw that one of the tubes in my belly did not have any fluids, only a little blood. These were good news since my head doctor approved its removal.

While the doctor checked my abdomen, without telling me what he would do, he pulled the tube. I was really surprised; the doctor had just pulled a foot long tube from my intestines, without any warning and without giving me anything for pain. Are not wounded victims supposed to be given something to ease the pain and if there is nothing, those helping out are supposed to make the patient bite some wood, so he or she does not scream? What about the team of people that are supposed to hold me down to my bed, so I do not go crazy and kick everyone due to my terrible pain? Had not these doctors seen any of these situations in films or television?

To be honest, I did not feel any pain, perhaps a mild cramp. Yet, having the tube pulled like that from my belly left me concerned and when I looked at the area where the tube used to be, expecting to see a huge hole, I was even more amazed to see the only trace of the process was a small scar that emerged almost instantly, right in front of my eyes. Only a little bit of blood surrounded the new scar. My skin had blended back, to my astonishment, in less than a second. This gave me great joy since I did not have to wait for weeks for it to heal; also, having one less tube in my body increased my chances of leaving the hospital.

## 140. Your goal is to win, not to compete.

My goal was the same most patients had, to win the battle. The saying, "it's not whether you win or lose but how you play the game," is not applicable here; you win and live or lose and die, as simple as that. I felt that if my rehabilitation took place in my house my probabilities of survival increased. Because of it, I tried to impress the doctor, pretending to be in better health condition than I actually was so they would discharge me.

When the doctors saw me by chance in the hospital hallway while doing my daily walks, I improved my posture and walked as straight as possible. Not even beauty contestants try so hard to keep their posture. It was really hard for me to keep my body straight. Fortunately, doctors only glanced briefly since they were busy with other patients. As soon as they looked away, I could let go of the pose and assume my non-glamour hunchback posture, which came about because of my abdominal pain and the weight of the tubes in that area. I also went back to gasping for air.

Whoever believes being a beauty pageant contestant is easy, certainly has not had to pretend being one. My weight was the only thing that qualified me for one of those pageants. Since I had lost so much weight while in the hospital, I was skinny for human standards but perfect for beauty pageants. I was working really hard to get rid of that skeletal body that only looks good in front of a camera.

By then, my doctors had approved a normal solid diet. I never ate sweets. I knew they would make my pancreas work too hard. By night, I was so exhausted from trying to get better that I went to sleep as soon as visiting hours were over at 8:00 p.m. I knew sleeping time, so necessary for healing and winning the battle of life, was not guaranteed in this trauma room where anything could happen to the patients already there or the new ones.

## Chapter 8:

## Find allies; enemies will come uninvited.

**141. Find someone who can inject, or you will spend more time at the hospital.**

Most great stories have a good character that represents everything that is good. In the Wizard of Oz, Glinda is the good fairy Godmother that unlike her sister, the wicked witch of the west, rejoices in making people happy. If there were Glindas in my story, the traveling nurses would certainly fit the bill; they were like the fairy Godmothers for patients. If only one of them could come to my house to inject me, I would be sent home right away, but these employees are the Lamborghini of nursing, unattainable for the ordinary patient. They only work at the hospital and do not make house calls, so I had no other choice but to search for another alternative.

I insisted to my doctors and nurses that I was ready to go home and that my mother would take care of me. They were not sure my mother could take care of the open wound, collect the pancreatic liquids, feed me with the pump and inject me three times a day. One of the nurses, noticing my urgency, asked my mother if she could really take care of me. My mom rapidly said yes, knowing that this was what her daughter wanted more than anything. Suddenly, fairy like music filled the air. I was convinced that my devoted mother would take care of me better than Glinda did for Dorothy in the Wizard of Oz. -So you are the one who will inject her? The nurse asked my mom. The music in my mind stopped sharply; I knew the answer to that question, my mother would do anything but inject me.

By suggesting that my mom injected me the nurse had unknowingly activated my mother's innate security system. Had my mother being a house, her alarm system would have been heard all over town; a red light would have started flashing, any light: the ambulance, the patrol police or an intermittent red light of a secrete place that has hidden merchandise in it and has been infiltrated illegally. This was the moment when her emergency system would have alerted the authorities of a serious intrusion.

My mother almost always has an open mind and open arms to help but this was precisely one of the very few things that went beyond what she was willing to accept. Injecting her daughter was as unthinkable as lighting up a tank filled with gasoline. Not only did she not know how to inject but also she had always refused to do it throughout her life. When her mother had diabetes, this was the only thing she did not do: inject her with insulin. Needles terrified her. Even when her husband needed injections at home, she went looking for a neighbor to do it; injecting her daughter was simply out of bounds. She had seen her daughter suffer too much with all the injections received in the hospital and was not planning on increasing that pain with more needles. Come to think of it, that was smart. My mom did not want me to associate her with pain. What for? A nurse could carry that burden. Absolutely brilliant! If Jackie had to be injected, it would be a nurse and not Violeta who would do it.

**142. If you lack patience, find more; you will need it.**

After the nurse left we felt sad; mom because she did not feel at ease with injections, her daughter because it was my impression that once we were home I would no longer need injections. The next day, both of us asked the nurse if the hospital had staff that went to people's houses to inject patients. She confirmed there were nurses that made house calls, but they had not found any in the area where I lived. I urgently needed to find that nurse, so I would not have to listen to the yelling and demands of the car accident patient. The last thing that crossed my mind was that the nurses had also reached their patience limit with this noisy roommate.

That night while Gyolonda, the visiting nurse that did everything to help her patients, changed the dressings that covered my wounds and tubes, I noticed she was sad. I could not help asking her what was wrong. She explained to me how she had gone to a service at her church and had asked God to give her more patience. Did I hear right? I asked myself silently. Patience? My mind did not know how to interpret the information. We are talking about a woman that every other day cleans my wounds, changes my diaper, feeds me and injects me more than 3 times in less than 8 hours, and I am not even related to her and after that she has to do the same for over 20 patients, and she is asking God for patience? Now girl: that is just being selfish. Do you want God to give you all the patience left in the world? Seriously, you already have more patience than most people I know, including me.

Can someone tell me: what planet is this woman from? Because she is certainly not from the same one I have been living at. Without hesitation, I told her that she behaved more like an angel than a human being that her patience amazed me, especially when she treated high maintenance patients with a commitment I never thought possible in a human being. -Thank you. Gyolonda replied with her usual humility, so uncommon in this side of humanity. After a beat, she explained how some patients wore her down, and she felt like she was letting God down because it was hard to be patient with those patients.

I was upset, not at her but at the person that was causing her so much pain. Gyolonda was teaching me something, without even meaning to, and I was so busy being upset that I totally missed her point. She was tormented because she did not want to feel any negative feelings towards anyone; she was practicing a commandment that many repeat but few people practice: "love thy neighbor as thyself." I loved how that sounded, in a romantic kind of way. In real life, however, I admit I have to pray harder because every time I hear the screams of Miss Selfish I feel many things but "love thy neighbor" is not one of them.

I have so much to learn. Luckily, I had a great teacher right before me. This incredible nurse was so devoted to her call that even though others around her created a terrible environment, she felt it was her responsibility to understand them and accept them the way they were. -I am sure Jesus must be very proud of you. I thought as I witnessed the tears in her eyes that showed how tormented Gyolonda felt for not being practically perfect.

Only a perfect soul would feel more could be done for someone as inconsiderate as Miss Selfish. Here I go again. Why can I not let go of that girl? I guess some students have a harder time learning a lesson. That is why I admired

Gyolonda. Other people would have ignored or screamed at someone as headstrong as the car accident patient but not this traveling nurse. Gyolonda felt that if she had negative feelings for any patient it was her fault, and she needed to ask God for more patience.

### 143. In a room, you can object to the air conditioner being turned on.

Maybe one day I would be like Gyolonda, the heaven sent visiting nurse; it seemed this was not going to be that day. I urgently needed to get better in order to be sent home, and Miss Selfish was jeopardizing my health and the health of all the patients, by sending someone to turn on the air conditioner, which in our delicate conditions could increase the possibilities of us getting colds or even worse, pneumonia. Miss Selfish felt hot even though it was November and winter had already started. She never asked for permission from anyone in the room to turn on the device. There was a villain in this room and something needed to be done about it. Miss Selfish was a dangerous adversary, the witch with the rotten apple. Her "venom" was poisoning everyone, yet no one said a word to stop her.

When a nurse attendant turned on the air conditioner, following the petition of Miss Selfish, I spoke loud and clear for the first time since being admitted to the hospital. -Turn it off. I said with authority. The car accident patient rapidly reacted from her bed. -I'm hot. To which I rapidly responded: -and there's other patients in this room, and we are all cold. Phrases of support to me, from the other patients, followed. It was a liberating moment; women who never complained before because of their weak conditions, united to defend their right to get well, all at the same time stood up for themselves and their rebellion paid off instantly.

Without the need of a prince, to awaken us from the poisoned dream with a kiss, these maiden had awaken and this time longing for justice. I did not look like Snow White or The Sleeping Beauty, but I felt like them, brought back to life after a long dream and ready to take back my kingdom. Even if I was in this small room made of curtains, inside a bigger concrete room filled with beds of ill women, I was going to behave like this was my castle, and they were the princesses I now had to protect.

The nurse attendant rapidly turned the air conditioner off. Actually, she was glad to since the patient who wanted the air conditioner on was the one that always mocked her when she spoke English. Sooner or later you pay for what you do. The screaming patient had been disrespectful to this assistant and perhaps that resulted in her losing this assistant's support. Besides, the rest of us patients outnumbered our oppressor and the majority rules. We were sick, that was a fact, but we were not willing to compromise our health any longer, nor for Miss Selfish nor for anyone who tried to impose anything that made us feel worse.

For the first time since our admission to the hospital, we had some sort of power and this felt great. Our first achievement had been to keep the air conditioner off but from now on we would be alert to everything that worked against us, and we would no longer allow it.

### 144. Stay away from bad influences so they do not contaminate you.

The car accident patient was surprised with our rebellion and finally shut up, at least for two hours. Unfortunately, she never took no for an answer and when all of her attempts to turn the air conditioner on failed, to the point that the other patients told her to leave to another room, she asked the guy who brought the food to turn on the fan on her side. It was a huge fan that blew air mainly to two beds: hers and the one that belonged to Maria 2. My poor friend, and I am not referring to Miss Selfish but to Maria 2, which not only had to deal with being diagnosed with cancer on that day but also had to endure a huge fan blowing cold air on her already cold body. Since Maria 2 could stand up and Miss Selfish could not, she rapidly turned off the fan, but the car accident patient did not stop complaining about how unfair we were all to her, how hot she felt, how she was going to complain to the hospital, and she went on and on; blah, blah, blah. Is she ever going to stop complaining? Oh mine! Am I sounding as selfish as her? I have to get out of this hospital soon; I think her poisonous behavior is contagious.

Maria 2 finally got so tired of the complaints of Miss Selfish that she allowed her to turn the fan on for an hour or two. Very wise are the words: "ask and you shall receive." Maria 2 gave the car accident patient what she wanted, not because she liked her but to get rid of her. Once the car accident woman fell asleep, Maria 2 returned to her bed after turning off the huge fan. At the end of the day, all patients were exhausted, the car accident patient from trying to turn the air conditioner on and the rest of us from trying to keep it off.

### 145. Low spirits in a patient come from being tired not from having lost faith.

Several volunteers had the mission of cheering the patients up, by taking them to the religious service of their choosing. To me, attending these celebrations was an excellent excuse to escape the chaos of my room. I needed help from up above to be able to deal with humans below. This time, even though I was physically stronger than on previous occasions, sadness had taken control of me. I could not help crying several times. Some people approached me, during the celebration and after it; they gave me prayer booklets and kindly offered to pray for me, assuming I had lost my faith.

I was too weak to explain to them that even though my

faith was still solid as a rock my body was very tired, and I just wanted to go home. I did not let them know; I simply smiled at them, accepted their booklets and thanked them for their support. How could I be mean to them if they just wanted to see me happy? This time, not even their good vibes were enough to lift up my spirits.

In my heart, I knew things were going to be all right but my body was too tired to understand that. Not even a lady, whose job in the hospital was to cheer patients up by giving them magazines, books, hair brushes and many items more, free of charge, was enough to bring a smile to my face. When I met her, I was impressed that a hospital would employ someone just to give gifts to patients. At that moment, I thought it was genius; I felt like a kid who had been given candies. My mother was with me on that day, and she got really happy when she saw my enthusiasm while picking up the magazines I liked. That day, however, the lady with the cart full of goodies was not enough to cheer me up; the only thing that would lift up my spirits would be going home, but my doctors had not approved my discharge yet.

### 146. Consenting mothers are the best personal nurses.

-They want to send you home, but they still have not found a nurse to go to your house. Said Ade, the loving African nurse. -I don't need a nurse. -Mom can take care of me. I answered with evident enthusiasm with the possibility of going home. -You can? Ade asked her. Mom rapidly agreed. –Yes. My mom confirmed. -Including injections? Ade continued. Here we go again! Did not this nurse know that mom was terrified of injections? Scared and opening her eyes wider than an owl, mom quickly said: -no, no injections. Trying to ease my already anxious mother I intervened: -I can have a nurse for injections, right? Ade responded quickly: -that's the problem; they still cannot find one in your area.

-I can teach you. Ade said while looking at my mother trying to cheer her up, but mom replied with a nervous smile: -no. I have to give the employee credit for trying, but the author of my days was already turning pale. Fortunately, the nurse noticed. -That's okay. Ade said, wanting my mom to relax. So that Violeta would calm down, I added: -she can change my dressings and everything else. Brief silence. -I'll teach you to change the dressings. Those words said by Ade finally calmed down my mom. The thought of injecting her daughter with a needle disturbed her but not healing an open wound that exposed the inside part of the stomach or emptying the pancreatic liquids, channeled through tubes embedded to the abdomen, or changing diapers. If elephants fear ants, then my mom's fear of needles is not a big deal.

Leaving injections aside, Ade chose the change of dressings as the first nursing lesson for my mother. Since

English is my mom's second language and she does not speak it fluently, she was a little nervous of learning the process of changing my dressings. Luckily, Ade also spoke English as a second language and communicated with my mother wonderfully. Mom turned out to be a great student. The only step that took her longer than expected was to put the sterilized gloves on. She was determined not to let germs near her daughter's open wound. But once she got over her beginner's nerves, everything flowed perfectly.

That same day, by the third time, mom was changing dressings like a pro. The training she was getting resembled the one experienced by small villages in any part of the world when moved by the shortage of warriors, the villagers decide that the teacher of the town or the bravest person must train ordinary people to defend themselves. In my case, the teacher that taught the amazing skills was Ade, the nurse; her student was my mother, and I represented the village. The enemy was my condition. Yes, I admit it, this sounds a bit corny but with so much time to spare I had to get creative to not get bored.

The following day, the learning process continued and Violeta was soon helping her daughter like any other nurse. There were no swords included in the treatment but scissors felt like the necessary weapon to cut the gauze, which in turn would contain the dangerous liquids that threatened our "village." My mom's commitment to helping me was admirable. She did not have to learn physical moves to face the enemy, but she could move her hands without a problem when the time to give me a massage came. Like a good soldier, nothing was beneath her. She was aware that while in battle she would have to do things like cleaning bowls and artifacts used to help the wounded, in this case her daughter, but she did not seem to mind doing it.

By mid-week, no nurse had been found to go to my house to inject me every six hours. In order to be discharged, I needed someone to do it. We had a wounded soldier and there were no nurses to help her. Then I spoke to my mother; I did not lie to her, I did not promise her a land free of war if she accepted to be a soldier. We both knew that even if she became my nurse in this uncertain battle, there were no guarantees of a happy ending.

I also told her that the only reason I was not allowed to leave was because of the injections. She looked at me, always with that compassionate look that only loving mothers can give their children. I really was not expecting anything; I knew how mom felt about needles. That was the only skill Ade had not been able to train her in. Then, out of nowhere, a small but crucial miracle happened; Violeta agreed to inject her beloved daughter Jackie. Great joy overwhelmed me. No wounded soldier would be left behind. My mother would be my personal nurse, so I could leave the hospital. Let the triumph trumpets be heard; this warrior was going back home!

### 147. The needles you are injected must be small.

I quickly set a plan of attack in motion. I would speed up my departure, first by notifying the nurse about my mother's acceptance to inject me and after that, by making sure my mom was trained as soon as possible. I called Ade and with joy notified her: -my mom will do it; she will inject me. Ade was one of my best allies; without having to ask her, she was always at our service. –Great. Ade replied. -Do you want to start now? She asked my mom. This ally knew that at war there is no time to lose. My only concern was that Violeta would panic again.

Fortunately, my mom accepted, with or without panicking she would live up to her word; she would inject me. That was how the final and more important of the trainings for the battle, against my bad condition, started. Ade showed mom the position the needle needed to be in so it would hurt less. Mom felt relieved when she realized the needle was smaller than another one used by a nurse previously. Back then, that employee had injected me with the same medicine but with a huge needle. I remember when we complained about the size of the needle, the nurse alleged it was the one I had to get. We had a feeling she was not telling us the truth but did not argue with her since we did not want the staff to think we were not cooperating with the treatment.

When we commented this to Ade, she told us that this

nurse was not supposed to use that needle to inject me. The employee had two needles, a small one and a big one; the big one was to break the seal covering the medication. After that, the nurse had to replace the needle with the small one so that it could enter the delicate skin. The needle had to be changed since the tip must not had been used so that it had a sharp edge and entered my skin easily; besides, the thickness of the small needle was substantially thinner to cause less pain.

    Luckily, the one training my mother would not be the careless nurse but Ade. Contrary to her colleague, she used the small needle and taught my mother to inject me correctly and despite the fact that mom was nervous, because she did not want to cause me pain and because Ade was watching, she overcame her anguish and injected me. I did not feel as much pain as I had felt with other injections and next to the martyrdom I had suffered with the nurse of the big needle, my mother's injection felt like a caress. I happily notified my mother and Ade about it. My days at the hospital were close to an end; my mom was ready to be the new nurse in charge of this patient.

    I would no longer experience the pain I suffered for two days, due to the careless nurse that used the big needle. That was a beginner's mistake and I am not only talking about that employee, which was too inexperienced at her job to the point of not knowing something so basic, I am also referring to me as a patient. Never again will I believe any employee that assures me that a big needle is the same as a small one: let them inject themselves with it, and we will see if it is the same.

### 148. No matter how much you plan, get ready for the unexpected.

While I fantasized with the idea of finally going home, another set back occurred; the Korean nurse I liked was trying to clean my feeding pump but the soda did not want to go in. My pump was unclogged with soda because it is so abrasive that it cleans the tubes better than detergent. Good heavens! I think this is what doctors mean when they warn us not to drink colas because they are bad for your health. Truth being told, the nurse tried several times with a huge plastic injection, without a needle, to have the soda go into my feeding tube but it seemed to be clogged.

It turned out the milk I was fed with, through the feeding pump, was so cloying nurses were not surprised when the tube got clogged. -It's clogged. The nurse notified me. -Let me bring someone. She kept saying while she went to look for another employee, to help her unclog the tube. If it is clogged, I thought, maybe it is because my body does not need it anymore and I can go back to eating regular meals. My pushing brain quickly designed a plan to get rid of that bothersome feeding pump; not having it embedded to my stomach sounded too tempting as to let go of this opportunity without trying to get rid of it. Then I suggested: -why don't you leave it like that until tomorrow? -I already ate enough by mouth. I added, hoping my sweet face would mislead them.

The nurse, unaware of my real intentions, accepted my proposal and removed the pump before leaving the room. The villain in me had won another battle, concealing my real intentions. Had I been working in a soap opera, this would be the part when staccato music would emphasize my evil behavior. I must clarify I did not do it to be evil; the pump was such a heavy load for my weak body that not having it attached to my stomach would make me feel lighter, literally; smile of a villain once more and staccato music emphasizes it.

Next morning, when my doctors arrived, they put an end to my triumph as a villain; I was just not ready for a normal solid diet yet; my pancreas was not ready for it. The more I ate by mouth the more dangerous liquids were produced by this organ. There was no option; I had to be fed through a tube. This meant having the clogged tube removed and replaced by a new one. Who is the villain now? But this time the "bad" news came accompanied by some good ones. My new team of female doctors let me know that as soon as the procedure was completed I would be sent home, as long as someone was by my side taking care of me 24 hours a day, 7 days per week and that I kept my appointments until a date was set for my next surgical procedure.

To me, this sounded just like when a kid is sent home for summer vacations with too much homework but if that is what is needed for me to go home, let it be. By then, I had gotten used to the idea that I was not the writer of this story. As much as I planned, the divine plan had precedence over mine. I had no other option but to accept that I was not the director that proposed the scenes of my own life. Even though I had already made plans to leave the hospital, I had to stay, at least until the procedure was completed.

## 149. Weekends are dead: do what you have to do during weekdays.

It was Thursday, and I knew that if the procedure was not done Friday I would have to wait until Monday and this was simply unthinkable. Doctors presented the possibility that I stayed until next week, but I begged them to do it before the week was over. It worked; the procedure was scheduled for next day. Staying at war zone for a whole weekend? Only a fool would think that is a good idea.

Few are the accomplishments during weekends at a hospital. Working days are from Monday thru Friday and any patient here, wanting to survive, learns it quickly. During weekends there is less staff and no relevant surgery happens then, unless it is an emergency. Since I was no longer at the emergency phase, I knew that one more weekend would only mean to put up with patients I urgently needed to leave behind. I was set on not counting myself among the patients at the trauma room. Everything was ready back home: my hospital bed, a new feeding pump, my milk, the nurse who would teach my mother to use the new feeding pump, and much more; the only thing missing was Jackie, and I was determined to fill that void right away.

### 150. Even doctors disagree; use that in your favor.

The idea of getting a new procedure, to put a new tube through my stomach, did not appeal much to me but since this was the only way I could be allowed to go home, I pretended to totally agree with the process; any ruse that helps you win the war is valid. I was actually happy to see an attendant come for me to take me to the gastroenterology surgical room. A huge smile decorated my face, knowing this would be the last time I would see those hallways on a bed as a patient.

Along my way, to the floor of the procedure, I recognized many of the faces of the attendants and nurses I had met during my lengthy stay at this place. I waved my hand happily at all of them, with the certainty of someone finally going home. At least I had something in common with all the beauty queens of the world; all of my teeth could be seen. Proudly, I waved my hand like a trained beauty pageant contestant: left right, left right, repeat. I had won the most important contest of them all, surviving, getting a second chance at life.

Even the gastroenterologists performing the procedure

were quite surprised with my energy. To them it was the end of the day, and they were visibly tired with a long day's work. They were not happy to know I was fed not only with the tube but also by mouth. I then understood how many clashes my head doctors must have had with the gastroenterologists, due to the small quantities of food this patient ate by mouth.

Both, my head doctors and my gastroenterologists, wanted the best for me, but they had different approaches. The gastroenterologists did not think I was ready to eat by mouth. My head doctors, however, had the last word regarding this matter. They believed their patient desperately needed to gain weight, in order to have the necessary strength to get better. At feeding time, my belly was glad it was the head doctors and not the gastroenterologist's decision the one that prevailed.

But now I was inside the gastroenterologists' territory, and I had to keep those opinions to myself; it was safer. After all, they were the ones in charge of replacing my feeding tube. So when they told me about their annoyance over the food I ate, I remained neutral and simply listened to the doctor, without confronting him in the slightest bit. A soldier knows when not to contradict the general. What this doctor did not know was that this patient used every possible ruse to convince my other doctors to give me the privilege of eating by mouth. The fact that doctors disagreed, on how to give me treatment, worked in my favor: divide and rule. I cannot take credit for dividing them, but I did use their difference of opinion in my favor.

## 151. Once you make a decision in the surgery room, there is no going back.

I needed some anesthesia for my surgery, but the anesthesiologist was already gone. Another option was to perform the procedure without anesthesia. The doctors did not think I would accept this second option but when it was offered, I rushed to answer: -do it without anesthesia. I said it even before they finished asking me the question; that is how desperate I was to leave the hospital. -Without anesthesia? One of the nurses replied surprised. -Yes, I can handle pain. I replied with great confidence and even with a hint of arrogance, so they would not hesitate to grant me what I asked for. Immediately, the entire staff began to prepare for the procedure.

-I can handle pain! Was I out of my mind? Was it morphine talking again? Wait a minute, I had not had any morphine; I was totally clean. No meds were in my body on that day. Why then was I behaving so dumb? I had agreed to have a minor surgery without anesthesia. What was I thinking? As soon as I saw the nurses and doctors getting ready, I realized the magnitude of my words.

What did I do? Sanity finally kicked in but once you make a decision in a surgery room there is no going back. I briefly thought about the consequences of my words and right away found an answer to this new worry: -don't worry, God will take care of your pain again. I reaffirmed myself. Yeah, yeah, when you cannot handle it give your mess to God. But at that moment I could not do anything else; I had messed up big time. The doctors were setting everything up to grant my wish, so it was too late to back out and there was no other alternative but to give my problem to a higher force.

## 152. Prayer will calm you down: concentrated prayer will bring you amazing responses.

I started to pray with great devotion but my prayers were almost as fast as the doctors and nurses who were setting everything up for my procedure. I prayed and although my faith was strong, I was a bit concerned with the big decision I had just made. Why didn't you wait until Monday to get anesthesia? I wondered, knowing that once more I had allowed desperation decide for me. Too late for second thoughts now: the tube replacement was already a reality, so I prayed and thanked God for taking away my pain throughout my stay at the hospital and asked for help once more. I was asking for help from anyone that could intervene from heaven, my angels, especially Archangel Raphael, the spirits of light, especially the Virgin Mary and when the procedure was about to begin, I could not believe who came to answer my call.

Right there, before my eyes: Jesus, the son of man himself, was standing in front of me. I wanted someone to answer my call but to see Jesus Christ looking at me with the most compassionate expression I had ever seen was beyond words. I had not taken any medicine in hours; I had no anesthesia and was totally awake. It was not a dream; I was clearly seeing Jesus, dressed in a beautiful bright white robe. Another white and equally shiny fabric covered his beautiful long and very black hair.

Physically, he looked different than many images I had seen of Jesus; his hair was not red or partially blond, it was totally black, a bit longer than shoulder length, flat with a few waves. His skin was white and he had a black beard. He was excessively skinny; the bad shape of his face shocked me. I had no doubts it was Christ, but I was surprised his face was extremely swollen, as if he had been beaten badly. I did not ask about it; for some reason, his physical aspect was the most evident but the least important thing; his great presence was what really mattered.

I simply understood that Jesus was presenting himself just the way he looked when he was punished while on his way to his crucifixion: he was confirming he shared my pain. But what called my attention the most was the incredibly unconditional love this being was offering me, by taking me in his arms and caressing my hair, wanting and achieving the disappearance of my pain. I had prayed to get help but never would I have imagined receiving such an incredible response.

## 153. Ask and you shall receive.

Without losing a second, I mentally asked him: -why are you here if you can be anywhere? Jesus responded: -y ahora estoy aqui contigo. Spanish for -and now I am here with you. -Besides, you know I can bi-locate. I understood what he meant; he can be in multiple places at the same time. I had read about this concept many times in my life but my human condition never really understood its meaning until now. Jesus was there with me but at the same time he was also taking care of many people around the world. This is obviously impossible for us human beings but not for the Son of God.

I did not question Christ about it anymore; I accepted the incredible blessing I was receiving and rapidly bombarded him with questions, recognizing the unique opportunity I had been given. Jesus replied to all of them without reservation; the responses confirmed that the best way to communicate with God, other than positive deeds, is to pray and that the Almighty gives us enough time and opportunities to find him. We are not alone and there is no reason for self-pity because God is taking care of us so diligently that he sends his own son to protect us.

## 154. Pain can be a blessing in disguise, use it in your favor.

Now that I was finally in a better health condition and on my way to rehabilitation, I felt immensely blessed to have next to me the being I admired and loved the most. What an incredible way to finish the most difficult time in my life. Jesus himself had come to comfort me and reassure me that God is always with us, especially when we call through our prayers and especially when we are suffering the most.

God gives us only what we can handle; it is up to us to understand that. Pain will always be around the corner; it is how we react to it what matters. Only when we suffer can we relate better to other people's pain. We can be more humane, more understanding and less judging when we know exactly what others feel, not because we have read or been told by someone about it but because we have experienced it first hand.

Now everything made sense to me; Jesus accepted the pain he was offered because he loved humanity. He could have avoided the suffering but decided to experience it and in doing so he set up new levels of tolerance. Chances are our pains are not even close to what Christ felt while dying on the cross so whenever we feel any kind of self pity, remembering this can put us back in perspective. Someone has already suffered more than us. Pain is not as bad as it seems and it might even be a blessing in disguise, an opportunity to truly understand what others go through when they experience hard times.

I was happy to get such great message from God. I finally understood the use of pain, its reason to exist. All of my life I have always wanted the happy ending, the happily ever after, you know any concept that involves the word happy. I doubt many people want a painful ending or a painfully ever after story. But now I finally understood the role of pain in our lives; it is simply our training tool, just like a soldier has to experience a great deal of physical pain in combat training so that when real pain comes he can resist it, we have to master pain so when suffering comes we can overcome it. Moreover, the more we can overcome pain, the better trained we will be for our next life, the spiritual one.

### 155. If you do not think about your pain, you will suffer less.

Happy tears rolled down my cheeks. I had my eyes closed and yet what I could see was amazing. I did not open my lips but what I could ask was revealing. To my doctors and nurses it seemed like I was silently crying in pain because of the procedure. But the reality was so much greater than that; I was having the most important conversation of my life with Jesus Christ, standing right there in front of me; I could see him as if we were seeing our reflection on a mirror.

When Jesus lovingly answered the last of my questions, I

heard a male voice say: -that's it, we're done. It was the voice of the doctor who had performed the procedure. A tube had been removed from my stomach and a new tube inserted, penetrating my belly until it reached my intestines and I did not feel a thing. As the doctor announced they were done, Jesus slowly disappeared in mid-air, and I happily realized what had just happened. Christ kept me busy, so I would not pay attention to my pain and therefore did not have time to suffer, and he achieved his goal with unsurpassed compassion.

## 156. Your health is improving if you can go to the restroom.

Next day, the sweet memory of my encounter with Jesus was still drawing a great smile on my face, which did not go away despite my anxiety to go home. I was so energized that I tried, on my own, to do things I would usually do with my mom's help. I brushed my teeth, my hair and cleaned my face as best as I could while sitting on my hospital bed. Every movement was still a major achievement for me and still painful. But I felt great and in high spirits after my great encounter with Jesus the day before. After I had a few bites of my breakfast, my feeding tube was disconnected, so I could walk with my walker around the hospital hallways.

I was determined to prove my doctors they had made a good decision by allowing me to go home on that day. With this in mind, I went to the room's restroom and was able to use it. This endeavor was quite painful because I still had my tubes penetrating my belly, but I wanted to prove I could survive outside the hospital. The idea of not being allowed to go home was out of the question. I had to "graduate" and be the patient who now left other patients, like the girl from Bangladesh, behind. I was concerned for this patient because she was still in critical condition; she was extremely skinny.

The only thing I could do for my roommate was to pray, so she would get better and soon "graduate" like me and go home. When I came out of the restroom that day, the girl from Bangladesh asked me how it went and was happy to find out that I was able to do "number two." In a hospital, for patients in a trauma room, going to the restroom and being able to perform "number two" is a clear indication that you are getting better and are on your way to recovery. I definitely needed to get out of the hospital. Who would have thought I would actually celebrate going to the restroom? Both, the girl from Bangladesh and I, seemed like little toddlers who celebrate when they are potty trained. The nurses also celebrated this event by using words an ordinary person would only use with a baby, and us patients reacted with the same joy of little kids.

## 157. It is always safer to walk accompanied by someone.

I felt so happy with the improvement in my health condition that I decided to take my walker and walk around the hospital on my own. It was already visiting time, and I would probably meet my family along the way so that was another incentive. With that in mind, I slowly grabbed my walker and headed outside the room. Along the way, I saw some of the nurses and attendants who were like cheerleaders motivating me to keep walking. Move over Beckham, LeBron, Ronaldo, Pacquiao or Woods the crowd is cheering for me! I might be way slower than all of them, but my audience seems to be happy. Everyone is so caring during the morning shift: the nurses, attendants, doctors, even the lady or the guy who deliver the food. They all gave me big supportive smiles and cheered me along the way.

As I kept moving forward, the staff returned to their tasks, and I was glad they did. I did not want them to realize I no longer felt good. I had used all of my energy reserves and had no strength left to keep walking. I had always being accompanied by my relatives in case I needed help but now I was alone in the middle of the hallway, was breathing heavily and felt like I was disappearing, running out of batteries. I almost fell on a chair that to my convenience was left in a corner of the hallway. I tried as best as I could to keep my posture so no nurses or doctors would realize I was feeling so weak and perhaps leave me at the hospital for a longer time.

I concentrated on my breathing to relieve the fainting sensation I felt. I could not allow others to see me like that; this would compromise my departure. Little by little, taking deep breaths made me feel better. Yet, I could not walk back to my room by myself; I would probably fall on my way, then they would leave me at the hospital. Had I only waited for my mother to help me walk, I would not be in this mess. I had no other option but to wait for my relatives, seated at that chair in a corner of the hallway and trying to cover up how bad I felt.

A few minutes went by, and I heard some voices I recognized: my mother, my husband and the nephew of my good friend Manuel, Gustavo. My face lit up, they would hold me, so I could go back to the room to pick up everything and go home. They were all surprised to see me in the hallway. I told them I was a little tired so they would not get alarmed; I actually felt terrible, but I did not show it. Convincing everyone to let me go home was a really hard task for me, so I was not willing to lose what I had earned. Under no circumstances, reasons or motives would I want to stay at the hospital any longer, so I showed my best smile; the actress in me was working over time and it seemed to be working. My family and friends helped me to stand up and with their help we were able to go back to the room.

## 158. Hospitals get rid of many things they use to take care of you: keep them.

Immediately, the preparation for my departure began. My husband and Gustavo picked up some of my belongings, and they headed back to the car. My mother was in charge of cleaning everything her daughter had used. We found out nothing of what I had personally used was recycled by the hospital for another patient, rather it was disposed of, so we decided to take all of that with us. To us, using the same devices that were used in my treatment meant great savings. Many patients do not take any of this and go home empty handed even though the hospital allows them to not only take them but also take additional things with them, as long as they request them. Chances are this does not sound exciting, but someone wanting to recuperate from physical trauma will find this help priceless.

Every item used in rehabilitation has a physical and spiritual value. The physical value is the evident one; bowls, for example, are to collect liquids. But those bowls have a bigger value, the spiritual one; that is the value each article acquires for the person who survives. In a religious celebration each article used has a sacred meaning that dates back to centuries and millenniums. As I watched my mom cleaning the bowls I had used to get rid of my phlegm, or the ones where she put the water, or the portable toilet, the walker and every item she used to take care of me I felt as if a very sacred ancient ritual was taking place; it was a ritual of remembrance and celebration.

Every utensil meant something, a moment, a battle and a conquest. Yes, they represented the hard times, but they also represented the joy of overcoming those hard times. Ade, the wonderful nurse from Africa, gave us some supplies: a few milk cans, gauze to cover the open wound and the leaking tubes, tape to put those in place and a few items more. What to anyone else would be ordinary items to take care of the sick, to the ill and those who take care of them they are necessary artillery to win the war.

### 159. If someone can help you with the health insurance paperwork, you will have less stress.

My mom and I knew, however, keeping me at home was not going to be an easy task or a cheap one. Come to think of it, what war has been cheap? With the bills at home growing by the second, due to my lengthy stay at the hospital without working, the idea of increasing my debt with the supplies needed to treat me was not an appealing one. Yet, going home certainly felt like the right choice. Besides, thanks to my friend Elba, I found out about and applied for the state's health insurance. If approved, I would only pay a fraction of the cost of my stay at the hospital or even pay nothing at all. My chances of getting the insurance looked good since I had not worked while at the hospital and would be disabled for a long time after my departure. This meant that being in such bad shape was not so bad after all.

I was supposed to be covered by my health insurance for my work as an actress, but the spokespeople of that health plan claimed some paperwork was missing from some employers and until that was cleared, I was considered uninsured. If my plan did not cover me, the state would take care of the charges. Since I qualified for both health insurances and all the applications had been made and sent, I just had to wait. Besides, to heal I had to avoid thinking about the hospital bill because if I did, I would have probably died for real!

## 160. You will go home once your discharge papers and prescriptions are ready.

Just like Dorothy in "The Wizard of Oz" I kept telling myself: -there's no place like home, there's no place like home. I did not have her slippers to take me straight home, but I had my wonderful family that would do precisely that. I wanted to go home right then, but I had to wait until my prescription was ready. Every time I saw a new nurse coming inside my room, I felt the same fear Dorothy felt of the wicked witch of the west. Even though nurses were far from being evil witches, I was extremely afraid that one of them might put an end to my journey back home and would tell me I had to stay at the hospital.

I could not stay at this far away kingdom any longer; like Dorothy, I had traveled so far to earn the right to go back home. I convinced my mom to go to the discharge room in the first floor of the hospital and wait for my discharge papers there. I reasoned that if they did not find me in the room, chances were they would not look for me in any other place. By then all of my belongings had been taken to the car so my petition to leave the room sounded acceptable to my mother. I do not know if she realized I was desperate to get out of there. The fact is I was placed in a wheelchair and my journey to freedom began.

As I was departing, I had a huge smile on my face. I bid farewell to everyone I had come across in this distant kingdom. I also wished the woman from Bangladesh got better soon. As my wheelchair progressed, I saw some of the nurses that took care of me; they looked liked the characters from the Wizard of Oz when they bid goodbye to Dorothy, at least I wanted to feel that special. The truth of the matter is they briefly said goodbye and kept doing their tasks. I had experienced so much anxiety because I thought they wanted to keep me there indefinitely, and they had already removed me from their case list. Such is life; the one that matters is the newcomer, not the one that is retiring. To me those were great news. They would follow their own path and this ex-patient hers. Now let's look for my prescription, sign my discharge papers and go home.

## 161. Make friends among staff members, and they will accelerate your departure.

Once on the first floor, we went to the discharge room. I had been told most people wait for hours in that room but it was my intention to shorten that waiting period as much as possible. It was already mid-afternoon, and I knew that if my discharge papers were not done quickly the staff would soon go home, increasing the possibility of me staying one more day to complete the discharge procedures. That was unthinkable for me so when I saw a familiar face in the room I found my salvation.

The lady I saw was an African-American woman I had met the day before while filling up some paperwork for my departure. It was a good thing that I was very polite to her then; I was counting on that to help me speed up my departure. -What are you still doing here? The lady asked me. Her friendly tone was my indicator that yesterday's sociability was bearing fruit. Had I hired her intervention it would not have been so timely. My own fairy Godmother had arrived, and she would grant me the wish of going home.

Using my sweetest tone of voice, I activated my last plan at the hospital: leave this far away kingdom as soon as possible. -I need the discharge papers to go home. I said while showing my harmless and innocent face to the nurse. -Your discharge papers? The lady inquired with an equally tender voice; my plan was working. The nurse immediately asked some of the employees in the office some questions and offered to fill out the papers herself. My mother had to prove she was ready to take care of me by answering some questions correctly.

That is how, after giving me some additional items, the hospital employee signed the document that gave me my freedom back. I was going back to Kansas, well not that far, more like North Hollywood, California but the outcome was the same; I was going home after a long and challenging journey. I gave the lady a kiss and a big hug, and she was moved. Somehow this moment felt like graduation day, right when the student gets the long awaited diploma from a professor and both hug each other or exchange a handshake.

## Chapter 9:

## What to Expect During Rehabilitation

**162. Every movement hurts those with recent surgery: drive them gently.**

I HAD FINALLY "GRADUATED" and was going home. I wished my wheelchair went faster, in case anyone changed their mind and sent me back to my room. But my relatives pushed the wheelchair cautiously; they knew every movement would be felt amplified in my ill-fated body. When we reached the parking lot, I felt safe. The hospital employees would probably not come back here for me. My relatives accommodated me with great care for the trip. Several pillows and blankets made my seating position more comfortable and contributed to cushion any movement during the journey.

My relatives drove the vehicle as if the patient were made

of porcelain and would break with any abrupt movement. It was a blessing to count on so much prudence since any irregularity of the road was highly felt by my weak body. My whole being was exhausted; I had pretended to feel better during the entire day, so I would not be left at the hospital, but on my way home I could barely stand the pain and weakness I felt. I thought that maybe it was not such a great idea to leave the hospital but decided to quickly erase that thought. I was determined to get better at home and that was precisely what I would do.

### 163. There are no easy rehabilitations but they can be made more bearable.

Rehabilitation at my home was, without a doubt, much more bearable than at the hospital: I did not hear the screams of high maintenance patients nor did I have to wait for pain medication, the temperature in my room was perfect, and my mother and my husband took care of me better than if I were at a 5 star hotel. Nevertheless, there are no easy rehabilitations; there is pain and unexpected situations a hospital could deal better with. Every day at home was filled with learning experiences. I had to polish my patience skills and accept the constant care I got from my relatives, and they in turn would polish their unconditional love skills like never before. It was like having a grown up baby at home. Not only did they have to take care of me like a baby, but they also had to put up with my adult tantrums.

I started to feel better as the days progressed. After some time, my body expelled two of the tubes: the feeding and the pancreatic one. The doctors had warned me to come to the emergency room if any of my tubes came out. Twenty days after been discharged that is exactly what happened. I did not feel worse; actually, after the great care I had received at home, I felt better and stronger. So the idea of going back to the hospital, even if it was for a few hours to deal with the tubes, was not so appealing to me. Would Dorothy go back to Oz after being in her perfect Kansas?

## 164. The ER is a war zone, come ready to face it.

The liquid coming out of my pancreas burned my skin and its terrible smell convinced my relatives and I to go back to the hospital, specifically to the emergency room. Just like the day when I was first admitted, the place was overcrowded. What an intimidating place this is! We had spent so many days in our gorgeous kingdom that we did not remember this was a battlefield; there were addicts, crazy and homeless people. On one corner, there was a man with extremely dirty clothes, unkempt hair and a smell that only he could stand; he was having a loud and serious conversation with himself. At another corner, some homeless took several chairs to sleep, leaving a lot people without a place to sit down. At another place, a woman could not stop coughing. It was "déjà vu" all over again.

Fortunately, we found some chairs at the most distant place we could find but almost everyone surrounding us could seriously affect my health; there were people with exposed wounds or sneezing or coughing. Mom and my husband protected me by seating on each side of me, to keep certain distance with the other ill people. They also brought everything needed for the wait. Mom had brought baby food for her grown up adult, water, a blanket and many pillows to make my wheelchair more comfortable. Mario brought magazines and books for the three of us. We were convinced we had come ready to face this inhospitable place and we had covered all of our bases but the wait was more than this patient could take. I needed to lie down to stop hurting my pancreas. After nine hours in a wheelchair in this unhealthy place, without having received treatment, we opted for going home and try to make an appointment for another day.

As we grabbed our belongings to leave the room, the name Jackie Torres was heard on the intercom. Play the triumphant music once more! Perhaps we had not wasted our day. We rapidly answered the call. Mario rushed to pick up our belongings while mom rapidly pushed my chair to get to the reception area before they gave my turn to another person. Not even a hurdle racerunner would have handled my transfer as skillfully as my mother did. She turned my chair from one side to another, dodging sick people, their relatives, bags, and chairs just like a champion. I made it to the lobby without a scratch and in record time. I do not know how my mother managed, but I guess practice makes perfect.

A short distance from us was Mario carrying our belongings. Since only one person was allowed to enter with me, the three of us decided it would be my personal nurse, mom. My poor beloved husband had to stay in this pathetic room for a longer time while I was transferred to a much better one.

### 165. To endure the long wait in the ER, equip yourself as if you were taking care of a baby.

Once inside, I was assigned to a room that had a little bed. By then, the long wait had taken its toll on my body; I felt very weak, my abdomen hurt, and I felt nauseous. On top of that, the dressings that covered my wounds had to be changed. Mom quickly laid me down, with the help of three big pillows she had brought and a blanket. Little by little I felt better, to the point of falling asleep while my mom remained alert to every movement I made. Mom was also concerned about the gauze that covered her daughter's open incision, just where the pancreatic tube used to be. By now that gauze was very wet and had to be changed or my skin would be badly burned.

Even though I had been in an emergency room only two

months ago, I did not remember the wait there is too long. Because of that, if the patient's condition is delicate, it is advisable that whomever takes him or her equips herself or himself just like a person who takes care of a baby would. Bringing things such as diapers, blankets, medication, food, liquids, and anything necessary for treating the patient will make the wait more tolerable for everyone.

In our case, mom had brought some of what we needed: food, liquids, a blanket and the pillows. What we did not think we would need in a hospital was my medications and the items mom used to heal me. Had we known our wait was going to be so long, we would have brought everything this patient needed. But since back then we did not know this simple rule of survival, the author of my days had to search for the healing items in that hospital room, in order to be able to heal my wounds, in case whoever attended me was not ready to do it.

Being as she was a trained warrior, my mom immediately started to analyze the battlefield. The first thing she spotted was the gauze. That was a good omen, the first weapon had been found. But the battle was a fierce one so more weapons were necessary to defeat the enemy. My mother kept scouting the place. Only doctors and nurses were allowed to search those drawers and compartments, but my mom had been wisely trained; she knew how to keep an eye on anyone that came near and at the same time look for the much needed ammunitions to win this war. She continued her search and spotted other items she was familiar with to cure her daughter: the sodium chloride liquid to get the gauze wet for the open wound, the surgical tape, the scissors, the nose and mouth mask, and the gloves.

A strike of luck! The entire arsenal had been found. She knew what to do and where everything was. She also knew her daughter was overdue for her dressing's change, but Violeta was in a hospital now and had to wait until given permission to take care of her Jackie.

### 166. If there is an option, avoid going to a hospital after a holiday.

Two hours after I was placed in that room the doctor finally arrived. Thank goodness it was an emergency; I only waited 9 hours outside and two inside, 11 hours total. I guess it is an incentive that during that time I did not die so this was an indication that my health was much better. The doctor apologized for the delay, even though it was not her fault. She had been at the hospital since early morning but there were simply too many patients on that day.

It was November 27, right after Thanksgiving Day and everybody seemed to have gotten sick on that day; either they got sick today or perhaps they, just like me, did not want to miss the delicious meal of Thanksgiving Day and waited until the day after to deal with their health issues. The last thing they expected, and I am daring to speculate based on my own experience, was that this place was going to be so crowded. I guess they were as sorry as I felt now for not having come to the hospital on another date.

I imagine the other patients, just like me, thought that it was no fun to refrain from eating on Thanksgiving Day. Because of it, they waited until today, so the doctor would not have the opportunity to limit their diet on the day when the best delicacies are eaten. Apparently, most of us had made the same decision. The sweetness of the delicious food and the great company we had the day before was something nice to think about while waiting the long hours spent at this emergency room. However, I think we all learned it is not healthy to come to a hospital after a holiday.

### 167. Feel proud to be alive and you will have more strength to keep on fighting.

A female medic, one of my head doctors, checked the area where the tube used to be and cleaned it up. -When did it come out? She asked. -It started to come out yesterday. -I mean, the day before yesterday. -We have been here for 12 hours now. -But it fully came out yesterday. I replied. I should have said they were 11 hours but felt so bad that I thought they were 12. Three more doctors came inside the room to check on me. They had heard about my condition and wanted to know more about my case. I felt so important with the presence of these doctors, which in a way was a bit odd; my importance relied on the fact that doctors found my condition a little out of the ordinary. I guess they saw it like this: how in the world is she doing okay? But my ego wanted to translate it like this: -how special this girl must be to have survived such incident.

One of them, a young handsome Caucasian resident doctor, was surprised by the fact that this patient had not developed diabetes even though my pancreas was split in half. -We've had many cases here but a pancreas fully split in half, this is the first time I see it. Said the doctor with admiration. See how even doctors think I am special? I had been in a bed for some time and during that time I did not have the opportunity to brag so this was my moment for stardom. Move over Oscar hopefuls, the doctor made his choice and the award to the most special patient goes to me. He said it; the evidence speaks volumes. Thanks my dear audience for tuning in.

### 168. If your caretakers forget to do something needed for your treatment, remind them.

I needed no more proof that I was a living miracle. Another doctor, also very young and quite handsome, told me that they would place me on a bed in a section of the hallway until I could get a CAT scan test of my pancreas. I was not precisely thrilled that my bed was parked in the hallway; that was another combat zone where I had already been in my first visit to this hospital and that brought me very bad memories. Just like my first time, this hallway was full of patients but since I would go home after the test I did not complain. I was not in a position to get picky and ask for royal treatment, like asking for a private room for me until I got helped. Behaving so demanding would have probably gotten me the opposite. Employees in this room work over 12 hours daily, and they have no time for divas.

One thing was certain, my mother had a petition and it was not related to demanding luxuries but with taking care of her daughter in a matter long over due, the change of my dressings. Violeta never lost sight of the ammunitions needed to cure her daughter and as soon as she thought it was prudent to do so, she requested that my dressings be changed before moving me. The few nurses available at that time had not performed the procedure, so they were not ready for this battle but my mother was. Her daughter urgently needed her intervention.

By then, I was supposed to have had the dressings changed three times and because of that they were soaked. I told the doctor that my mom had been trained in the process, and he approved it. My mother rapidly changed my dressings with the artillery found at the room and this made me feel much better. It is difficult to win the war when you are wet. Besides, the liquid coming out of my pancreas was burning my skin. Once the dressings had been changed, I was ready to keep on fighting.

### 169. Bring something to keep you warm: the ER is an igloo.

I returned to the battlefield with my best soldier, my mom. A nurse assistant moved my bed to a hallway, next to several patients who were waiting for a test or a bed in the hospital. The hallway was very cold. I understand hospitals should keep cold temperatures so germs do not survive, but do they have to kill patients in the process? I am freezing! I guess the fact that my defenses were low, due to the wait and fatigue, made the cold feel stronger.

I started to feel extremely weak. I imagined this must be how it feels to sleep in the open during war. Mom was also very tired, and both of us worried about Mario, who was still waiting in that smelly crowded room outside. I asked my mom to check on Mario. That is what she did; mom went outside and found my husband at the hospital's pharmacy. By then it was 3'o clock in the morning, and my poor husband seemed to have had enough experiences for the day. Not only was he freezing, he also had to move from the emergency room to the tiny lobby of the pharmacy next to it, because it was less crowded and definitely smelled better. That place was a little colder than the other room since it had less people; however, resisting the low temperature was safer than surrounding himself with so many people in such bad physical and mental state.

### 170. The pharmacy, at a hospital, is a magnet for drug addicts.

The last thing Mario expected was that at that precise moment some patients, that looked more like drug addicts than regular patients, came to the pharmacy to get their medicine. When it rains, it pours! They did not behave like average patients who are weak due to their illnesses. They demanded their medicine talking, rather screaming, quite loudly and moved around restlessly. "Beggars can't be choosers"?

When Violeta came to see her son in law, he was more than eager to leave. I do not blame him; one thing is to deal with a drug addict when they pass by you in a busy urban street and another one is to face not only one but several with an attitude and acute sense of entitlement. My husband was finally able to leave this overwhelming place after my mom came inside my room once more to check on me, and I told her to go to rest since it was already 5 in the morning and it seemed like I still had to wait for hours longer. At least I was at a safe place, surrounded by patients. That was not my husband's situation at that time of the morning. At that time, all of society's vampires came out to suck every drop of medication they could from the public health care system.

## 171. The ER is for emergencies: special needs will have to wait.

At that precise moment another young and handsome Caucasian doctor came to my bed; I let him know that the contrast liquid I had drunk for the test was making my stomach go wild. The doctor closed some curtains and immediately improvised a small room in that hallway. He checked my feeding tube and confirmed that the contrast liquid had upset my internal organs; a yellow liquid was coming out through a small opening on my skin, next to the feeding tube.

The actress in me spotted another opportunity to get away with what I wanted, which was to have the tube removed. I put on my tender smile; it was excessively sweet, not as evident as the smile of the cat from Shrek but it was quite moving. -Are you going to remove my feeding tube? I asked the doctor with the most innocent tone of voice I could come up with. -It is also coming out. I assured him. To convince the doctor to remove my tube, I described how uncomfortable it was, how painful the gases provoked by the feeding pump were and how I believed I did not need it, since I was also being fed by mouth and was already eating complete healthy meals.

I do not know what made me forget that the one I was talking to was a doctor. These doctors really know their stuff;

not only have they studied more than anyone else, but they have also treated hundreds of people and probably many of them have tried to bribe them, with the same technique I was using right now. But since at that moment I was so determined to fulfill my special need, I did not have the time to use common sense.

I was convinced I had covered all my bases; I sounded convincing and harmless and my petition was based on facts, so I was already enjoying my victory when the doctor, much to my surprise, got out what seemed to be a thread and needle and started to make some stitches on my stomach so the feeding tube would not come out completely. Oh no, you're not using that needle and thread to keep that tube attached to me! That is what I wanted to tell him, but I had to keep quiet and observe the not so pleasant event. I was certainly not expecting this.

-This is going to hurt a little. The doctor remarked and made three stitches that hurt me considerably. Why is it that when they say: -this is going to hurt a little, what they really mean is: -brace yourself because this is going to hurt like hell. Of course, once you have been warned you do not want to look like you do not have manners so no matter how much it hurts you hold it and even manage to look elsewhere, pretending it did not even call your attention. When he was done, I could finally breathe relieved. Goodness gracious, that really hurt. Either way, my special petition will have to wait.

## 172. No matter how tired you are chances are the doctor has had less rest.

The doctor then changed my gauzes, which were fully wet again, now with the yellow liquid provoked by the contrast solution in the area around the tubes. I have to give him credit for that, at least having dry gauzes covering my wounds made me feel better; being dry again felt so good. That night something called my attention more than my own condition. I was concerned about the doctor; He looked very tired. I could not resist giving a prescription to the doctor: -you need to take care of yourself now. -You need to rest. I told him, not with the intention of becoming his doctor but with real concern because he looked with less energy than his patient. -Not yet. He kindly replied. -I have to be here for a few more hours. I asked him how many hours he had worked on that day and found out he had already been there for fourteen hours. No wonder he looked drained, yet he did not care about himself; his patients came first.

-How many hours do you sleep? I asked him while he cured me. -Five, when I'm lucky. He responded. 5 hours? That is practically half of what many people I know sleep. As tired and sick as I felt, I was lucky to be taken care of by someone who has had less time to rest, not just today but almost every day.

## 173. At the ER everyone is busy: if you need help, ask for it.

After telling me that they were still waiting to get me in for a CAT scan, the doctor left. Chances were the test would not happen yet so I had to wait until it happened, without the assistance of my mother or my husband. Without them I felt lost but letting them go was the healthiest choice; my soldiers needed to recharge their batteries to be ready for another battle. Meanwhile, I tried to get some sleep but could not. The upper part of my bed was in an upright position, and I did not have enough strength to change it.

I tried to spot a nurse but there were none around. It felt and looked like "déjà vu." Once more, I was in the middle of a minefield with no allies to help me. At that moment I needed to go to the restroom; my body had such bad timing to take care of its needs. I had not been to a restroom in over 12 hours, since I did not want to use restrooms that were so visited, for fear of infecting my open wound. Something told me I had waited for too long; this was now a red alert. I had to get someone quick, so I tried to stop anyone that would pay attention. As much as I tried, I was not able to stop any nurses and opted for stopping a young volunteer; he accepted to push my bed until we reached the restroom.

Those were good news; I had managed to find an ally in hostile grounds. Good thing there was not an ounce of shyness in me. I do not want to imagine how difficult it would be for someone shy to survive here. Every employee is busy saving someone else so if you do not speak up and ask for what you need chances are you will not get it, unless you are dying. The same volunteer pushed my bed back into the hallway. He was going to leave right away, but I was faster than him and asked him for another favor: to lower the upper part of the bed so I could lie down. The volunteer did as he was told. I thanked him and accommodated myself. When I was about to ask him for more help, he had already left. Now this has got complicated. The only ally I had managed to get deserted too quickly. I could have called him again, but I felt sorry that he was working for free, very late at night and obviously wanted to leave. That meant that once more I had to manage by myself.

**174. The ER is noisy; bring music if you want to sleep.**

I had gotten used to being accommodated in my bed by my relatives to be able to sleep. Without their help my probabilities of falling asleep were not good. I felt too weak to be able to take care of myself. I closed my eyes, trying to get the much-needed rest but there was too much noise in the hallway. There were no bombs exploding nor the sound of rifles and guns was heard but the bustling of beds, doctors, relatives and patients was equally deafening and maddening to me.

I had gotten so used to the peace in my bedroom that I just could not fall asleep in this chaotic place. Everyone who came to the ER, at that time of the night, walked in front of my bed. It was a pity I did not bring the mp3 my husband had given me; it would have done wonders for me. But without headphones or a device to play music I could hear everything and started to feel the urgency to go back home.

### 175. The CAT Scan feels like a ball of fire but it is harmless and very helpful.

I certainly felt great relief when a nurse attendant finally picked me up for the test. He knew how long I had been waiting and told me they kept bumping me for later because there were a great deal of accident victims on that night, and they had to be attended first since they were in life threatening situations. As the assistant pushed my bed while talking to me, we left behind the noisy emergency room and arrived at a huge hallway, totally empty, where no sounds could be heard.

Waiting here was not inconvenient at all. The attendant parked my bed next to the door where the CAT Scan test was done and told me: -I want you to wait right here, so they see you and finally let you in. -Otherwise, they will just keep leaving you for later. The nurse attendant was right; as soon as the technicians saw me there, they decided to do my CAT scan.

I did not like this test. Come to think of it, I did not like any test but this one was especially unappealing. I have had it several times while at the hospital; it provokes a burning alive sensation. You feel like a living torch and this feeling increases as more contrast liquid is injected into your veins through the IV. This extra dosage of medicine, I was told, allows a clearer view of the organs. That way, whatever is wrong can be discovered. This liquid, used to clear the visibility of organs, provokes the sensation of being burned alive. Every time I had this test done I felt like my entire body was on flames.

I remained calmed but felt like I was going to explode; it was as though I was a big ball of fire but since I already had experienced the test, I knew this sensation only lasted a few moments. I was also aware of the priceless value of this test for my treatment. At that time, its importance rested on it revealing the condition of the pancreas and any harm the liquids coming from it were causing to the rest of my body. I was certain that my prayers had been answered. I seriously believed my pancreas had started to heal by itself, and doctors would witness this miracle with this CAT Scan.

### 176. It can only work in your favor if doctors want to analyze your case further.

Once the test was over, I was taken back to the ER hallway; there, I waited four more hours for the test result. I was exhausted; I had not been able to sleep. I was also starving and just wanted to go home. At 11:00 am three doctors came to see me: a woman and two men. Though tired, I was alert because I was expecting they would release the news of my miracle rehabilitation. The female doctor was the first one to tell me the result: -we have decided to leave you at the hospital for a few days. She said. I was speechless but my mind was thinking about a thousand things at the same time. Did I hear right? She was supposed to tell me I had been healed and could go home. You are kidding, right? For a joke is a pretty lame one. I thought.

But the doctors were not laughing or even smiling. I could not believe my luck and cried while with a broken voice tried to convince them to not leave me there. -But why? -I feel better. I told them, trying to change their minds. -We have to place you under observation and do more tests. One of the male doctors replied. I was heartbroken, metaphorically speaking of course; I guess it is good to clarify this when you speak from a hospital. I had so many mixed emotions. On the one hand, I knew that whatever doctors decided was for my own good but on the other, going back to a hospital room really frightened me.

### 177. Returning to a hospital might not be as bad when you have already experienced it.

I was pondering about my return to the hospital when my mother, God bless her, came in with a homemade soup. I felt relieved by her presence. Rapidly, I ate the delicious soup with the urgency of someone who has not had food for too long; this was my first meal in over twenty hours. I explained to my mother, with tears in my eyes, I had to stay at the hospital and that a bed had just been assigned to me. I guess I was expecting my mom to join me in my tragic soap opera, but she gave me another lesson with her relaxed way of handling the most difficult situations; serenely she explained to me that at least now we knew what to do.

I expected mom to feel sorry for her poor daughter. Perhaps I expected a tear or two, in solidarity for my misfortune. Instead, the earthly author of my days was so cool about it that I started to see the situation as an acceptable one. My husband was allowed to enter, to carry some of my belongings that had been brought from home. He was equally relaxed; there was no drama and no joining me in my self-pity attitude. Since I found no one to join me in my self-pity moment, I gave up feeling sorry for myself. Feeling sorry for yourself is not as much fun if no one seconds you. Besides, the delicious soup I had just eaten had calmed my irritable mood.

Mom is right, we already are experts in hospital stays and know where everything is and also know what is coming. The ones that are at a disadvantage are the new ones; we are already veterans. With that encouraging perspective my husband lovingly helped me to sit down in my wheelchair and the three of us departed to our new room on the 10$^{th}$ floor.

## 178. If you focus on your achievements instead of your failures, you will heal faster.

As I entered the room, I felt a little more relaxed. The environment felt more peaceful than in my previous room. Even patients seemed to be in less critical conditions than my previous roommates. A big TV set was on; a sports event was being broadcasted. Maybe going back to the hospital was not as terrible as I had thought. My mom and my husband stayed with me until visiting hours were over, and they took care of everything; they cleaned me with towels, brushed my hair, healed my wounds, fed me, and more. I could now brush my teeth on my own.

Mario also brought my mp3 device, with many songs that helped me during my most critical days. My cousin Glorita had sent me two CD's with religious music, and my sister Carmen had sent me a Mozart CD and a CD with religious music that motivated me a great deal. Mario also brought the laptop our friend Lucio had loaned me, so I could check my e-mails if I got bored. Violeta brought magazines in Spanish that she bought at a store on the first floor of the hospital and a bag filled with baby food, natural juices and pain medication for her Jackie. She also brought a figure of Archangel Raphael, so I would remember angels were protecting me.

Can someone refresh my memory, why was I feeling sorry for myself? If anyone of the post-apocalyptic stories found the amount of food I had with me, they would be euphoric. Not only did I have more food than I could eat but also had entertainment, celestial protection, a family and a hospital taking care of me. All of the sudden, I was no longer a victim. There was an entire kingdom on my side as if I were a great queen.

Maybe the tears I shed, when I was notified I had to stay at the hospital, responded to a reality that was no longer mine. I was still weak and in delicate condition, but I was certainly better than two months ago when I was first admitted to the hospital after my accident. Back then I was at the brink of death. Now I could even talk and walk, slowly but surely. Once I realized this, the idea of being back at the hospital was not as frightening after all. I had overcome many obstacles; my achievements were evident.

Once my relatives left, I met my new roommates and realized I was in better shape than at least one of them. The lady had a car accident; she was seriously injured and could not move from her bed. A car accident patient, oh no! Did this mean I had to brace myself for another noisy night? I observed her closely, and she seemed very civilized. She was awake but did not make noises. She did not complain once, even though she had all sorts of equipment keeping her in place.

She certainly looked in really bad shape. On the other hand, my physical condition was much better than the one of that roommate. Even though the other patient could not move a finger, I had the luxury of not only walking but also being able to go to the restroom. Even more fabulous was the fact that with the help of my toilet seat riser, I could even sit down without hurting my pancreas and the best of it was that I did not need anyone's help. It would take me some time to reach the restroom but at least I could do it on my own. Thanks car accident lady for reminding me that I am doing just fine. This is not such a bad day after all. With that thought in mind, I received the last injection of the day and went to sleep after thanking God for helping me to survive such long day.

### 179. If you are not at intensive or the trauma room, there will be fewer emergencies.

I closed my eyes and my heart was filled with joy when I opened them again and realized I had slept the entire night with only a brief interruption for my injection. No one had moaned in the middle of the night; no patients were admitted in critical conditions and there was not a single emergency. Apparently, this room has ill people in better health condition than the intensive unit, the emergency room or the trauma room. Additionally, even visits to the restroom were possible for me at this room; contrary to the previous one, here I did not have to wait for anyone to change my diaper.

That morning, when the doctors came, I was happy to

report that I was feeling better. They seemed surprised to see my body reacting positively even though my pancreatic liquids were not contained yet. A new young and handsome doctor, tall, with white skin and black hair, Dr. Boland, would be the new head of my new medical team. He came with some other medics, including one of my original head doctors, Dr. Hammond.

### 180. Trust a hospital with a medicine school: professors always supervise their students.

Dr. Hammond is very formal; maybe this is his way of promoting respect among his medical students. In my case, I am not very conventional and was so happy to see one of my former doctors attending me, I did not resist kissing his hand, to express my appreciation. His red cheeks gave away the fact that the gesture took him by surprise but he seemed satisfied; at least I concluded that when I saw his timid smile. In my hometown, regardless of whether we are related or not, it is so normal to hug, kiss or take the hand of the person we are fond of that too often I am just unaware I am no longer in Kansas (Kansas being Puerto Rico, of course).

Truth being told, in order to avoid loosing the attention of his students, the professor started to talk to them about my condition in a very didactic way. Dr. Hammond asked his students what had happened and what was being done with the patient. He also asked what precautions would be taken in order to contain the pancreatic fluids that were coming out of the hole left by the tube. Not even an expressive woman, kissing his hand, would mess up his disciplined way of teaching his students.

Later on that day one of his students, which was also my new head doctor, came up with an idea. Accompanied by another beautiful and skilled female doctor, they both placed a small straw in the void left by the tube and around it they placed a cardboard with glue and adhered it to my body. The cardboard had a plastic bag with a sealing cap that was perfect to remove the liquids that came from the pancreas. The professor inspected the procedure and everything done by resident doctors. To me, it was a great relief that contrary to the bags that previously collected my liquids, the new ones were small and therefore did not occupy much space. This made my movements less restrictive. The students, the professor and the patient were happy to realize this invention worked.

### 181. If you have been prescribed pain medication, keep it close to you.

I was in a much better condition than when I first arrived at the hospital but that day I started to feel acute pain where the straw had been placed. I asked the nurse for some pain medication, but it was taking her a long time. Fortunately, my mom had left several pills, of the ones I had been prescribed, inside the nightstand. So after I had waited a reasonable time (about five minutes) to make the whole procedure "legal," I took my own medicine. In a few minutes I felt great. I was happy, relaxed with the medication and ready for the remaining tests and injections of the day.

Gone where the moments when I had spent six hours in chronic pain because of a torn muscle. Now I did not have to wait for anyone. By the time the nurse came back four hours had gone by, and she only came to inform that she could not get a hold of the doctor who would approve the pain medication. I do not know how she did not notice this patient was cheating and was "tripping" already. Could she not notice my happy face? I told her I was fine and no longer needed the medication. After the nurse left, I even joked with my new roommates, letting them know I had pain medication for sale. The other roommates laughed but thankfully none asked for the medication. Although I was flying high, my travel plan was a responsible one.

I only took one pill. I knew those medications make you feel high for a while but later on they get even with a vengeance for a longer time. I was not really looking forward to the side effects, especially the cramps in my legs; therefore, for the reminder of my stay I preferred to bear the pain.

## Chapter 10:

## Mastering the Art of Being PATIENT

**182. A second stay at the hospital could show you how far you have come.**

BY THEN I HAD BEEN IN THE HOSPITAL for almost 40 days: 35 the first time and almost 5 this time around. 61 days had gone by since my accident, and I was doing way better than the first time; I could eat, walk, breathe, talk, brush my teeth, and more; all of them slowly but I could do them. I could also advise my roommates and "coach" them on the procedures they were about to experience. How could I not spread my words of wisdom? What is the fun of a major trauma if you cannot give the world good unsolicited words of encouragement? I could give them the inside scoop given only by those who have experienced hell and live to tell about it.

Who would have thought that my traumatic experience would bring me so many positive things? My pain would serve to tell others how to survive it and how there are always people willing to help us when we are down. This was, after all, a great place to be in, a place to learn and teach at the same time, to receive and give, to slow down and think about what you have achieved in your life and what you wish to accomplish before you die. Was I still under the influence of medication? That was not the case but my positive philosophical way of seeing everything was a little funny to my relatives. They love me so much and listen to me even if I am being philosophical and if there is an audience, I keep talking.

Being back at the hospital was not a coincidence; it was meant to happen. Only by going back to that place could I realize how much I had gained from this painful experience and how much more could I get by sharing it with others. That is why when a nurse in training told me to write everything that had happened in a book, the accident started to make sense to me. I had "graduated" in pain and was ready to help those around me and around the world with the newly found knowledge. Coincidentally, I never saw that employee again. Was he really a nurse in training or an angel in disguise giving me a clear message?

An angel sounds more poetic and even supernatural. I cannot confirm either one. All I saw was a human male nurse that I never saw again. His words motivated me to write this story, destined to cheer up those who read it and let them know that even the most painful events can be survived because we will always count on help along the way.

### 183. Be nice to everyone; hospitals are small, and you will see the same people again.

Next day, I had several tests done. My mother waited for me in a waiting room on the $2^{nd}$ floor. There, nurse attendants picked up their patients after these tests. It was there where I saw the girl from Bangladesh once more; the same girl I had met while we were both at the trauma section. What a pleasant experience was to see her accompanied by my mother, who recognized her walking down the hallway. I had wondered many times if she had won the battle if she had survived the aftermath of her tumor. If she was here, it meant that at least she had not lost the battle yet and those were great news.

The girl told us she had been released two days after my departure but since she was still throwing up everything she ate, she had to return to the hospital and this time was placed in an isolated room. I felt sorry for her; she was still in delicate condition. Long gone were the days when her calls for the nurses annoyed me. It was a good thing that I never told her how uncomfortable her screams were.

Having been prudent earned me a new friendship; seeing her alive made me very happy.

## 184. Helping someone in worse condition than you could help you feel better.

I felt a little guilty; I knew that if the girl's mom would have been there chances were she would have been fed right, and she would be in a better condition. At that moment I had an idea, her mother was not here but mine was. What if my mom prepared some of her magic soup? Maybe the girl from Bangladesh would start eating again, without throwing up. After a few minutes talking, the girl had to return to her room, and we all exchanged hugs.

My mother and I remained a little longer at the waiting room, and I shared with her my new brilliant plan to save the world, well perhaps not the entire world only the girl from Bangladesh but that was a good beginning. -We have to help her. I told my mother, letting my strategist side make plans. -I'm sure your soup is what she needs. It will make her stomach stronger. I told the author of my days with a tone of complicity as if not wanting any possible spy to find out about my brilliant master plan.

Just like the great comrade she had always been, my mother immediately accepted. Right away she planned how she would bring the soup the next day. Her plan was simple but quite effective; she would bring the soup in a thermos so that it would remain warm for an entire day, just brilliant. I just love the perks of having such a sharp comrade. Spy stories aside, we were both happy with our plans for the following day.

### 185. If someone keeps you company, waiting for forgetful employees will be history.

Soon we realized that my nurse attendant had forgotten to pick me up. Something that in my previous stay would have been quite sad, due to my fragile condition, was not such a big issue this time around. I was in a better health condition so waiting was not as painful. Besides, my consenting mother was with me, so all we had to do was ask for permission to return to the room with the earthly author of my days.

As mom pushed the wheelchair, to pass by the nurse's lobby next to my new room, they realized no one from the staff had picked me up. They apologized concerned, but I told them not to worry while pointing at my mom who smiled at them satisfied. I tried to make it look like it was no big deal, but I actually felt as proud as an athlete after getting the highest score at the Olympics. I showed off my trainer, my mom. These two family members showed they could run a stretch and take the lead towards getting better, even if the other team members (the nurses) had stayed behind.

My mom also had a million dollar smile. She was not reproaching oblivion but we knew that after that reminder the probabilities of such mistake happening again were few. This time around nothing seemed to bring the mother and daughter team down.

## 186. All roads lead to Rome and therefore to any room in a hospital.

The dynamic duo was able to help someone else the next day. Well, at least I wanted to see it that way; I wanted to think I was helping even though my mom was the one who did all the work. Nevertheless, she is my mom so that has got to count for something, right? We went to the floor where we had seen the girl from Bangladesh, with a thermos filled with homemade soup. That morning Mario had taken his mother in law to buy the thermos; there she put the soup that God allowing would help the girl to eat again.

We did not know in what room the girl was but since we remembered the floor, we dared to ask around. With the help of my walker, I walked slowly but happily next to my mother, looking for the room where the girl from Bangladesh was. We found the room after asking a maintenance African American middle-aged man. -Sir, do you know where the isolated rooms are? I asked the kind looking man. -Who are you looking for? He replied, ready to offer help. -I cannot recall her name, but she is from Bangladesh. I said, ashamed of not knowing her name. -Maybe it is the lady who walks a lot with a pole. The man wondered while consulting with another man next to him. At least I was not the only one who did not know the girl's name. -She is in the room next to the nurses. Said the kind man and after thanking him, mother and daughter headed towards the room.

We entered a room next to the nurses lobby, but the girl from Bangladesh was not there. I asked a nurse, and she took us to a room with a glass window. Inside, we were able to spot the girl from Bangladesh. -Is that her? The nurse asked us. —Yes. I replied, happy for having found her.

### 187. Isolated rooms are meant to protect the patient, not the visitors.

Before entering the room, the nurse instructed us to put on gloves and a mask. As soon as the employee left, mother and daughter looked at each other briefly, worried about the girl from Bangladesh; if she needed so much isolation, we thought, she must be in a very delicate condition. We did not know if so many security measures were to protect the girl or us. We entered the room, and the girl was happy to see us. She was touched when my mom gave her the thermos filled with homemade soup. She looked for a container to place the soup, but mommy quickly told her: -it is for you. The girl from Bangladesh was thankful and got even happier when we clarified I was also staying at the hospital. She was under the impression I had come only for an appointment the day before.

Now that she knew we were only a few floors apart, she promised to visit me on the next day. She also clarified us that the infection control measures were to protect her as a patient and her healthcare workers.

### 188. A person in delicate health condition needs motivation to eat.

After a brief conversation about our conditions and our families, the young woman's husband showed up. He had brought several food items, to the girl, from a local health food store. Some were foods I was able to recommend to her when we spoke the day before and that could easily be heated up at a microwave oven. I was so glad she had paid me so much attention the previous day when I told her about the things she could eat without affecting her stomach. Knowing that someone listens to you, especially if you are trying to help by sharing what helped you, is gratifying.

An employee of a health food store recommended some items; the young woman's husband was delighted to show what he bought there. The girl from Bangladesh seemed motivated to eat, now that we had talked about how I regained the desire to eat. These foods were destined to create the same effect on the girl from Bangladesh and the possibility of having his wife eating again, without throwing up, really excited the girl's husband. We were all giving our best to find a way in which she would eat again, without throwing up.

There was hope in the air for her and this made all of us happy. -Start little by little. -Six spoons are okay to start so you don't throw up. I told her, regarding the soup, with the "been there, done that" attitude. An ordeal like mine had to be good for something, right?

It was my intention to spread my newly found knowledge and since I had a captive audience, I took advantage of the occasion. -Then, little by little, increase your servings until your stomach gets stronger. I told the girl with the wisdom and confidence of someone who has already gone through the same incident. After a few moments, I started to feel a bit weak and needed to rest. This motivational speaker had the cheering spirit but lacked the physical energy to continue. We all said goodbye, with the promise of visiting each other again and find out if this effort, to motivate the young Bangladesh woman to eat, worked. We would talk about it the next day; now I needed to recharge my own "batteries."

### 189. Helping others when feeling physically better will make you feel useful again.

That day my mother and I felt very happy; not only did we help someone else but also this new duty seemed to infuse more strength in me. Almost without realizing it, I had been able to walk with my walker from the $10^{th}$ floor to the second floor. Of course, there was an elevator to take me between floors but I felt as if I had conquered the biggest feat because in my still delicate condition walking from my room to the elevator and after that to another room was really amazing.

For someone healthy that is not a big deal but for someone in such delicate condition it was as admirable as climbing Mount Everest. Well, perhaps not so spectacular, at most my walk was the same as climbing a simple hill but that does not impress anybody so whoever asks me about it, I will tell them that I am an athlete in my own right. I was so happy with my new mission that to me my effort was worth as much as if I had brought a gold medal home. I felt useful again and that made me feel better.

### 190. Someone by your side can mean the difference between life and death.

When my mother and I reached my room, there was a big commotion in it. Mario had noticed that the patient, who could not move because of several fractures, was choking. Knowing he was not allowed to assist other convalescent people, he immediately called the nurses, whom changed the bed's position since the patient was choking on her own saliva and was also unable to change her posture or call for help. A few more seconds and she would have choked, had Mario not seen her and alerted the nurses. I do not even want to imagine what would have happened had my husband not been there. Having someone watching out for you in a hospital is one of the best ways of preventing catastrophes.

What a day for the entire family this was; we had come to the hospital searching for help and ended up helping others, almost without realizing it. Spiritually, this hospital is like a university where through tough real life experiences and depending on the choices made, anyone can obtain a degree in "betterment of the soul." The doctors, several nurses and some nurse attendants had passed the test with the top of their class; my mother, my husband, and I were certainly on our way. With their example, all of them taught us that by helping others we are helping ourselves.

## 191. Knowing your roommate's conditions benefits everyone.

That night I felt happy even after my relatives were gone; I knew my body was responding well to treatment. I made friends with everyone in my new room and asked them about their conditions, just in case there was an emergency. An old lady who only spoke Spanish was admitted to the hospital after falling from a ladder in her house. Another one that fell from a ladder, see how I am not the only clumsy one? In fact, I must admit I am clumsier since the woman is about 30 years older. Poor lady, she had dislocated the lower part of her leg but seemed to be relaxed. She could not move from her bed. All she did was pray with her rosary day and night, until 2'o clock in the morning when everyone was asleep.

Next to the sweet old lady was the Hispanic woman that almost choked on her own saliva. She was probably in her late 30's to early 40's. She could not move, due to her fractures after a car crash. Either the freeways of Los Angeles need some fixing or we have to send a lot of people back to driving school. This was the third patient in my room who could not move thanks to a car accident, two in my previous room and one in this new one. The rooms with men had even more patients of this kind. Fortunately, this woman was not like the other two car accident patients from the previous room. She was not a crying baby. Many times she was in pain, but she was very blessed to have a huge family and friends that constantly visited her and helped her to eat, among many other tasks.

Next to her was another Hispanic woman in her 20's who worked at a department store. She told me she had asked God for vacations but promised to be more specific in her prayers next time because she got a vacation, the hospital, but she would have preferred a different destination. This young woman was here due to acute pain in her abdomen. Her first big test would take place next day, and she was quite nervous. I tried to make her feel better, by telling her that I had that test done and it was painless. The young woman was not too convinced but my reassurance gave her some relief.

The truth of the matter was I had not had that test done;

it was the test with the small camera the gastroenterologist had decided not to perform on me. I knew the young patient would feel better if she heard from someone who had experienced it. I lied but did not feel guilty about it because I knew the young patient needed all the cheering up she could get, since she was afraid and had never had tests done in a hospital before in her life.

Now that I knew the conditions of all the patients in the room I felt more at ease. At nighttime, when there are no relatives or employees nearby, we were our best help since we could ask for help in case the patient in need could not do it.

### 192. Bring equipment to entertain yourself but hide it while you sleep.

The patient in her 20's and I had something in common: we had come to the hospital ready to beat boredom. In my case, I had an mp3 device while the young woman had an mp3 with a Bluetooth headset. I had the laptop computer my friend had loaned me; the young woman had a DVD player with its own screen. We both had many DVD films and exchanged them when the other was done. It was so surreal to see these two patients, their beds facing each other, with technology's latest gadgets in a hospital room.

We had been warned by a nurse attendant to hide everything while we slept since unscrupulous people take advantage of the patient's sleeping time to steal. We paid attention and luckily none of our belongings disappeared.

### 193. Knowing that others are in worse shape will make you realize how lucky you are.

Next day I faced a situation I had faced many times in my previous room; my next bed roommate was going home. She was a middle aged Hispanic woman who had developed a hernia while carrying heavy turkeys to be cut in pieces for sale. Apparently, she carried more than she could take and her body decided she needed a break from that job.

Intuition tells me preparing turkeys for sale, in freezing temperatures, did not make her top ten list of dream jobs to have when she made it to the United States. Unfortunately, the financial situation in her house seemed to be extremely harsh and her plans were to go back to work at the same place that had provoked her hernia. To the queen of common sense in me that was an absurd plan. I tried to convince her to change jobs, to do something that was less physical. However, my kingdom does not look at all like this lady's reign. I am a US citizen; I can leave and return as much as I desire. My roommate, on the other hand, cannot leave for if she does, she may never return. Her legal status in the United States is still pending. Therefore, she has to accept the jobs other Americans reject, the hardest ones, the less paying ones, less glamorous and highly physical.

Her education also is not the best. As far as she can

remember, she has to work so education is a luxury she has never been able to afford. On top of that, this patient does not have the same support I get from my family. Her family would help but up to a certain degree which did not seem to include giving her the necessary time to heal and to find a better job. Whereas in my case I had one hundred percent support from my family, my next bed roommate was not so lucky even though she had a husband and sons over 21. Without meaning to, this patient showed me that my problems were small next to hers. Some say other's worse condition should not be our incentive, but it should be a reminder that if others in worst situations have the courage to keep on going so can we.

### 194. –This too shall pass.

That day my roommate left the room to wait for her relatives at the first floor. They were late, and she knew her bed was needed for another patient, so she bid me goodbye and left to wait for her family at the lobby. I did not feel sad to see my new friend go while I stayed at the room. This time I was not so desperate to go home. I was still in delicate condition but was much better than when I got here. I could handle staying in the hospital until my doctors discharged me.

That day, my mom and my husband came at 11:00 am, as

sharp as usual. By now they were extremely proficient in the healing routine: mom cleaned my body with towels, Mario brought new DVD movies for me to watch with the laptop, and I was in charge of brushing my teeth and my hair. Later on, the three us exchanged conversations about those who sent their greetings or any new incident. When we had spoken enough, each one had a book or a magazine to read; just like the family we had seen when we first came to the trauma room. Back then, we could only dream of the day when I would feel good enough to just sit down and read.

I remember that during those days my sister had repeated to me a phrase we both like: -this too shall pass. How wise is that adage, how prophetic and profound its teaching is. The worse was over; I had come full circle and my family with me.

### 195. In a hospital everything can change in seconds.

That afternoon the girl from Bangladesh paid me a visit. She came with her pole, carrying her IV and medications and was wearing a mask on her face and gloves on her hands. She looked like a character straight from a science fiction film; yet, she did not seem to notice or mind. My mother and I were happy to see her again. The young woman told us she had eaten six spoons of soup and her body had accepted them. It was a great beginning, and we were all happy about it. Yesterday she could not eat anything and today her body had accepted the food. I told her that now she had to increase the dosage little by little, so her stomach would get stronger like mine did. I spoke to her like a mother to a little kid; I felt it was my responsibility to get this young woman to eat again. We chatted a little longer and soon it was time for the girl from Bangladesh to go back to her room to rest. We promised to see each other again the next day.

Little did I know one of my new doctors would pay me a visit, only twenty minutes after the girl from Bangladesh had left. -Would you like to go home tonight? The blond and beautiful young female doctor told me. Surprised I looked at mom and Mario. -Of course. I was quick to reply. The doctor quickly exited the room. A few seconds before I had promised to receive the visit of another patient the next day but in a hospital making plans is not too wise. I looked at my mom and tears covered our eyes. There was no need for words. Could this be it? Had my ordeal come to an end? Had my test shown that a miracle had happened and an organ that is not supposed to regenerate, like the pancreas, had done it? I had always dreamed big, why stop now?

Others would have been happy with just getting out of the hospital alive, but I craved for the main course; I wanted to be the first person to report that I had a pancreas that regenerated itself. While I cried happily next to my mother, Mario could not understand the reason for our tears. -¿Y por qué lloran? (And why are you crying?) He asked. Men just do not get it. Women cry, and we know exactly why and if we do not, we cry anyways to show solidarity. My husband was supportive, but he was not a woman and therefore was not in the same line of thinking, so I had to explain. -Es que hemos pasado tanto y... (It's just that we have been through so much and...) I answered while I started crying, so much for my ability to explain what was happening to my husband. Mom joined me in my emotion, so she could not explain either. Mario looked puzzled and his face only made us laugh even more while happy tears covered our eyes. My destiny had changed in seconds and we could not be happier.

### 196. If you are asked: -do you want to go home? Get ready; you are leaving.

We all knew what we had to do and would gladly prove how good we had become at it. So with our imaginary music and in fast forward motion we started to pack everything up as fast as we could. Mom put everything in bags. Mario put the laptop in its case. I put my mp3 device and my brushes in a bag and rapidly changed my clothes. Wasting no time, my husband took everything to the car and returned with my wheelchair. Had we been in one of those game shows where you compete to do everything in a minute or less, we would have won.

By the time a nurse came to let us know I had been discharged and my next appointment would be in two weeks, I was already sitting in my wheelchair, with my own clothes on and with that cocky and at the same time relaxed look of an experienced patient. My mom and my husband had the same attitude of those with plenty of experience in the subject matter. We could not resist showing off to the nurse that we knew what she was going to tell us. Of course, we were not dumb; we let her do her job, we simply did not jump up and down in excitement. We were the "cool" bunch. We had the "been there, done that" attitude without having to rub it.

The nurse smiled; she also had the "been there" attitude and recognized ours. The employee gave us plenty of healing supplies, so my mom could change the open wound dressings at home. Since the doctor did not tell us what the test results had been, we could only speculate about them; however, we were surprised to find out that the dosage of my injections had been doubled. We would not discover why until my next appointment, but we were happy to go home, not because I wanted to leave the hospital as much as I did last time but because leaving it this time meant a better health condition.

### 197. Hospital cares + family + patience + positive attitude= HEALTH

We were not told what the status of my pancreas was. Everyone who knew me was praying for a miracle; we all wanted that organ to heal fully and to be back together as one, not a split pancreas. We never stopped praying for it. I was convinced God had healed me and only waited for the doctors to confirm it. I did not ask my medics about the status of my pancreas. I guess I had learned to be patient. For now I would keep up my cool attitude and just go home with my family to continue our healing routine.

The increase in medication I was given came with a high price tag; my skin was dry and my hair was falling out so drastically that we all started to wonder if I would soon have to shave my hair like cancer patients. But this did not worry me so much; what mattered was that my health was improving. Go figure, in the "normal" world I would not be an acceptable lady unless my hair and skin looked healthy. I was not suitable for exposure in our regular society and somehow that did not bother me in the slightest bit.

Advertisers who feed on people's need to "look good" would have gone bankrupt with me at this point of my life. I now had another way to measure who "looked good" and it had nothing to do with anything that can be advertised or bought. My goal was to be healthy again and the means to achieve it, hospital & family cares aside, were patience and a positive attitude, none of which comes in a can.

**198. Good care can eliminate the need for other surgeries.**

One day, I went back to the hospital for a check up; there, my new head doctor examined me. I wanted to know when would my next operation take place. In a secretive way, the doctor told me that I might not need another surgery. I thought it was odd that he had to give me such good news as if he did not want anyone else to hear. It is so sad doctors have to spend their valuable energy in making sure they are not sued. As a society, we ought to be ashamed of the existence of so many people focusing on earning money when they did not work for it; such is the case of those who sue doctors for anything. The making "easy money" mentality of so many people, in this part of the world, is really shameful.

The doctor continued his conversation by telling me I would not need another surgery; it all depended on the liquids coming out of the pancreas. If they stopped, the surgery would no longer be needed. This "confidential and off the record" message was great news to me, since I was not precisely thrilled about another surgery. Yet, I was a bit confused; I was under the impression the surgery was to fix my pancreas, but I had now found out it was to dry the pancreatic liquids instead. What then was the status of my pancreas? There were no answers for that yet, and I did not push for them either. My recently acquired patience skills were fully at work here. What I did know was that I was doing so well that I would not need another surgery and this was a good enough reason to celebrate.

## 199. If your doctor and caretakers approve something, do not mind what others think.

With that positive outlook Christmas came, and I was blessed enough to spend it with my family, whom pampered me constantly. I was still rehabilitating; walked slowly, with the help of a walker, had to be very cautious with everything I ate and was still cured twice a day by my mommy, Violeta. I was happy to spend such a great occasion with my family. We even went to the mountains for New Year's Eve. Others friends and relatives were very concerned about this; they did not think I was ready for a trip.

Why does everyone love to share non-requested opinions? Do not get me wrong, I appreciated their concern, but it was my time to finally get some control over my life, and I was not going to give up that right just because someone else thought I should stay home. Go and stay in a hospital bed for two months and then try telling me what to do. It is always easier to tell someone else to do something we do not even know we could handle. I was feeling a little rebellious. Luckily for me, both my mother and my husband were a little tired of being home as well. So their approval and the doctor's permission was all we really needed. Anyone else's concern was appreciated but not taken into consideration. We needed to go as far as we could from any hospital environment.

We headed north in a trip that lasted about eight hours. I

was so happy to see the mountains of California filled with snow that it was worth it. We had to stop mid way because a snowstorm had started; we stayed in a small hotel that was about an hour away from our destination: Lake Tahoe. I was excited about everything, even about the snowstorm. Mom stressed out, she was concerned about me; she had no clue that her daughter was super excited. Moreover, had it been for me, that same night we would have crossed the mountains in the middle of the snowstorm. I assure you, this time there was no medication in my veins, but I was so happy that the adrenaline kept me going. After being locked up in a hospital, coming out and seeing those mountains filled with dangerous snow fuelled my desire to exist.

Fortunately, my mom saw disaster coming and decided that we stayed at a small hotel we found, right before the mountains. By then my dressings needed to be changed; something my mom was able to do as soon as we got to our room. Without wasting time, my mother and my husband transformed the hotel bed into a hospital one; they placed pillows all over and prepared the area to clean my wounds. They were concerned about me, but this patient was having too much fun.

## 200. Every cloud has a silver lining: the same is true about your life.

Two days later our family celebrated New Year's Eve at a cozy restaurant surrounded by mountains. My clothing is a festive yet elegant red suit, my first civil attire in a long time. I felt so elegant; I had worn pajamas for too long. My make-up wonderfully hides the traces of my accident. Under my colorful clothes are my tubes and the open wound, covered by dressings, but I was so skinny that everything fit in without a problem. Luckily, the only thing people saw that night, in this holiday picture-perfect restaurant with a breathtaking view of Lake Tahoe and snow filled mountains surrounding it, is a vivacious woman with a huge smile on her face and a crown on her head that says: "Happy New Year."

I was sharing this special moment with my husband and my mother. After two storms, last night's and the one of my accident, being at this place celebrating was a clear indication that "every cloud has a silver lining." Our smiles are worth millions. My twin sister, her husband and his parents joined us. It was a cold winter day at the mountains between California and Nevada, in the United States, but the warmth and happiness felt at this cozy restaurant was incredible. The place was filled with enthusiastic families sharing New Year's Eve with their loved ones.

## 201. Being self-sufficient is one of the main goals of anyone in a delicate health condition

Today, more than ever, I was happy to have my doctor's permission to eat food by mouth. I would be able to taste the mouth-watering delicacies the chef had prepared for this special occasion. I was feeling so much joy that night that I barely felt the painful gases provoked by food, liquids and medications in my now fragile stomach. Proudly, I told everyone I would go to the restroom without the help of my walker. My relatives supported my commitment to live a "normal" life as soon as possible but could not avoid watching over me as I slowly made my way to a nearby restroom.

I was using the walls I found on my way to support myself when a mature man in his sixties spotted me and with a complicity tone said: -happy New Year, ah? Then he winked his right eye at me. I smiled, no translation needed; he obviously thought I was drunk and that was the reason why I walked slowly and used the walls to support myself. I did not feel the urge to explain. I was happy to find out people saw me as "normal" again. "Happy New Year," the old man's words resounded in my mind while a satisfied smile covered my face, and I completed my task. How great was to be one more member of society and even greater to be self-sufficient, knowing that, at least for this task, I would not have to bother anyone else. This would be, after all, a better year!

## 202. If you wish to have a tube removed, ask your head doctor.

I returned to the medical center early in January, with infused energy to face the rehabilitating months still lying ahead. In this visit I requested the stomach tube to be removed. The female doctor who saw me had Middle Eastern facial features and belonged to my new team of doctors. She was willing to take the tube out but needed permission from my head doctors, and they did not give it to her. This discouraged me since the tube hurt me when it rubbed my skin and affected my every move. Besides, it had no use since it was placed there in case of another operation.

My next appointment would be in another month, and I did not want to wait so long carrying such a heavy tube in my stomach. When mom, my husband, and this patient were about to leave, our friend Elba showed up; she came to help with the paperwork to apply for the state's health insurance for me. By then my hospital bill was more than I had made in my entire life. Elba knew this, so she went to the hospital's first floor to make sure my application had been filled.

At the elevator, I told Elba about my unused stomach tube and how the hospital staff refused to remove it. Elba suggested talking to my head doctor and without thinking twice we went to his office; there, Elba found one of her old friends from her hospital days, whom luckily turned out to be my head doctor's secretary. Dr. Salim was not there, he was with his students going floor by floor to visit his patients. I left a note for the doctor with his secretary and gave up on the idea of seeing him today.

We were exiting his office when I saw Dr. Salim with many of his students in front of the staff elevator. I do not know where I got my strength from but as fast as I could I walked with my walker towards them and reached them, right before they entered the elevator. -Dr. Salim. I said while getting closer to make sure he would not get away. -I know you're busy but can I ask you something really quick? I asked, almost forcing him to get out of the elevator. Dr. Salim got closer to me while the other doctors took the elevator. Dr. Boland, my new head doctor, accompanied him. This was my great chance, a once in a lifetime opportunity; it was now or never. I had to be quick to convince him to set me free of those bothersome tubes, so I spoke as fast and clear as I could. -The tube in my stomach is really hurting me. -It gets stuck everywhere. -Can you remove it please, please, please? Sweet face feature activated to move the doctors. -If anyone can do it, it's you guys. I told them with a soft convincing tone. Then I added: -also, my feeding pump has not worked in more than a week. I have been eating full meals for quite some time and my body has reacted greatly. Please! I begged them once more.

Dr. Salim looked at Dr. Boland; they both shared information about me. They communicated using medical terms that to me sounded like they were speaking an alien language. They were not sure on what to do. I knew that if I convinced the professor the student would agree. —Please. I continue begging Dr. Salim with the sweetest tone possible. Student and professor exchanged more details with an emphasis on the pancreatic liquids. The only thing I could make out of their conversation was that Dr. Boland was telling Dr. Salim, using medical expressions and measurements, the liquids were constantly diminishing. -Okay, take them out. Dr. Salim said. I smiled happily and my family with me. Orchestral music of triumph filled that quiet hallway in my mind. That's what I'm talking about! This patient would be released with two less tubes from the hospital.

### 203. The tubes in the stomach come out easily.

Without wasting time, Dr. Boland took me to the intensive care unit, which was right next to the hallway where we were talking. It was the same one this patient had been at for the first ten days at the hospital. I entered and sat down at a chair while the doctor asked for scissors. One of the female nurses offered a private room for the procedure, but the doctor said he did not need it. I was a little worried; he had scissors in his hands and was putting on gloves. Would he perform the procedure right there and without anesthesia? I did not question anything, since I wanted the tubes removed.

The doctor told me to hold my shirt, and I thought he was going to take a look at my abdomen. Suddenly, I felt something pulled out of my stomach. It was my tubes! They had been pulled at the same time; it hurt a little but it was the impact of seeing them suddenly coming out of my stomach what shocked me the most. The doctor was a good one, there was no doubt, but he certainly was so used to doing this sort of procedure that I could only wonder if he had the slightest idea of what it was to be on the patient's side.

All he had were scissors in his hands, and a patient's mind can travel to mysterious places very fast. I thought the doctor was going to cut my skin in some way. Do not blame me; blame Jason, Freddie Krueger or any of those famous murderers on the news that with a knife or any sharp object, like scissors, cut their victims. Therefore, the few moments prior to the doctor pulling the tubes I felt like screaming; I contained myself because my need to be without them was stronger than my need to ask for help. I am glad I did not scream; imagine how ridiculous I would have felt when I realized the scissors were only to cut two stitches that held the feeding tube. Fortunately, there was nothing to be sorry about. As soon as the doctor pulled the tubes out, he announced that was it. I worried about the open wounds left by the tubes and asked the doctor what should I do to cure them, lest them get infected with any virus in this place. The doctor, without meaning to, showed me how unfounded my fear was when he brought my shirt up to show me that the skin, where the tube used to be, had already become a small scar. I felt so ashamed: even my body seemed to be making fun of my worry. In a split second it healed itself without any drama, just like someone waiting for intruders to exit to quickly close its doors. Once those hoses were removed, only a small drop of blood was visible in one of the incisions; the other scar did not even have blood.

I mistakenly thought my blood was going to splatter everywhere but do not blame me, with so many serial killers around, my fears are rightly conceived, right? The good news was that I was alive, without a scratch and felt great. No wonder the other doctors asked me if I had pulled my tubes; I never did it but now I knew how easy getting rid of them would have been. Probably I would not have had the courage to remove them, both hurt even with the slightest movement. My head doctor, Dr. Salim, had removed another tube in a previous occasion but it never crossed my mind I could do it by myself. The doctors, however, were another story; pulling a tube was an easy task for them and they knew the faster they did it the less it would hurt their patient.

The movement was so fast I did not even have time to think about it; it was like removing a band-aid from your skin if you pull it slowly it hurts more, the fastest you do it the less it hurts.

## 204. With time you will look better: do not pay attention to the way you look know.

My health was improving daily but my skin, weight and hair continued to get worse with the medications. I was perfect for the role of an extra-terrestrial in a movie: skinny legs, very thin body, short height, a huge head thanks to the weight loss, and the baldness so common in Hollywood's aliens. Many of my acquaintances could not hide their surprise when they visited me unannounced and saw my fragile body. Even a first time producer who had casted me for his first movie, before the accident, could not hide his surprise when he saw my thin body the day he visited me at home. He did not hide his concern. I am glad I have never had self-esteem problems; otherwise, this person's opinion would have seriously affected me.

A friend that was also going to be in the same movie quickly told me to not pay attention to that producer since I was perfect to model in Milan, his hometown. I know he was exaggerating; models in Milan are taller, younger and extremely beautiful but his eloquent compliment was just what my ears needed to hear. If someone needs words of encouragement to keep going that is what he or she must get. This actor knew this simple law of life and that made me feel better.

## 205. Water over a wound is one of the best methods to heal it.

By mid January I returned to the hospital, this time to announce that the pancreatic liquids were no longer coming out and to have my open wound checked at the wound clinic. With the pancreatic liquids gone, the doctor told my mother she could now allow the open wound to close by itself; she no longer had to stuff the wound with wet gauze since the infections were gone. I was also encouraged to take a shower and get the wound cleaned with water pointing directly at it. I was not so convinced about soaking the wound with water but once I tried it, I only wished I would have done it earlier.

It was a pity that none of the nurses or doctors had told me something so simple but so valuable previously. I guess the hospital staff assumes the patient is aware of this type of information since to them is so basic but to the convalescent it is not; the sick tries to follow doctors and nurses orders verbatim. Therefore, health professionals must always advice their patients about what should be done to care for their health at the hospital and at home, even if such advice could be interpreted as common sense. My skin appearance improved dramatically with every shower and seeing the incredible transformation of my dermis I could not avoid wondering how much faster I would have healed, had I known something as simple as the benefit of pointing with water towards a wound.

### 206. Man proposes, God disposes.

As the days went by, I started to slowly but surely gain my weight back. Next time I saw the doctor was in February, a date I had eagerly been waiting for months; it was then when I would find out the results of my recent CAT scan. Finally, I would find out the status of my pancreas. This was the final showdown, my whole being had waited for it. My heart was beating like crazy; it felt like it was going to pump out. My belly felt butterflies. After so many months of diligent care, all of my friends and family had been praying for a final miracle.

Had my pancreas miraculously regenerated itself even though this organ does not regenerate? Would it need another surgery to help it do its work? The answer came from one of my original physicians: Dr. Pierce. I was truly honored to see him once more. What a perfect person to give me the news.
-Is there going to be another surgery? I was quick to ask him.
-No, unless you start lifting things up and give yourself a hernia. Dr. Pierce replied with a wide comforting smile.

A miracle, a miracle! I thought, anticipating the CAT Scan had revealed a regenerated pancreas. With my heart beating as fast as my emotions were telling it to beat, I continued my questioning. -What's the status of the pancreas? Did it regenerate itself? Suspenseful music while I wait for a response. -No, the pancreas does not do that. Complete silence from my side; shock attitude while I listen to the doctor and his voice seems to disappear in the distance. -It is still split but it seems to be working. Dr. Pierce kept talking in a casual and friendly way.

I looked at him surprised; I could not believe my fate. I had mixed emotions; all the prayers, care and wait only to find out my pancreas was still hanging inside my body and split in two, and I did not even know which half was working and which was not. I admit it; the drama queen in me could not quit feeling like a victim. I guess what the doctor was telling me was good but this was my story; I wanted my own happy ending, the one my relatives, loved ones and I had written, not the one I had been given without my consent.

## 207. Even though you cannot control your destiny, you can control how you feel about it.

What did this mean? I was confused. Someone else wrote another ending for my story, and I had not been consulted about it; this was not how I envisioned this moment. I was experiencing so many feelings at the same time; it was as though right at that moment I felt everything I had experienced during my days at the hospital: the uncertainty of my condition, the compassion of the doctors and nurses taking care of me, my faith and the faith of my loved ones in a miracle cure, the pain of my darkest moments, the happiness of my survival and the gratitude towards everyone that had helped me, now represented by Dr. Pierce.

I felt so blessed and so overwhelmed at the same time that I started to cry. My friend Elba was next to me and cried with me. Remember what I told you before? It is called female bonding and if it is not named that way, I officially proclaim authorship of the concept. My friend Elba cried with me and had no clue why her friend was crying. But she understood women and us girls simply need someone to share our pain. The doctor had the same puzzled look my husband had when my mother and I cried during my last discharge. He was a doctor, but he was also a man, so this girl did not expect this man to understand. Elba, on the other hand, was a woman and she understood and because of it she decided to explain my tears to the doctor: -doctor, the thing is my friend... my friend... Elba said eloquently, just before she joined my choir of tears. With this concert of crying women, who would remove the doctor's panicked face? Poor man, between our crying and our Spanglish (Spanish and English as if it were one language) so normal between Elba and I but so strange for the doctor, we were driving him crazy. Elba then decided to take control since her friend could not stop crying. She said I had been crying a great deal, and she thought it was because of the medications I had taken during my treatment. She also told the doctor how difficult and painful was still for me to perform basic things like walking; how things as simple as sneezing, coughing or even yawning were quite painful.

Dr. Pierce understood everything; he truly knew the human condition and had treated hundreds, if not thousands, of people with every sort of illness. With a compassionate smile, he explained to me that I could go back to do whatever I did before the accident, but I had to give my body time to heal, inside and out. -Listen to your body. He told me, before extending my disability time. A few days later, a state doctor reaffirmed my need to allow my body to heal; it was the last step needed to approve state health insurance.

My family, friends, and I had prayed for a miracle; we all wanted my pancreas regenerated. Yet, God who is pure light and wisdom answered in a different way. The Almighty left my pancreas split but somehow it was working as if it were complete. The miracle had been performed, not exactly as my family, friends, and I had prayed for, but who are we to decide how God makes miracles? The truth of the matter is I am living day by day with a broken vital organ that is somehow working as if it was a healthy one.

I had another surgery; just as Dr. Pierce predicted I developed a hernia, not because I had lifted anything up but because of the dramatic incision made to save my life during the first surgery. I was mentally and physically ready for this second procedure. I was not scared; I knew I was in the hands of the Almighty. With that thought in mind I had another surgery, a year and a month after my first procedure. The surgery was a success. The hernia was fixed; the pancreas is still split, but I am finally at peace.

I know life will never be the same for me, but I feel like I can handle more than I could before the accident. My "tragedy" had transformed my loved ones and I into stronger people. The incredible work of the doctors and nurses of my miracle hospital, along with the love and care I have received from my friends and family and even the support of a state that had so often been so cold and was now caring enough to give me health insurance so I could heal, have jointly achieved what seemed impossible: giving me a second chance to live. Who cares if life is different now? It has changed for the best; every wound, stitch, scar and every moment spent in medical treatment has been the greatest gift I have ever gotten, a gift directly from God's hand, a gift of love and survival, of pain and healing, of patience, of understanding the human condition a little more and in the process becoming more compassionate. Some day the physical ailments will no longer be felt but the wealth gained by my spirit will live within me and with my loved ones throughout eternity.

**THE END**

*Rather... and they lived happily ever after.*

## My gift to you

Since you shared with me a very special book, I wish to invite you to enjoy valuable offers in my web page: www.jackietorres.com

## About the author

Jackie Torres is a film, TV and theater writer. Universities use her films to analyze the Hispanic reality in the United States.

Her TV shows have been number one in ratings. She is a speaker, university professor, producer, director, member of the team of actors for the training of medical students in a world-renowned university, has an Associate Degree in Theology, a Bachelor's Degree from the University of Maryland and a Master's Degree from the University of Puerto Rico in Communications.

## Dedication

Dedicated with all my love to my mother, Violeta, for giving me the happiness of taking care of me once again, just like when I was a baby. And to everyone who prayed for me and helped me through the toughest time of my life so far, especially my sister Janet, Carmen, Omayra, and my husband Mario, who has healed almost as drastically as I have.

## Acknowledgements

Thanks a million to those that read my book in its different stages and provided me with their wise advices: Violeta Milagros Rolón, Janet Torres, Heidi Horst, and my greatest critic and essential partner for the publication of this book, Mario Ramirez Reyes.

Book Cover: Mario Ramírez Reyes

www.ingramcontent.com/pod-product-compliance
Lightning Source LLC
LaVergne TN
LVHW051541070426
835507LV00021B/2359